Sonoran De[sert]

Understanding, Insights, and Enjoyment

Gerald A. Rosenthal

Library of Congress Control Number—2007909462
ISBN Number—978-0-615-18671-9

REVIEWER'S COMMENTARY

"Dr. Gerald A. Rosenthal, a world-renowned American biologist and biochemicc entomologist, has written a fascinating book on the flora and fauna of the America Sonoran Desert. This work will be of keen interest to high school teachers, college professor and their students, and individuals interested in arid land biodiversity.

The book will also be of considerable value to amateur desert lovers and adventuresom tourists, especially those outside of North America, who are seeking answers to the meanin of bizarre desert life forms, and adaptations to a harsh environment. It is an informativ field guide that can aid the family in understanding and enjoying the fascinating intricacie of the Sonoran Desert.

A unique aspect of the book is the role that beetles, bugs, bats, and bees play i maintaining genetic diversity by dispersing pollen and assuring that eternal life thrives in the Sonoran Desert."

Eloy Rodriguez, *James A. Perkins Endowed Professor*, Cornell University. His areas c expertise are in Environmental Tropical and Desert Biology and Natural Biomedicine: of the Amazon Rain Forest, and the Sonoran and Chihuahuan Deserts of the Americas

---

"The author provides excellent images of more than 300 plant species from the Sonoro desert in this compact volume. Each image is complemented by a clear, brief description an practical observations about the plant and its identification. A series of practical notes an photo insets help the reader to relate the species to the environment. Dr. Rosenthal's boo provides valuable information about the natural history and ecology of the Sonoran deser in large part based on his extensive field experience. I will certainly carry this outstandin and convenient field reference with me on future visits to the Southwest."

David Seigler, *Professor of Botany*, University of Illinois at Champagne-Urbana.

"The author has admirably achieved his goal of guiding both the casual and more seriou minded desert enthusiast toward a more sophisticated, more accurate, and ultimately more enjoyable appreciation of the Sonoran Desert."

John Adcock, *Regents' Professor of Biology*, Arizona State University, and Author o Sonoran Desert Spring and Sonoran Desert Summer.

CONTENTS

OPENING IMAGE CREDITS

Saguaro (Gerald Rosenthal), great horned owl (Gerald Rosenthal), Sonoran Desert afternoon (Gerald Rosenthal) and sunrise (Ed Mertz), Harris' Hawk [Ed Mertz (top) and Linda Covey (bottom)], Sonoran Desert sunset and cirrus-studded sky (Linda Covey).

SETTING THE STAGE: THE SONORAN DESERT

The Sonoran Desert is a vast, arid region covering some 120,000 square miles, most of it located in southwestern Arizona and southeastern California as well as Sonora and Baja California in Mexico. It is the hottest of our North American deserts, and, in places, one of the wettest deserts in the world. It can receive 20 inches of precipitation each year, but at the other extreme, some regions of the Lower Colorado River Valley (see map, p.

9) obtain only 2 inches. An annual precipitation of 3-16 inches is a reasonable estimate for the overall desert. A well-established upper rainfall level that sustains a typical desert is 10 inches per year[1]. The high annual level of precipitation experience over much of the Sonoran Desert coupled with a two seasonal distribution pattern has resulted in the greatest plant diversity o any desert on Earth. Plant inventories record at least 2,500 species of flowering plants.

Virtually all rainfall is delivered either in the winter months (December through March or as part of summer monsoons (July through September). Summer rains, generally deposited by powerful storm cells, are localized often in narrowly delineated areas, and accounts for 30 60% of the annual precipitation. Winter rains form typically from moist, tropical air masses moving out of Baja California or coastal California that can create violent, thunderstorms with potentially destructive winds. These winter rains, often emanating from the North Pacific nourish a much broader area and they can last for days, providing a sustained precipitation that penetrates deeply into the soil; summer rains, however, tend to be short lived, but fa more violent and torrential. Much of the water runs into arroyos and washes.

When autumn and winter rains are adequate in amount and properly distributed throughout these seasons, the resulting spring floral display is nothing less than spectacular Dominated by annuals and non-woody, herbaceous perennials, the landscape fills with a vas sea of color that rivals a desert rainbow.

Freezing temperatures occur at night but their appearance is infrequent; winter weathe

is moderate. This can be a hot desert, with summer, temperatures over 115 degrees (often more) that can persist fo days on end. Typically summer days exhibit a diaphanous sky from horizon to horizon that can be devoid of even a hint of a cloud. Solar radiation is always intense and this combined with desic cating winds and a relative humidity that

Saguaros, palo verdes and ironwood trees, chollas, prickly pears, and hedgehog cacti are all characteristic members of the Arizona Upland Subdivision (Tonto National Forest).

often does not exceed 10 percent combine forces to deplete available moisture. Coupled with nighttime lows that can be in the 90s, plants and animals experience continued and sustained summer stress.

---

[1] During the markedly wet winter of 2005, parts of the Sonoran Desert received more than an average year's supply of rainfall in less than two months.

Subdivisions. The plants described in this guide are most abundant in the Arizona Upland Subdivision. The most distinguishing feature of this portion of the Sonoran Desert is the presence of large, columnar cacti such as the saguaro; barrel cacti; many bean-bearing or leguminous trees that account for the bulk of the woody perennials; and numerous succulents. Overall, it is surprisingly arborescent in composition and the only North American desert with trees. Much of this desert subdivision rests on upward-sloping topography; thus, the term upland. The Arizona Upland Subdivision has a landscape of small mountains and hills and much of this vast area drains into the Gila River.

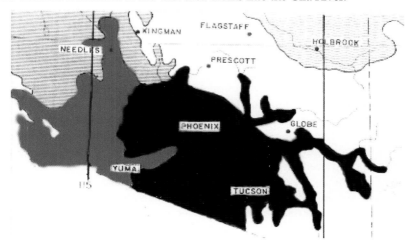

Arizona Upland (green) and Lower Colorado River Valley (red) subdivisions of the Sonoran Desert.

The other subdivision considered in this book is the Lower Colorado River Valley subdivision that extends west to California and south beyond Puerto Peñasco in Sonora and into Baja California. The latter subdivision is characterized by creosote, bursage, ironwood, and chollas. It is an area of bajadas and desert plains; far drier than the Arizona Upland, it houses a less diversified and robust flora. In this work, the focus is on that part of the Sonoran Desert within the state of Arizona.

Annual Plants. The Sonoran Desert annual flora is incredibly rich in its abundance and diversity. Annuals make up about half of the flora with about three-quarters growing in the winter season. The remaining plants are either non-seasonal or part of the summer assemblage.[2] Plant cover in this habitat can be surprisingly limited. A recent detailed study of the flora of Pinnacle Peak Park in Scottsdale, Arizona demonstrated that the entire perennial and ephemeral annual flora covered only one-third of the total surface area[3]. This availability of space for growth due to the limited ground cover creates favorable habitat for annuals. When water is not limited, this available space fills quickly with many annuals.

Research of D.L. Venable et al.
Research of G.A. Rosenthal et al.

Winter annuals have a few months to grow, unfold flowers, and develop fruit and seeds they enjoy a more favorable climate. For summer annuals, however, the growth season is far shorter. Being measured in weeks, changes in the vegetation happen quickly. Once the soil dries and cloudless, hotter days set in, conditions for these delicate plants worsen; soon, only their shriveled tissues are left.

The infrequency of freezing conditions, intemperate summer nights and days, moisture distributed sporadically through much of the year, chronic aridity, violent rainstorms, and a long growing season, have molded a highly specialized, well adapted, and diversified population of flowering plants that tolerate desert extremes. Under harsh conditions, plants languish, but they rebound spectacularly with the return of favorable conditions.

Desert annual seeds can remain dormant for many years until adequate moisture for both seed germination and development becomes available. One means of delaying germination is the presence of growth-inhibiting substances in the seed coat that prevent germination until sufficient rain has fallen to leach away these materials. Development of mechanisms for delaying seed germination until conditions favorable for the success of the seedling have occurred has obvious survival value for any plant.

Many annuals grow a hard and impervious seed coat that requires time and physical activity to etch slowly their tough exterior. Rainwater tumbling, grinding, and moving seeds particularly in sandy washes, prepares seeds for germination.

When the required needs of the seed are met, the desert can become a sea of diverse color spreading out as far as the eye can see. Such favorable circumstances fortunately do occur periodically in the Sonoran Desert. Another benefit of abundant rainfall is that rarer annuals make their appearance, and the numbers of a given plant in a particular area can reach into the many tens of thousands.

Annual plants have soft body tissue and lack woody materials. In general, they are far less massive than perennials. This is not to say that an annual flowering plant cannot reach significant stature; some are taller than most hikers are. But they do not accumulate a large mass of woody material.

Perennial Plants. Perennial plants are persistent, surviving the long, hot summer months by a variety of strategies. Many are succulent, having the ability to store water in most of their tissues; for example, a of the desert cacti. Another effective

Velvety pubescence creates the silvery sheen to the foliage of brittlebush, *Encelia farinosa*

strategy is the loss of water-wasting plant parts—particularly leaves. Many desert plants such as the ocotillo, exhibit episodic loss of foliage in response to moisture stress. When the rain returns, a new burst of leaves appears; this cycle can be repeated several times during the growing season. Other desert inhabitants are drought resistant. The leaf size, thickness and pubescence of brittlebush, *Encelia farinosa*, can increase significantly according the availability of water. Plants, supporting smaller leaves, simply sacrifice less water.

Because there is more time for development by perennials, these plants can grow and flower at prescribed times of the year. Thus, there are distinct waves of spring, early summer, and late summer perennial flowerings. Many perennials are herbaceous. They do not produce long-lasting, woody tissues; their softer tissues generally die back at the end of the growing cycle. Perennials send up new growth the following year. Some flowering plants are biennial—geared to a two-year life cycle; many plants that adhere to an annual life cycle can also experience a two-year cycle.

Other desert perennials, such as the desert trees and shrubs, are woody and far more persistent than herbaceous perennials. They attain much greater size and experience a significant yearly increase in mass. There is no formal delineation that distinguishes a small tree from a large shrub. In general, trees tend to be far more massive as they accumulate more woody tissues than do shrubs—even large ones.

Finally, many desert perennials have conspicuous hairs (pubescence) on the leaves. Their presence adds to the ability of the plant to reflect solar radiation and they may also break up the air mass moving over the leaf surface and thereby impede evaporation. Hairs can also be a deterrent to animal feeding. Clearly, having a longer life span than that of an annual requires more complex strategies for long-term survival.

Desert Soils. Desert soils are usually shallow and of limited fertility. This property reflects the scarcity of organic matter caused by the slow rate at which dead material is recycled back into the soil. Most of the soils are sandy and gravelly. Biological activity, leading to enhanced fertility, is also reduced by periods of desiccating temperatures and associated drought.

Calcium carbonate can accumulate in the soil, often producing an impervious layer known as caliche (*left*). Caliche is created when such deposits of calcium carbonate harden; often gravel, sand, clay, and/or silt are incorporated into this hardening structure. Typically, caliche is found at the soil surface but it can rest beneath the surface.

One way it can form is from materials brought to the surface when water pooled beneath the surface raises (driven by surface evaporation) and carries minerals with it. When plant transpiration depletes desert soils of moisture, carbonate deposits can be left behind. Additionally, the weathering of Paleozoic limestone and dolomite rock formations eventually provided calcium carbonate and fostered caliche formation. Atmospheric carbon dioxide, dissolved in rainwater, also enhances carbonate formation. This hardpan limits plant establishment and productivity.

Many finely textured soils are stabilized by a community of blue-green bacteria [4] and green algae as well as lichens[5] that form a stabilizing crust over the desert floor. This delicate cover creates an invaluable barrier to erosion and further loss of precious soil.

---

[4] Often called blue-green algae, these unusual bacteria synthesize chlorophyll and are capable of producing their own food via photosynthesis.

[5] Lichens are created by a symbiotic relationship between an alga and a fungus.

Sonoran Desert flora varies significantly in relative abundance from place to place. Large groupings of a particular plant or plants may be found along certain soils or slopes; yet, be far harder to find in other places in the Sonoran Desert. While plants described in this field guide were selected primarily for their relative overall abundance, they were included to provide commonly found representatives of the major groups of desert plants of the Arizona Upland and Lower Colorado River Subdivisions (up to 4,500 ft.) of the Sonoran Desert. This assemblage of plants adds beauty, complexity, and inspiration—especially to the pristine places that remain in our Sonoran Desert.

HOW TO USE THIS GUIDE

Most beginners will simply thumb through this work hoping to find a picture that resembles their plant of interest. This simple method can work, but far too often the plant is not identified correctly because photographs often do not provide adequate information for a correct identification. Photographs seldom reveal the seeds, or tiny hairs, or the interior structure of the flower, or lack sufficient detail—some, or all of which, may be required to determine the identity of the plant.

A better approach is to begin by taking the time to inspect carefully the plant. Begin with the flower and enjoys its beauty and form, and then move onto the other principle parts before even opening the guide. In time, you will come to know the features to look for.

Flowers. Of course, you will note the color of the flower, but then go beyond and look to see how many petals are present, are they solitary or fused, do they form a long, tubular structure? Is the flower divided into upper and lower portions with one or more lobes? Can the flower be divided into two parts along many or only a single plane? Examine the sepals for their properties and characteristics[6]. How are the flowers arranged? Are the flowers clumped at the head of the plant, supported individually or distributed in a recognizable pattern (inflorescence)? Within each of the plant descriptions, the floral section generally opens with the primary flower color, details the corolla, examines the nature of the inflorescence, and ends with a description of the calyx.

Leaves. Note the shape of the blade (this is the opening descriptive for the leaves), and examine the margin of the blade. Look at the leaves and decide if they have a petiole or are sessile. Are they simple or compound? If compound, what is the level of complexity? Are they alternate or opposite?

Is the leaf form uniform along the stem or are the basal leaves different from leaves higher up on the stem? Are the leaves distributed along the entire stem or concentrated at the base of the plant? Note if the basal leaves persist once flower development has occurred *Within the plant descriptions, all of the leaf arrangements, unless described otherwise, are alternate.*

Examine the plant for fruit; this is a truly valuable diagnostic tool. With some practice, you will come to know the various types of fruit. Gently touch the plant, is it smooth or does

---

[6] Occasionally, petals are absent; the showy structures are sepals.

t support some kind of hair? Botanists have many terms to describe plant hairs, but the term pubescent has been used exclusively to cover the various types of hairs. Handling the plant may also reveal the presence of spines or thorns. The presence and location of these appendages may be a helpful clue to their identity. Crush a leaf or two and take in its smell; odor can also be a helpful clue.

The botanical description is written to enable you to answer the above questions. With practice and gained knowledge, the process becomes much easier, and your confidence that you have made a correct identification will be justified properly. It is not necessary for all of the described properties of a given plant to match the sample you are observing; there is natural variation. But if the discrepancies are numerous, you have to continue your search.

Due to the significant variation in the size of plant parts as well as the plant itself, limited dimensional data have been provided. Instead, emphasis is placed on the properties and features that are immediately apparent to the careful observer. All of the plant descriptions contain information intended for the beginner reader. However, additional descriptive information for more advanced readers is provided as well.

The overriding objectives of this work are to enable a motivated person to successfully identify the desert inhabitants with a high degree of confidence in their own judgment; to enhance enjoyment, insight and understanding of the flora and fauna of one of the Earth's unique and truly special ecosystems; and to gain greater understanding of the ecological and evolutionary factors that play out so importantly in desert daily life.

Botanical terms have been limited, but most are practical, justified, and worth learning since they place many different descriptive conditions under a single umbrella. For example, the term: pubescent or pubescence is used to describe a variety of hair-like coverings. *The Glossary is comprehensive and written plainly. It has sufficient details to help effectively with the task of learning new terms and concepts. It is a valuable resource and learning tool. Care has been taken to ensure that if a technical term was used within a given definition it was also included within the Glossary.*

Finally, all of the annual and herbaceous perennial flowering plants have been organized into colored assemblages. Within each group, the plant families are arranged in alphabetical order, and finally the species within the family are alphabetized by their Latin name.

Simplified dichotomous keys, requiring the reader to a make a choice between two alternative descriptions, are provided to aid in distinguishing between genera within a family. In addition, the basic botanical features of the commonly encountered plant families are available to help the interested reader. These materials are intended to enable the reader to gain increasing skill and confidence in plant identification.

As your ability improves, try to begin identifying your plant by determining what family it belongs to. The main characteristics of the most abundant families of plants are provided in this guide[7]. If you have the ability to identify plant families, then the task of making the correct plant identification is far easier. Get in the habit of taking your handlens with you; it is an invaluable tool that makes the whole process so much easier and more enjoyable.

See: Plant Family Characteristics, p. 290.

THE BOTANY THAT IS HELPFUL TO KNOW

Plant Names. Simplified common plant names, often intended to aid in remembering them, are important; one cannot reasonably call a wild heliotrope "the plant with the blue flowers and hairy leaves" without quickly running out of meaningful descriptions that differentiate one plant from another. Plants typically carry more than one common name; worse, the same name can be used for more than one plant. In fact, it can be daunting. The name peppergrass is used to describe more than one hundred species of flowering plants. Two *Hymenoclea* are *both* known by the *same* two common names. A legume, *Melilotus indicu* generally bears the common name of "annual sweet clover" but it has been referred to as a "sour clover". Well, it seems that taste is clearly in the tongue of the beholder.

Recently, I asked a fellow hiker what she called a very tiny, white-flowered plant growing close to the ground. "Why that is obvious", she said. "It's the belly flower because you have to get down on your belly to see it." It was an amusing and reasonable response that may have solved the naming problem for this plant, but what about all the other tiny flowered plants that required the same vantage point? Belly

flower number two! A recent inquiry to a riding cowboy about a flower's name, elicited— "it's a PLF, pretty little flower".

Obviously, a naming system is required that is wholly unambiguous— meaningful to everyone, everywhere. Botanists use a binomial (two elements)

system for naming plants; that is, two Latin names for each plant. The first name is the genus (plural: genera) that design-nates a group of plants that share significant common genetic characteristics. This system of binomial nomenclature, in which the concept of a species and genus was formalized, was first codified by Carl Linnaeus, a Swedish scientist *(right)*. For example, there are three commonly found members of the genus *Phacelia* through much of the Upland Subdivision. *Phacelia crenulata (left)*, *Phacelia distans*, and least often, *Phacelia campanularia*. Each plant is unique but they also share many common characteristics with one another. Thus, they are all housed in the genus: *Phacelia* The second name is the plant's specific epithet; it provides a distinguishing label for each plant within the genus. This second name is typically descriptive; for example, *"crenulata"* for the fact that the leaf margins are crenulated or scalloped in design. Many Latin names honor an individual who made a noteworthy contribution to or was a supporter of some aspect of botanical sciences. For example, *Opuntia engelmannii* recognizes George Engelmann[8]. Often, they contributed to or supported the process of finding, identifying, and ultimately organizing the vast inventory of flowering plants.

Phacelia crenulata may seem to be a mouthful, but it does provide a unique, name that everyone worldwide agrees refers to single, specific plant and none other. The current system of botanical naming effectively eliminates confusion and error in referring to a given plant.

Given the bewildering preponderance of common names, and continual changes in the Latin binomial, appropriate nomenclature is difficult and subject to argument and debate. In the end, the selection of common and Latin names represented a reasoned compromise between common usage, the authoritative Integrated Taxonomic Information System (ITIS)[9], and the Flora of North America.

Generalized Flower Parts. Flowering plants typically have colorful, showy petals, often with distinctive shapes, forms, and coloration. It is this part of the flower that we respond to aesthetically.

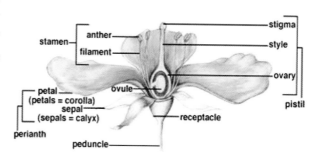

The evolution of these flower parts was driven by differences in reproductive success among individuals. Those features that best promoted reproductive success, such as increasing visitation by animals able to transport pollen, are what we enjoy today. Petal (a segment of the *corolla*) color, size, and shape can vary dramatically from plant to plant and therefore it is an important feature in identifying a given plant. Usually, a ring of nondescript, often green, sepals (sepal: a segment of the *calyx*) protects the internal flower parts. The term *perianth* is used collectively for all of the sepals and petals.

The *male part* of the flower, the *stamen*, consists of a supporting structure (*filament*) upon which the *anther* rests. The anther houses the individual *pollen grains* that transport the male genetic compliment. Thus, pollen grains carry half of the genes for the new plant. Often, there are a number of stamens that surround a solitary pistil. The pistil is the *female part* of the flower. At its base is the ovary that houses the *ovule(s)*. The ovules provide the remaining

---

[8] An avid plant collector, his herbarium served in the organization and naming of much of the flora of western America.

[9] The ITIS was created by a partnership of federal agencies to meet their mutual need for scientifically credible taxonomic information. While an important source of information, it is not the sole authority.

genes for the new plant. Fertilization of the ovules by the pollen grain initiates wondrous cellular processes that result in fruit formation and seed development. *The ovary will grow into the fruit, and its ovules will become the seeds.*

Strategies for Reproductive Success. In most desert plants, both the stamens and pistils are present within the same flower; such flowers are complete sexually and are said to be *perfect*. However, it is possible that a plant produces flowers only with stamens (*staminate flower*) or only with a pistil(s) (*pistillate flowers*). If these *imperfect* (sexually incomplete) flowers are located on separate plants, such species are said to be *dioecious* from the Greek for two houses. Essential sexual organs are found in flowers located on separated and distinct (independent) plants. Pistillate and staminate flowers can also occur on the same plant, such plants are *monoecious* from the Greek for one house.

Monoecious and dioecious flower formation is an intriguing arrangement since it separates the pollen grain from the pistil. This would seem to make fertilization more difficult to achieve because the male and female reproductive elements are separated in space. However, when this partitioning does not occur, the process can be too efficient—the ovules tend to be fertilized overwhelmingly by pollen of the same plant. Lack of separation encourages self-pollination, and reduces the chance for introduction of new genetic materials, obtained from another plant.

A single plant can have both stamens and pistils, but if they reach maturity at different times, they are distinct functionally because they lack both viable reproductive structures at the same time. If one plant's flowers are staminate and another plant's flower is pistillate, then fertilization must occur between two independent plants. In this way, the chance for the introduction of novel and favorable genetic material is greatly increased. Long-term plant survival is linked intimately to inherent plant *variability*. It is this genetic variety that enhances the ability of a given species to adapt to new environmental and other challenges.

One of the most fascinating examples of avoiding self-pollination occurs with certain insect-pollinated plants that produce long stamens and short pistils while other flowers of this plant produce short stamens and long pistils. When a pollinating bee lands on the first plant, pollen is position on the bee's body where the long stamens touch. This pollen can be transported successfully only to another plant with a long pistil. This striking difference in morphology (form) avoids self-pollination. A still more complicated system of such avoidance is based on genetic incompatibility between the pollen grain and the stigma of the same plant. All of these mechanisms insure that the plant will receive genetic material from an independent source—thereby enriching its gene pool. In spite of the above factors, many highly successful flowering plants, that are aggressive competitors, self-pollinate. There are alternate paths in reaching the desired goal; a variety of successful strategies have sorted out over the long course of the evolutionary process.

Floral Inflorescence. Floral inflorescence, the cluster or arrange-ment of the flowers on heir *pedicel* or *peduncle*, falls into several categories. In a *spike*, the flowers are *sessile* and rest directly on the peduncle. It's an unbranched inflorescence without pedicles. A common nflorescence, the *raceme* is characterized by flowers whose supporting structure (*pedicel*) is attached to and supported by a *peduncle*. Thus, a raceme is like a spike, in that the nflorescence is unbranched, but differs in that the flowers are supported and arranged spirally. The peduncle continues to enlarge and new flowers emerge from the apical region.

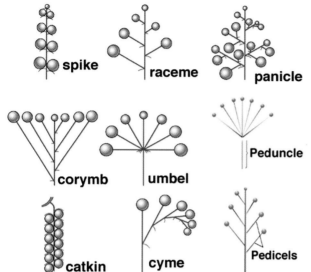

A *panicle* is a branched or compound raceme. The apex of the raceme has tissues capable of growth (meristematic) and it continues to lay down new flowers. Thus, the oldest flowers are those at the base of the inflorescence. In like manner, each branch tip of the panicle is capable of growth and it too continues to put down new flowers.

Cymes are flat-topped, branched inflorescence in which the flowers, supported by a pedicle, emerge at different points along the peduncle. The youngest flowers are located at the extremities; as one moves into the interior the individual flowers are older. This arrangement results from the fact that he terminal bud of the main stem forms the initial flower, subsequent flowers are generated from the lower, lateral buds. Finally, some cymes, producing flowers only on one side. It reminds viewers of a scorpion's tail; in such instances, it is referred to as a *scorpioid cyme*.

A *corymb* is much like a cyme except that the youngest flowers are in the interior while older members form the extremities.

In an *umbel*, all of the pedicels emerge from a common point on the peduncle. Thus, this flat-topped inflorescence is reminiscent of an umbrella. A *compound umbel* is where a secondary umbel forms at each flower position of the primary umbel. The oldest flowers are at the extremities of an umbel. Think of a raceme and a panicle as bearing the complexity of an umbel and a compound umbel. *Corymbs* are like an umbel in that the oldest flowers are at he extremities; it's also like a raceme except that the pedicles of the lower flowers are progressively longer. They expand to create a flat-topped inflorescence.

A *catkin* has pistillate or staminate flowers, and looks much like a spike, but a catkin is subtended with bracts. A head is discussed in the above section since it is an arrangement where flowers are supported by a receptacle as in the Asteraceace. *Axillary* flowers are those that emerge from the axil which is the angle formed by the stem and the leaf.

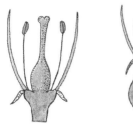

SUPERIOR OVARY   INFERIOR OVARY

Ovary. A final important property of flowers in plant identification is the nature of the ovary. If the other flower parts such as the corolla, calyx and stamens are part of a structure (*hypanthium*) that rests beneath and free of the ovary, it is a *superior* ovary. Alternately, if these flower parts are located above the ovary, this is an *inferior* ovary type.

Leaf Form, Margins, and Shape. Three physical features of diagnostic value in plant identification are leaf form, leaf shape, and leaf margin. Most leaves are *simple*; that is, the leaf *blade* is attached directly to the plant by a supporting structure known as the *petiole*. Leaves attached without a petiole are *sessile*. This is the simplest type of leaf form.

On occasion, the leaf exhibits a more complex form—it is not simple; instead it is *compound*. A compound leaf occurs not as a single blade; but rather, multiple components

PINNATELY COMPOUND

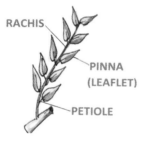

RACHIS

PINNA
(LEAFLET)

PETIOLE

BLADE   MID-VEIN
AXIL
PETIOLE   STEM

(*leaflet* or *pinnea*) that are attached to an accessory structure (*rachis*), that in turn connects to the petiole of the plant. This leaf form is called *pinnately compound*.

In summary, in a *simple* leaf, the petiole emerges from the plant and supports a single leaf blade. In a *pinnately compound* leaf, the petiole still emerges from the plant, but now the simple blade is divided into components called *leaflets* or *pinnae* (pinna: singular). The leaf is no longer simple; rather, it is pinnately compound. For example, there may be four pairs of leaflets (8 pinnae) that are attached ultimately to the plant via the petiole.

To make matters more demanding, there is a still higher level of compound leaf complexity in which each *pinna* is replaced by another group of leaflets (*compound leaflet)* **[A]** to create a *twice-pinnately compound* leaf **[B]**. Again, there exists a single petiole attached to the plant, but the individual leaflet or pinna is replaced by a compound leaflet.

TWICE-PINNATELY COMPOUND

PINNULA

COMPOUND
LEAFLET

[A]   [B]

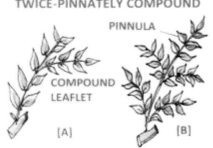

Now, the individual leaflet (fundamental unit) is known as a *pinnula* and the entire group as a *compound leaflet. There is no pinna in a twice-pinnately compound leaflet.*

Throughout the text, a particular twice-pinnately compound leaf has been described as "twice-pinnately compound leaf containing 26-34 pinnula with four compound leaflets". Yes, it is complicated and undoubtedly will require several readings; however, it is powerful diagnostic tool, particularly for leguminous plants, and well worth the effort taken in its understanding.

A source of confusion in leaf form results from the physical similarity of a *pinnately divided* and a *pinnately compound* leaf. In the pinnately divided leaf, the lobes are so deep that the blade appears to be pinnately compound. However, each of the lobes is connected directly to the midvein, there is no rachis.

PALMATELY COMPOUND

PINNATELY DIVIDED

In a final foliar arrangement, the leaves radiate from a central point like the fingers of a hand; this is termed *palmately compound*.

Additionally, the leaves may project from the branch directly *opposite* each other, or they may project from one side and then the other in an alternating pattern (*alternate*).

Observing if the leaf is alternate or opposite, simple or compound, margins entire or otherwise, and overall shape can aid greatly in identifying a flowering plant, and successfully distinguishing between similar appearing plants.

Fruit. Later in the growing season, the ovary of the fertilized flower will mature to form the fruit that house the new generation of seeds. There are many types of fruit and knowing them can assist in identifying a given plant. Fruits can be divided into two groups: *fleshy* and *dry.* Fleshy fruit have high water content, as do the many fruits of human consumption.

Dry fruit of various desert legumes. *Top*: **foothills palo verde** (*left*), **blue palo verde** (*right*). *Middle*: **desert sweet acacia** (*left*), **catclaw acacia** (*right*). *Bottom*: **velvet mesquite** (*left*), **hairy duster** (*right*).

Some desert plants produce berries, a fleshy fruit whose seeds are embedded within a fruit which does not open along a natural seam (*indehiscent*). The fruit of Fremont wolfberry, *Lycium fremontii,* is a tasty berry, and when opened looks like a miniature tomato (*above*).

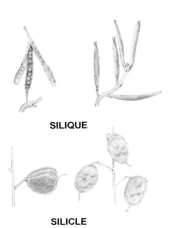

SILIQUE

SILICLE

Fruit of the Brassicaceae.

Dry fruits contain far less water and while the frui itself does not afford meaningful nutrition for deser dwellers, their seeds are an important dietary source of a food groups—particularly proteins. A *legume* is a dry frui that opens along two natural seams in the wall of the fruit.

The desert flora is particularly rich in members of the Legume Family (Fabaceae), all of whom produce legumes Most everyone eats legumes (string beans, snow peas etc.), but these plants have been bred for high moistur content and low fiber to enhance their edibility. Legume characteristically are *much longer than they are wide*.

A dry fruit that opens along two sutures, but is *less tha 3x as long as it is wide* is a *silicle*. This fruit is found amon members of the Brassicaceae or Mustard Family. Mus tards can also make a distinct fruit known as a *silique*. A silique is *more than 3x as long as it is wide*. These fruits car resemble superficially a legume, but they have membranous structure (septum) that divides th fruit.

Another dry fruit is the *follicle* which open along only one side of the fruit wall. All deser milkweeds, an important food resource for th monarch butterfly, produce follicles.

An *achene* is a commonly occurring dry frui Unlike fruit that open along natural sutures, a achene is a dry, one-seeded fruit that does not spli open when mature. Think of a strawberry, black berry, or raspberry; they are fleshy fruits whos surface is covered with closed achenes. Plants of th Asteraceae produce achenes.

Nuts have properties similar to an achene, bu they produce a thick fruit wall that protects th seeds. A large group of desert plants produce

Follicles of the rush milkweed, *Asclepias subulata*.

another dry fruit that is not elongated and bean-like. These fruits fall into a large grouping known as *capsule*s. Seeds are released through pores (poppy) or various openings in th wall of the capsule.

Smoketree, *Psorothamnus spinosus,* bears physical similarity to crucifixion thorn, *Canoti holocasta;* the former grows a legume while the latter produces a short and sharply-pointe capsule. Inspection of the fruit, that can remain on the plant well beyond flowering, definitively separates these two plants even in the heart of winter.

Dispersal. Desert plants disperse their genes in a variety of ways. Sometimes dispersal does not involve seeds. The chollas rely primarily upon barbed spines for moving intact plant parts. Far more commonly, however, seeds are involved. Seeds can bear their own winged structure as part of the seed itself; for example, the rush milkweed, *Asclepias subulata (left)*. Other plants utilize a wing-like structure (*pappus*) that is attached to and thereby facilitates seed transport by wind currents. For example, the hundreds of sunflowers whose seeds can fill the air with cottony white.

Some plants produce fleshy fruits that are desired by animals that eagerly consume the enclosed seeds. These seeds are released subsequently with animal defecation. Often the digestive process helps germination. Some fruits build significant internal pressures; the pods literally explode—projecting seeds away from the mother plant.

Seeds of *Asclepias subulata* carry their own winged structures.

Barbed and otherwise sharply-shaped fruit are caught in animal fur and thereby hitchhiked into new areas. The effectiveness of this reproductive strategy, whereby seeds are attached to passersby, is demonstrated by simple inspection of your socks after a desert hike.

A tiny seed has the advantage that it is moved easily by desert rains. Additionally, they are hard to spot and this can minimize loss to predation. Whatever the means, plants are highly successful in moving the next generation into a suitable habitat. Plant ability to colonize available habitats is demonstrated most dramatically by the many invasive plants that after gaining a foothold, now occupy vast areas within the Sonoran Desert. The salt cedar, *Tamarix pentandra*, has taken over so much riparian habitat along the Colorado River that this water-consuming plant diverts millions of gallons of water each year.

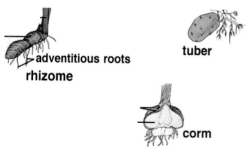

adventitious roots

tuber

rhizome

corm

Storage Organs. A large number of desert perennials are maintained during the winter with food reserves accumulated in specialized plant organs. One such organ is the *rhizome* which is actually perennial stem tissues that grows horizontally and pierces the ground. Once they are buried, stem tissues directly gen-erate the rhizome. In a modification of this theme, the stem can produce a root (that grows subterraneous and eventually forms (adventitiously) a root *tuber*. This tuber does not form from the tissues of the root responsible for growth; rather, it is derived from the stem. Another way of viewing a tuber is as a thickened part of an underground stem. We consume a tuber every time we enjoy a French fry. A *corm* is derived from a swollen underground plant stem.

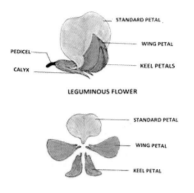

LEGUMINOUS FLOWER

Fabaceae. Many desert plants, belonging to the Legume Family (Fabaceae) which produces bean-like pods, have developed a particularly strong dependence upon insects, typically bees, to transport their pollen. These plants produce flowers with five, highly modified petals designed to accommodate visiting insects. The top petal is the *standard* or *banner* petal, there are also two lower *wing* petals on the side, and a final pair of petals fused to form the lowest *keel* petal. The calyx is also composed of five segments. Nectar is stored just over the filaments of the anthers inside the keel petals. When the bee enters the flower, its body weight moves the keel petals and this, in turn, causes the anthers to brush up against the bee's body depositing pollen onto the oblivious forager. The bee receives positive reinforcement, nectar reward, for this behavior, and the flower has an effective agent for transporting its pollen. The stamens commonly consist of 10 members arranged in two groups. Nine stamens constitute a common grouping, while the tenth and final member is more or less independent.

Asteraceae. Sunflower-like plants are grouped into a single family—the Asteraceae (named

after its most prominent member: the aster). The *solitary appearing* flower is actually composed of multiple flowers. The typically darker, central portion of the flower con-sists of *disk* flowers that are surrounded by *ray* flowers. Thus, what appears to be a single flower is actually a composite of numerous distinct flowers. Some plants of the Asteraceae produce only ray flowers (florets) others only disk flowers, and still others—both. Many members of the Asteraceae produce typically green bracts (*phyllaries*) which protect the flower head. All of the bracts are

Composite flower of the desert marigold, *Baileya multiradiata*, displaying both ray and disk flowers or florets

known collectively as the *involucre*. The features of the involucre are of prime importance in learning to recognize the many similar-appearing members of this family. Examples of the many properties of the involucre include their shape, their number, the number of series that they form, whether they are equally sized, their color, and other surface features.

CACTI

These signature plants of the Sonoran Desert are living testimonials to plant adaptation, perseverance, and the compelling power of evolution.

Saguaro, *Carnegiea gigantea*

Cacti. Leaf-bearing, woody plants such as oak or maple are generally familiar and well recognized. All cacti evolved from plants that share much in common with these forest giants. Thus, cacti are not isolated plants that evolved autonomously and independently from other woody plants.

If you look at a decaying suguaro, the large woody ribs running the length of the barrel stand out conspicuously. This ribbed barrel is the comparable to the solid, woody interior of a forested tree. Softer tissues surround the woody ribs; these tissues perform the same functions in both the suguaro and the forest tree. Moreover, some cacti, such as *Pereskiopsis*, share the property of having leaves. Nevertheless, a principle difference between these two groups of plants is the loss of leaves. So, what happened to the green leaves of the forest tree?

The woody materials (xylem) of the saguaro.

The true leaves of a *Pereskiopsis*

Loss of Leaves. Most cacti are leafless. Why the loss of these leafy appendages? A typical leaf contains a vast number of tiny openings (*stomates*) through which carbon dioxide gas enters the plant. This gas is the primary ingredient in making essential food-stuffs via photosynthesis. There is a problem: *in opening its stomates to acquire essential carbon dioxide, moisture escapes out through these same portals.*

A plant can avoid this harmful water loss by reducing its size or eliminating large leaves. Then where is photosynthesis to be conducted? How will the plant manufacture its food? The final strategy was to move all functions of photosynthesis to water-conser-

ving, non-leafy systems such as the branches and stems, and to retain small foliage that is shed when water become limiting.

Another water-conserving strategy of certain desert plants is to open their stomates in the cool of the night and trap the carbon dioxide taken in as stable, storage compounds. During the day, these storage compounds break down and release the carbon dioxide *that was taken in the cool of the night, not the heat of the day.* The plant does not lose valuable moisture in order to gain essential carbon dioxide. This is another fascinating example of adaptation by desert plants to the environmental extremes under which they must live.

Loss of Bark. Cacti have also shed the thick bark tissues of a forest tree since it obstructs the absorption of sunlight by the green stems. Loss of bark tissues also resulted in the loss o a barrier that protects the plant from the ravages of ultraviolet radiation. Cacti are remarkable in the ability of their surface tissues to avoid these adverse effects without a bark-like protective layer. In the case of *Opuntia*, their pads have a thick layer of calcium oxalate which offers protection from solar radiation.

Growth of a Lateral Root System. Trees and cacti both produce a root system that is responsible for uptake of water and essential nutrients from the soil. However, forest trees grow much of their roots straight down and deep, thereby anchoring the plant with great tenacity. In contrast, cacti rely on an extensive, lateral root system able to secure every available morsel of water after a rain. Roots spreading everywhere, but not deep is the price paid to maximize available water uptake before significant soil water loss to evaporation and runoff. On the downside of this strategy: a mature saguaro can be toppled by strong desert

winds. Employing an extensive, lateral root system also occurs in various barrel cacti. They are often found on the desert floor with their surprisingly feeble root system largely exposed. In a forest tree, the leaves develop from lateral growing centers or buds, structures packed with cells responsible for plant growth. In a cactus, these buds evolved into the *areoles* from which the spines and other structures grow. The development of spines is of enormous survival value because they protect the plant from animals that consumed its tissues not only for sustenance, but also as an invaluable source

A mature saguaro uprooted by windy, winter rains.

It is the areole, and their accompanying spines, above all else, that are the quintessential, de-fining structures of all cacti. Thus, simply speaking, the *bud and the leaf of the woody trees of our great forests have become the areole and spine of the desert cacti.*

Water Storage. A critical adaptation to limited water availability was the development of succulent tissues capable of significant water storage. The outer stem tissues of a cactus (cortex) have been modified to increase the size and number of cells. It is these tissues, as well as those of the inner portion of the stem, that

Areoles and spines were critical in the development of the modern cactus.

create the succulent, water-hold system of the cacti. Because cacti are an effective water-storing plant, desert animals can tap this valuable resource for their own survival. In response to such herbivory, cacti also developed sharply pointed spines and highly irritating glochids.

Cylindropuntia **and** *Opuntia*. Among the most ubiquitous of the Sonoran Desert cacti are members of the genera: *Cylindropuntia* and *Opuntia*. This assemblage of plants includes the chollas (*Cylindropuntia*)—*cacti with cylindrical stems or branches constructed of individual joined segments*. Most abun-dant of these chollas are the jumping chollas: the Teddybear cholla (*Cylindropuntia bigelovii*) and the chainfruit cholla (*C. fulgida*).

These jumping cholla are named aptly because they seem to jump out and grab onto every passing person. Facile release of segments of these cacti is essential because, to an overwhelming extent, they reproduce asexually. Asexual reproduction means that rather than relying upon fertilization between a pollen grain and an ovule, with the resulting mixing of male and female genes, the offspring develops *solely* from genetic materials of the mother plant. Chollas facilitate asexual reproduction by employing a barb that increases plant dispersal by attaching to a passing animal

Delicate, densely pubescent glochids, by being highly irritating, provide protection from cactus-eating animals.

Many of these jumping chollas may share a common genetic complement, having been cloned from a single mother plant.

In addition, the barb anchors the dropped segment into the desert soil. Detached segments grow into new, independent plants from tissues known as tubercles. No new genetic material is introduced in this process; the daughter is an exact copy (*clone*) of the mother plant. This method of reproduction explains why jumping chollas often occur in highly clustered groups.

Other chollas include the buckhorn cholla (*Cylindropuntia acanthocarpa*), the staghorn cholla (*C. versicolor*), the Christmas cholla (*C. leptocaulis*), and the pencil cholla (*C. arbuscula*). All of these cacti share the common characteristic of *jointed stems*. Chollas are unique for two reasons. Firstly, they are the only cacti with papery sheaths that enclose and protect the spines. Secondly, they produce *tubercles*—small projections on the stem that support the areoles and spines. Some spines of cacti are not connected to the lower tissues of the plant; their removal, like the thorn of a rose, does not rupture living tissues. Spines not only protect the cactus from a host of hungry animals, but also are sufficiently dense to shield delicate tissues from solar radiation and thereby lower surface temperature. Spines are also thought to break up flowing air currents, thereby lessening surface evaporation.

The remaining members of this group are housed in the genus *Opuntia*. They have conspicuous stem segments (pads) that resemble paddles. These cacti have thick and sharply pointed spines as well as very fine, hair-like members called glochids which are highly irritating and torturous, if they find their way into the eyes. The fruit of the prickly pear is edible once the spines are removed carefully from the skin. The juvenile stem segments are also edible and highly prized.

Saguaros—Their Juvenile Stage. The stately saguaro, *Carnegiea gigantea*, is the signature plant of the Sonoran Desert. Starting from the tiniest of seeds, it grows into a majestic plant that can reach 2 feet in diameter and 60 feet in height[1]. Most saguaros begin life in the shade and protection of another plant. Often this nurse plant is a desert legume such as a palo verde, ironwood or a suitable shrub such as a triangle leaf bursage. These mother plants offer a nurturing environment for the young cactus by shading the site, which reduces dramatically soil temperature, and thereby diminish water loss to evaporation. The leafy plant's many branches assist in breaking the flow of desiccating desert wind; thus, impeding water loss. These tree legumes are able

Many legumes serve as a nurse plant for a developing saguaro.

to fix nitrogen, a process are also rendering the nitrogen of the atmosphere usable for plant growth. Any plant residing under the canopy would gain an enormous advantage from this increased soil nutrition. Detritus, all of the dead material obtained from the mother tree, must eventually decay, and these materials area a principle source of organic matter—one of the most important components in overall soil fertility. While a young saguaro can grow successfully in the open, clearly its long-term survival for protected saguaros is vastly improved.

The cactus body is wholly green, reflecting its food-producing function. Its columnar stem is fluted heavily; areoles and spines adorn the ridges of the stem. Pleated stem construction facilitates expansion and contraction in response to water availability. A saguaro

[1] There is a claim for a 78 ft saguaro.

is capable of absorbing prodigious quantities of water, producing an increase in body mass well in excess of a 1,000 lbs. The ebb and flow of the ribs is an index of the water status of this giant.

Conventional wisdom states that around 75 years of age, *C. gigantea* begins to develop stately arms. Arm production continues throughout the life of the plant, generally about 150-200 years. Five to ten arms is commonplace, but on occasion one finds far greater limb formation[2].

Like virtually all desert cacti, its root system is not massive. A deep taproot is not present; it only extends about three feet into the soil. Instead, an extensive system of lateral roots permit rapid water uptake over an extensive area, even after a brief cloudburst. These lateral roots can reach nearly 100 ft. from the stem. On the down side, this adaptation for enhanced water procurement leaves the saguaro swollen with water and vulnerable to up rooting and falling.

A joyous sight in early summer is the appearance of saguaro flowers. These flowers arise overwhelmingly from areoles positioned at the apex of the main stem and side arms of the cactus. A series of creamy-white petals surround the yellow stamens to create a picturesque and stunningly beautiful flower. Since this cactus cannot self-pollinate, the plant provides sweet, sought-after nectar that attracts various birds, an array of insects, and even bats to the flower. These animals act subsequently as vectors in pollen dispersal to another flower. Saguaro flowers open at sun-down and remain open throughout the night but close with the heat of the new day. Thus, its flowers are ephemeral, typically withering within a day of opening. Successful pollination must occur during this short time frame. Older plants, typically supporting a greater number of arms, have the advantage of being able to provide a more flowers than their younger counterparts are.

The fertilized flower gives rise, over a period of 4-6 weeks, to a succulent fruit (cylindrical berry). When opened, the fruit reveals thousands of tiny, black seeds in its pulp, all housed within the scarlet-red walls of the fruit. This colorful fruit provides a clear visual clue to suitable animals to eat the seeds. Such feeding results ultimately in successful seed dispersal through eventual release of non-digested seeds during defecation. Seeds germinate within days, a period of weathering or leaching is not required to initiate germination. Some authorities contend that birds roosting on nearby trees, and their defecation while perched on its branches, places saguaro seeds in the protective surrounding of the mother plant. This is a plausible concept.

Seed production can be prolific. One study found approximately 2,200 seeds on average within a single fruit. Such profligate seed production is necessary since ant foraging alone accounts for the loss of about 90% of seed production.

---

[2]A colossus, said to support 50 arms, has been recorded.

An enormous host of desert creatures relies upon this colossus for some aspect of their daily needs. Bats, birds and numerous insects feast upon the flower's nectar. Foxes, coyotes, and many other animals are avid consumers of the fruit and seeds that are rich in oils and proteins. White-winged doves, gila woodpeckers and house finches move the seeds to new locations. One seldom sees a mature, open fruit that has not been totally devoid of its seeds.

Conspicuous holes are often excavated in the saguaro's barrel, they make a fine dwelling for a gila woodpecker (*Melanerpes uropygialis*, left), gilded flicker, owl, house finch, or cactus wren; abandoned nests are quickly commandeered by other shelter seekers. Great horned owls, Harris' hawks (*Parabuteo unicinctus*, above), and ospreys use the arms and summit as a perch for hunting.

Aberrant saguaros. Saguaros, particularly at the northern limit of their range, are susceptible to frost damage and attack by a variety of microorganisms and viruses (*top left*). These forces and others can damage delicate tissues, at the tip of the barrel, responsible for height growth. When damaged, striking aberrant growth can occur to yield *cristate* or crested forms.

Right. The cause of the grotesque growth form of this saguaro has not been definitively established, but most authorities believe it to be related to a viral or other pathogenic organism.

Middle left. Most unusual is the appearance of a cristate side arm on an otherwise normal individual.

Bottom left. This is an atypical aberrant individual because normal tissues have emerged from the crested region of the stem. Indeed, the current year of soon-to-emerge flowers can be seen on every terminal arm.

Top left. The abundant rains of the 2004-2005 winter season brought Roosevelt Lake to near record levels.

Lake water covered much of the base of the stem and slowly dissolved vital external tissues; food-carrying tissues have been removed, placing this individual in harms way.

Right. Being so tall, particularly in comparison to other desert dwellers, it is not surprising that a saguaro makes an excellent lightning rod. This plant, bordering Cave Creek in the Spur Cross Conservation Area, is said to have been hit by lighting during a summer monsoon. Heat generated by the lightning bolt literally cooked this giant. Over a span of about a week, it slowly dropped large amounts of fluid, and its vital tissues simply fell away.

Bottom left. An interesting theory suggests that there are exceptional years for saguaro germination and development. The similar physical appearance of many cohorts in this population lends credence to this speculative idea.

Top left. Under normal conditions, arm growth is regulated by tissues at the stem apex that are responsible for growth in height. When these vital tissues are damaged, arm formation control is lost; normally quiescent, lateral tissues become active growth centers. This can happen repeatedly resulting in a number of arms that develop simultaneously at the damaged site.

Bottom left. Sometimes, a particular place is just right—adequate moisture, desirable soil fertility, gentle exposure and luck; the resulting growth can be awesome to behold, generating a living giant whose mass measures in tons.

Right The bizarre appearance of this saguaro probably resulted from damage due to freezing. Much of the Arizona Upper Zone can experience freezing or near freezing night temperatures, a factor that establishes the northern limit for this desert inhabitant.

This saguaro is a testimony to desert plant ability to cling tenaciously to life even in a harsh environment. The dark material is callus which protects the internal tissues from desiccation, frost, and pathogens.

Of the many animals who use this plant as their home, few are as unusual as the bees who built their nest on its trunk.

Saguaros are home to many wild creatures. Two great horned owlets *(Bubo virginianis)* are protected by a parent while the other member hunts for dinner.

Its deep gaze—so piercing that it seemed to see right into my inner self. The owl, comfortably pierced on a mesquite limb, appeared oblivious to my presence; it sat obligingly while I photographed. Finally, bored with my intrusion, it alighted; no auditable sound could be discerned.

Barrel Cacti. After the saguaro, the various barrel cacti have the thickest stems of the desert cacti. These plants, belonging to the genus *Ferocactus* (fierce or wild cactus), include the fishhook barrel cactus, *Ferocactus wislizenii*, and the larger compass barrel, *F. cylindraceus*. Barrel cacti have massive, cylindrical, or barrel-shaped stems, with many prominent pleats; they are protected with great effectiveness by clusters of strong, sharply pointed spines that can be curved like a fishhook. Indeed, they have been used for exactly this purpose.

When young, they are spherical, but attain their columnar appearance with age. Flowers form at growing centers that are always located at the top of the stem. Most barrel cacti display yellow flowers, but they can range from yellow-green, through orange, to red flowers that bloom generally in the summer. Fertilized flowers produce a yellow, barrel-shaped, scaly fruit whose persistence

Spiral orientation of the spines and areoles is typical in *Ferocactus*.

offers a long-term food source for deer, rodents and other animals. Suitable habitat for these cacti is found west into Texas and south to Sonora.

Due to differential growth of the stem, barrel cacti incline to the southwest. When this lean undermines stability, it is not unusual for the barrel to be toppled and uprooted.

Hedgehog Cacti. This group of cacti, comprising about three dozen species, belongs to the genus: *Echinocereus.* This is not a solitary cactus, but one that occurs as a cluster of numerous cylindrical, erect stems. These stems house areoles with very long, sharply pointed spines that effectively protect vital tissues.

Engelmann hedgehog, *Echinocereus engelmannii* is the most abundant of this group. Flowers are a brightly colored purple to lavender. Other hedgehog cacti range in flower color from green to yellow, pink, orange and red; their cup-shaped flowers remain open throughout the day.

Pincushion Cacti. The cacti described previously in this section mostly have distinct ribs that support their areoles and spines. Pincushion cacti, grouped within the genus: *Mammillaria,* lack such ribbing. Instead, spines project from *tubercles,* elevated areas upon which the areoles are borne. These spines can be straight or curved; typically, they are numerous—covering the entire stem.

The handful of central spines is the largest; lateral spines are smaller and far more abundant. Pincushion spines are elongated and soft; this creates an illusion that the stem is covered in soft hairs. This group of cacti is also unusual in that often the flowers emerge as a ing that encircles the stem. The flower buds of the *Mammillaria* are formed in the summer, but remain dormant over the long winter; summer monsoon rains unlock the flowering process. Several cycles of flowering can follow sequential periods of summer rain.

SAGUARO (*Carnegiea gigantea*)
CACTACEAE (cactus)

Saguaro, the signature plant of the Sonoran Desert, is a massive, multi-armed, columnar cactus. Its floral tube lacks distinctive sepals and petals, but a horde of stamens, and an inferior ovary that is fused to the perianth is produced. The fruit served as a medium for fermentation, its thorns as an implement in tattooing, and the ribs as splints for setting broken bones. Favors rocky hillsides and gravelly soils.

Male cerambycid beetles (*Trachyderes mandibularis*) grow formidable mandibles which they employ in establishing and holding their territory in a fruiting saguaro. In this insect, males who cannot grow these clasping mouthparts become nondominant males. Nevertheless, they are successful in copulating with females who descend to relish the ripen fruit. How? Simply because this cactus invests so much resources into flower production; more fruit is created then the dominant male beetle can patrol and monitor and monitor. It cannot be everywhere at once!

Top: right and left. A massive limb was severed from the main trunk sometime in April 2004; note the succulent, healthy tissues. *Middle:* considerable decay and degradation have occurred in only 1.5 years. *Bottom:* photograph taken in October 2006.

This picture sequence demonstrates that the decay and turnover of some stem tissues, under arid desert conditions, can be a rapid process. However, the durable and indurate xylem (wood) shows little evidence of decay.

BUCKHORN CHOLLA (*Cylindropuntia acanthocarpa*)
CACTACEAE (cactus)

Flowers: yellow to amber, to orange, to deep red; positioned at the apex.

Stem: thick, cylindrical, jointed trunk, and main branches that become woody with age. Covered with many elevated tubercles.

Tubercles: elongated, white, and oval areoles; short, yellow glochids; and pale yellow to red-brown spines.

Fruit: light brown, pear-shaped, and non-persistent; many *spines*.

Notes: forms a highly branched, tree-like plant; some spines protected by straw-colored sheaths.

PENCIL CHOLLA (*Cylindropuntia arbuscula*)
CACTACEAE (cactus)

Flowers: yellow-green, to reddish, to brown; occur at the joint tip.

Spines: each areole contains as many as 4 stiff, piercing spines; one spine is elongated and angled downward. Protected by a yellowish brown, papery sheath.

Stems: slender, uniform thickness.

Tubercles: thin and inconspicuous.

Fruit: pear-shaped, red, and green but becoming yellowish brown; protected by persistent spines.

Notes: shrubby, segmented cactus with many branches, some close to the ground. Reproduces primarily from dislodged stem joints.

Can be confused with C. leptocaulis. *The latter has jointed stems that are 1/8-1/4 in diameter while* C. arbuscula *has larger jointed stems (1/4-3/8"-can be 1/2")*.

TEDDYBEAR CHOLLA *(Cylindropuntia bigelovii)*
CACTACEAE (cactus)

Flowers: pale greenish-white, to yellow, to purple.

Stem: segmented, jointed cactus with a central, upright stem and short, compacted branches; not spreading.

Tubercles: quadrangular in shape, about as long as wide.

Fruit: pear-shaped, yellow, typically with unfertile seeds.

Notes: white areoles with yellow glochids and horrific, sharply barbed spines that typically can be difficult and painful to remove. These spines, covering virtually the entire stem, have a pale-yellow, papery sheath.

There is a glistening sheen to the spines which is lacking in C. fulgida.

CHAINFRUIT CHOLLA (JUMPING CHOLLA)
(Cylindropuntia fulgida)
CACTACEAE (cactus)

Flowers: violet, but can be pink, magenta, or red.

Stem: areoles with short white or yellowish glochids; ovoid tubercles.

Spines: yellow or brownish, enclosed in a white, papery sheath; barbed tip.

Fruit: green, pear-shaped and spineless; produces sterile seeds.

Notes: a segmented, jointed cactus with an open look, long branches, and a trunk—giving it an arborescent appearance. Much of the fruit, occurring as part of a large, pendent cluster, is infertile.

CHRISTMAS CACTUS (*Cylindropuntia leptocaulis*)
CACTACEAE (cactus)

Flowers: yellow, green, or bronze; inconspicuous.

Stem: slender, bushy; segmented joints with a single down-turned spine per areole.

Tubercles: support small areoles with yellowish glochids.

Spines: lightly colored with a whitish-yellow to reddish-brown sheath.

Fruit: small, globose, numerous glochids but lacks spines.

Notes: short trunk and an overall shrubby appearance. Red fruit, persistence through the winter, is responsible for its picturesque common name.
Found in southern Arizona, New Mexico, Texas, and into Oklahoma.

STAGHORN CHOLLA (*Cylindropuntia versicolor*)
CACTACEAE (cactus)

Flower: variable color: yellow, greenish, reddish, or brown.

Stem: tall, tree-like cactus with a spreading, open growth form. Possesses a stout, gray trunk.

Tubercles: elongated; dark green to reddish-brown, but occasionally gray or yellow.

Areoles: reddish glochids.

Spines: gray-red brown, barbed and sheathed.
Fruit: *spineless*, smooth and never bright yellow; rather, green with tinges of purple. Oval to pear-shaped, can persist for more than one season.

ENGELMANN HEDGEHOG (STRAWBERRY CACTUS)
(*Echinocereus engelmannii*)
CACTACEAE (cactus)

Flowers: magenta; cup shaped, green stigmas embedded in a sea of yellow stamens.
Spines: elongated, 2-6 central spines and 6-14 radial spines.
Fruit: edible, green, spiny fruit that turns red upon ripening.
Notes: cylindrical clumped cactus with about a dozen ribs; grows as a community that encompasses dozens of members.
Alternate common name reflects the tasty nature of its fruit.

COMPASS BARREL (CALIFORNIA BARREL CACTUS)

(*Ferocactus cylindraceus*)
CACTACEAE (cactus)

Flowers: light yellow, forms a ring around the apex of the stem.
Spines: 4-7 white, yellow, red, or brown; central, hooked spines that often have a reddish tint. Largest members are curved downward or backward,
Fruit: spineless, yellow.
Notes: this barrel forms a long, cylindrical cactus at maturity; bighorn sheep, adroit at dealing with the massive spines, readily consume the armored barrel. Favors steep, rocky slopes. Part of the spring flora.

Arguably, the most difficult common name situation exists for the barrel cacti. Ferocactus cylindraceus and F. wislizenii are each known by a dozen differ common names. Both are often referred to as a compass barrel.

The highly succulent tissues of the decaying stem of a compass barrel are degraded rapidly—deflating it like a punctured balloon

The necessity of developing a root system that spreads laterally, but not deep makes the compass barrel susceptible to extreme leaning.

In addition, tissues on one side can grow more rapidly than on the other side. It has been suggested that such differential growth accounts for its tendency to recline toward the southwest.

An unusual sight is that of a saguaro and a compass barrel growing in such close proximity (*right*). This succulent cactus made a suitable meal for a desert inhabitant; imagine the adaptations required to make this a suitable foodstuff (*left*).

FISHHOOK BARREL CACTUS (*Ferocactus wislizenii*)
CACTACEAE (cactus)

Flowers: brilliant orange-yellow through red, forms a ring around the head of the barrel.

Stem: fat, barrel-shaped, solitary cactus; highly fluted with about 2 dozen ribs.

Areoles: elliptical, slightly depressed with fine brownish pubescence; widely dispersed.

Spines: 4 central spines: white to red; one is thicker than the remaining members, flattened and curved at its apex. Lateral spines are few in number.

Fruit: lemon yellow, spineless; about 2" long and edible.

Notes: typically 2-4 ft. but the barrel can reach over 8 ft. Cactus-specialist bees actively pollinate the flowers[1]. Birds, squirrels, deer, and javalina favor the fruit which can persist for more than one season. Commonly seen to lean toward the southwest. Flowers make their appearance in mid-June to August.

The top of the stem supports an abundance of distinctively colored spines. This conglomeration of overlapping spineage provides shade for vital tissues beneath them. These tissues, forming the apical meristem, are responsible for the growth in height of this columnar cactus. It can tower easily above a person.

In a technical study conducted with a comparable type of cactus, the apical spineage of plants growing at 30°N in Sonora was about 1/2 again as numerous as cohorts found at 35° N.

---

[1] *Diadasia rinconis* is a highly effective pollinator of both species of *Ferocactus*.

These comparative illustrations reveal the spinal structure of *Ferocactus cylindraceus* (*left*) and *Ferocactus wislizenii* (*right*). While admittedly they are very similar, *F. wislizenii* has one primary spine that is noticeably larger than the remainder as compared to *F. cylindraceus.*

GRAHAM PINCUSHION CACTUS (*Mammillaria grahamii*)
CACTACEAE (cactus)

Flowers: bright pink with white margins; borne just below the stem tips.

Stem: single or clustered, cylindrical, grows to about 6".

Spines: covered with a host of dense, white, radial spines. A far smaller number of central spines (1-3)—a single member is dark and hooked.

Areoles: located on nipple-like tubercles that are spirally arranged.

Fruit: bright red.

Notes: dormant flower buds awaken with summer monsoon rain; additional rains mediate episodic flower production.

Botanical note: flowers are not derived from the areoles but from a region at the confluence of 2 tubercles.

BEAVERTAIL PRICKLY PEAR (*Opuntia basilaris*)
CACTACEAE (cactus)

Somewhat smaller than the Engelmann prickly pear, it has bluish-green to bluish-gray pads and generally lacks spines. However, this low-growing cactus is protected by a formidable array of glochids and can be covered with a fine, velvety pubescence. There are numerous, closely spaced areoles each supporting a small tuft of glochids.

The magenta flowers yield tan and spineless fruit. The flower buds exude nectar that is sought after by ants. In turn, the ants protect the pads from assault by destructive feeders.

PANCAKE PRICKLY PEAR (*Opuntia chlorotica*)
CACTACEAE (cactus)

This is an upright prickly pear that can reach 7 ft and produces flat pads with densely packed, yellow, and translucent spines. It is shrubby or tree-like with a stout truck. The areoles support yellow glochids and 1-5 golden yellow, downward-pointing spines (on occasion, can be spineless).

Flowers appear in late spring and are light yellow with a red internal splash; they give rise to red-purple fruit that becomes gray with age. While the fruit is spineless, it supports glochids.

Another widespread cactus that can be found in California, Arizona, Nevada, Utah, New Mexico, Baja California and Sonora.

ENGELMANN PRICKLY PEAR (*Opuntia engelmannii*)
CACTACEAE (cactus)

Flowers: usually yellow to orange, but occasionally light red; solitary. Open flower dies after one day.

Pads: support widely dispersed areoles (1-4) and yellow or brownish glochids.

Fruit: edible, red to purple, pear-shaped, borne along the edges of the pads.

Notes: Javalinas, jackrabbits, and packrats are able to digest the oxalic acid (a toxic compound) stored in the pad. Native Americans rolled the pads along the ground to remove the glochids, and then eat them raw or sun-dried. Current human consumption of the pads, as nopalitos (diced nopales), is dependent on cultivation of

Opuntia ficus-indica, although the pads of almost all *Opuntia* species are edible.

The heated pad was applied to the breast of a new mother to stimulate lactation.

Summer monsoons in 2007 produced little rain. This scarcity, coupled with a record-breaking number of daily temperature highs of at least 110°, resulted in severe water stress for desert plants.

This condition is reflected in the highly shriveled state of the *Opuntia* pads, and demonstrates its capacity to store significant amounts of vital water.

SANTA-RITA PRICKLY PEAR (*Opuntia santa-rita*)
CACTACEAE (cactus)

Visually similar to Engelmann prickly pear except for the striking reddish-purple to violet color of the pads. The flowers are lemon yellow; generally, 1 or 2 long and brown primary spines per areole; and numerous glochids.

There is an upright, trunk-like growth pattern to this cactus.

NIGHTBLOOMING CEREUS (*Peniocereus greggii*)
CACTACEAE (cactus)

Flowers: white; corolla: funnel-shaped, about 3" diameter, dozens of stamens and numerous delicate and lanceolate petals.

Stem: gray-green stem with 4-6 ribs.

Fruit: red, succulent and elliptical; reflexed spines. Edible.

Note: night-blooming cactus that produces a stunning but short-lived flower. It opens at night and fades with the morning light.

Interesting fact: the population of this cactus blooms synchronously for only a handful of nights a year in early summer. The flowers bloom for 1 or 2 nights (occasionally longer); pollinators have little time to waste. This may account for its particularly fragrant blossom, which signals the onset of flower development.

Note: produces a stunning but short-lived flower. It opens at night and fades with the morning light.

Interesting fact: the population of this cactus blooms synchronously for only a handful of nights a year in early summer. The flowers bloom for 1 or 2 nights (occasionally longer); pollinators have little time to waste. This may account for its particularly fragrant blossom, which signals the onset of flower opening.

YUCCAS & OTHERS

Intrinsic variation, occasionally with a surprising departure from the expected, occurs in all plant communities.

Soaptree Yucca, *Yucca elata*

Young yucca inflorescence.

Yucca. Yuccas do not grow areoles or spines, and consequently form a group classified independently from the cacti; they are grouped within the Agavaceae, a plant family distinct from cacti. Yuccas grow fibrous, often thick, or fleshy leaves that are concentrated near the base of the stem. These plants produce conspicuous, creamy-white blossoms that are part of an elongated, erect inflorescence. Their flowers have six fleshy, petal-like structures. Some authorities call then *tepals* since the petals and sepals are indistinguishable.

Yuccas have evolved a fascinating relationship with certain desert moths—insects responsible for transporting pollen from one yucca flower to another.[1] When these plants are cultivated in the Old World, where yucca moths are absent, they do not produce seeds unless they are hand-pollinated.

Flowers of a given yucca plant produce a fragrance that is irresistible to a particular moth. This factor and others support a special accommodation between a yucca moth and the yucca it pollinates. In Arizona, *Tegeticula yuccasella* and *T. maculata* are the primary yucca pollinators. Yucca pollen is not distributed as individual pollen grains; instead, sticky materials are used to lump the pollen into a large mass known as a *pollinium*. A female yucca moth collects pollinia and then uses its prehensile appendage to produce a massive pollen mound that she transports faithfully to another yucca. This large pollen ball is inserted into a deep cavity positioned near the pistil. At the same time, the female moth oviposits her eggs into the ovary; these plant tissues provide nourishment for the emerging larvae. Most importantly, not all of the ovules are consumed by the voracious insects; sufficient numbers remain to provide seeds for the next generation of yuccas.

In this mutually advantageous interplay, the female moth gains sustenance from the flower and is assured of adequate food for her emerging brood. The yucca flower is also a rewarded participant. Its pollen is not carried just anywhere so that much of it is wasted; rather, it goes only to another fertilizable flower. This is the critical point: *pollen goes to a*

---

[1] Yucca moths of the genera: *Tegeticula* and *Parategeticula,* are all obligatory pollinators of yuccas.

compatible flower. Such restriction in the flowers that the yucca moth will visit subsequently enhances significantly the overall effectiveness of floral pollination. Development of such a close, specific relationship is one of the classical examples of *co-evolution*, organisms evolving together in response to mutual needs.

Yuccas are used by many desert animals. The soaptree yucca leaves have considerable nutritional value and are sought actively by many desert animals. Wood rats love this plant—they remove the leaves at their base and use this material both as a food source and for nest-building material.

Cattle, deer, pronghorn antelope, and other herbivores nibble on its leaves and relish the succulent, young flower stalks. Orioles and cactus wrens construct their nests within the dense leaf bundles. Yuccas provide perches for hunting shrikes and hawks.

Finally, the name soaptree yucca results from its production of plant chemicals called saponins. These materials can create a cleansing lather—much like soap.

Ocotillo. Ocotillos are unique and special plants. Their open growth form is created by numerous slender woody stems that project from the base of the plant; their massive bulk, spreading arms, and vivid red-flowered heads produce a visually striking desert dweller. They appear to be somewhat cactus- like because of

Flowers, foliage, and form: all contribute to the uniqueness of ocotillo.

their elongated spines reduced foliage, and overall appearance. However, ocotillo produces true leaves that remain on the flower stalk as long as water is plentiful. Drought induces leaf fall, the return of favorable moisture stimulates a new crop of leaves. The time required for this refoliation can be as short as two days. Ocotillo stems sprout roots easily and stems pushed into the ground can and do grow into a viable plant. Taking advantage of this property, desert people used the stems to build living fences and corrals (*left*).

Ocotillo flowers are tubular and bright red, features that favor pollination by hummingbirds. Another important pollinator appears to be carpenter bees who overcome the lack of large, probing mouthparts by moving over the petal and piercing the flower tube to secure the nectar. These flowers also are eaten by ants and antelope ground quirrels.

Ephedra. *Ephedra* are among the most unexpected of desert plants. Given the long, arid summers does not find trees such as pine, spruce, or fir because these are all conifers, an ancient lineage, that flourishes in colder places. They produce relatively inconspicuous reproductive structures that are not flowers. Gymnosperm seeds are borne *naked* and exposed in the interior of an *opened* cone (*left*). Flowering plants have seeds protected *inside* a fruit. What makes members of the *Ephedra* so fascinating is that they are conifers that not only grow in woodlands and grasslands at colder, higher elevations, but also at the lower elevations of the Sonoran Desert.

Ephedra leaves are reduced to tiny, dark scales at the joints

This open cone of eastern white pine, *Pinus strobus*, lacks its seeds; they would have rested exposed and naked within the depression of the cone scale

and photosynthesis occurs in the green stem. Certain *Ephedra* stems are rich in ephedrine and pseudoephedrine, pharmacologically active alkaloids, but the plant concentration varies. These plants must be consumed with great care; they possess potentially lethal stimulatory effects on the central nervous system and heart.

When combined with caffeine, the combination increases significantly the chance of adverse side effects. Fortunately, the *Ephedra* plants of the Sonoran Desert contain little of these substances; this scarcity is typically of New World taxa. There is a large commercial market for *Ephedra* preparations; they are sought after to increase energy, aid in dieting, and to enhance athletic performance.

Members of the *Ephedra* are difficult to distinguish; it is unnecessary for the reader to identify species. They are shrubby plants with jointed, grooved, and broom-like stems; reduced and scale-like opposite or whorled leaves (2 or 3 members emerging at the node); and dioecious, miniature cones. The staminate cones have 2-8 stamens supported by fused filaments.

The common name *"Mormon Tea"* has been used to name all locally occurring *Ephedra*. While most *Ephedra* look like modest shrubs, mature individuals can produce a significant amount of woody tissues.

BANANA YUCCA (*Yucca baccata*)
AGAVACEAE (agave)

Overview: heavy, stout plant with long, sharp foliage that can reach 6 ft.

Flowers: inside portion is creamy-white tinged with green at the base, reddish brown margin; corolla: campanulate. *Inflorescence*: a dense panicle.

Leaves: long and rigid, blue-green, and much heavier than those of *Y. elata*. Dead foliage remains on the plant, forming a dense mat at its base. Broad and coarse fibers borne freely on the margins. Sharp, terminal, spine-like tip.

Fruit: a green cylindrical capsule housing black seeds.

Handlens: Six stamens, white filaments; anthers curved at the tip. Pistil: tubular, pointed with ridges.

Notes: flower and seed production consume significant plant resources; perhaps, explaining why this plant does not set seed annually. A well used herbal remedy for treating arthritis.

The fruit of the agave is indehiscent (closed) and must first be eaten by packrats, rabbits and other animals to release the seeds. Can form densely clustered communities, particularly on open, disturbed sites.

Yucca baccata and *Y. schidigera* produce leaves that have loose fibers at their margin—*Y. elata* does not. The perianth of *Y. baccata* exceeds 2" while that of *Y. schidigera* is less than 2"

SOAPTREE YUCCA (*Yucca elata*)
AGAVACEAE (agave)

Overview: normally shrub sized; it can reach 20 ft. in height.

Flowers: ivory-white; corolla: cup-shaped, made from 6 ovate, petal-like structures.

Leaves: when young, the yellow-green, narrow leaves have margins that are entire, but they quickly split into slender, whitish strips that concentrate in the center of the plant. Simple, flat on the upper surface but curved beneath.

Highly fibrous leaves, that add great strength, coupled with its sharply pointed tip led to an alternate common name of Spanish bayonet.

Fruit: black, edible seeds fill an erect, oblong, 3-segmented capsule (2-3"). Capsules, from a prior year, often hang above the plant.

Handlens: six stamens and a hexagonal, 3-segmented ovary.

Notes. this plant thrives in open areas with full light.

MOJAVE YUCCA (*Yucca schidigera*)
AGAVACEAE   (agave)

Overview: a shrub with a simple or branched trunk that can attain small tree status.

Flowers: creamy white with a purplish tinge. *Inflorescence*: clustered as a panicle at the end of a small peduncle.

Leaves: linear, yellow-green, sharp spine (to 0.5") at the leaf apex; margins splinter to produce numerous coarse fibers. Copious, sword-like foliage project from many planes.

Fruit: edible and fleshy, oblong capsule that matures to a leathery texture.

Notes: component of the westward edge of the Sonoran Desert. Sole pollinator is the moth, *Tegeticula yuccasela*. As with *Y. baccata*, perhaps 3 years are required to build sufficient metabolic resources for flower production.

Excellent source of saponins (can reach 10% of its weight), plant compounds that are employed as simple soaps. Prevalent in the western portions of the Sonoran desert.

OCOTILLO *(Fouquieria splendens)*
FOUQUIERIACEAE

Flowers: bright crimson or brilliant red; corolla: elongated, tubular and 5-lobed. *Inflorescence:* deployed as a terminal panicle.

Leaves: ovate to spatulate, ephemeral—falling in response to drought or cold conditions.

Stems: multiple, cane-like, armored with thorns, project from a common basal region.

Fruit: dry, brown, 3-celled capsules house winged, wind-dispersed seeds

Handlens: 10 or more, exserted stamens; thickened filament base.

Notes: all other members of this group are found only in Mexico; *F. splenden* thrives in the northern most part of their range. An outstanding favorite of hummingbirds.

Point of interest: first-formed leaves provide the leaf stalks that develop into the spines. The remaining leaves arise from the base of these spines.

A closely related plant, native to Baja California and parts of Sonora, is the boojum tree, *Fouquieria columnaris*. Leafless most of the year, it never fails to hold the viewer in rapt attention and awe.

DESERT MISTLETOE (*Phoradendron californicum*)
VISCACEAE (mistletoe)

Flowers: dioecious, male and female plants bear white to reddish-pink, inconspicuous flowers.

Leaves: opposite, reduced to scale-like structures.

Fruit: white, globose berry that turns red as it ripens.

Notes: forms a large, clustered mass that typically hangs from a host tree branch. On occasion, it can be massive— relative to the size of the host plant. Desert mistletoe, is an accomplished parasite of many desert trees, such as ironwood and various acacias, mesquites, and palo verdes. When a viable seed is deposited on a suitable host, it can germinate and grow into host tissues, becoming a living part of the tree. Often, the infected plant cannot mount effective counter-measures; the mistletoe becomes permanently established— gaining sustenance by taking vital foodstuffs from the host plant.

One may think that the attacking mistletoe would be better served by being more conservative in its utilization of host resources, particularly since it has some food-making ability. Taking only what it needs, thereby insuring that the plant sustains the mistle-toe over the long haul, would seem a desirable mechanism for survival. Often this is not the case— mistletoe diverts resources to such an extent that the host dies. This is mutually assured destruction since the mistletoe also perishes. Have you ever seen live mistletoe on a dead host?

It may be that the mistletoe takes so dramatically from the host to insure a full measure of robustness to maximize its immediate reproductive output and success. Producing many red berries, as quickly as possible, enhances its *immediate* contribution to the gene pool.

FUNGI

Given the dry climate, it is not surprisingly that few free fungi are found within the Sonoran Desert. Often, a year passes without a single sighting. Even saprophytic fungi, which specialize on dead or dying organic matter, are not seen commonly.

An exception to this paucity is *Podaxis pistillaris,* a basidiomycete that is related to the more common puffball. It has been used to treat skin disease, sunburn, and inflammation. Although lacking in substantial caloric content, it produces a full spectrum of essential dietary components, and is a food source in certain cultures.

The picture depicts the reproductive stage of this organism. Its vegetative matter or mycelia can form a dense, underground network.

LICHEN

The rock surface is an excellent habitat for desert lichens. These symbiotic organisms, involve a fungus and an alga, have adapted to the harsh environment of exposed rock surfaces.

These organisms accelerate the processes of chemical and physical weathering of the rock which results ultimately in soil formation.

WHITE, WHITE-GREEN & GREEN

This section contains many with white flowers, but some are a mix of white-green, and finally green. Included in this group are many members with distinct and unusual floral structure and form.

Sacred Datura, *Datura wrightii*

ARIZONA CARLOWRIGHTIA (*Carlowrightia arizonica*)
ACANTHACEAE (acanthus)

Overview: slender, gray-green, and multi-branched perennial with fine, white pubescence. It can grow into a shrub-sized plant.

Flowers: white; corolla: 4 petals. Upper: yellow throat bearing purple to maroon streaks; middle: white, flat; lower: white with purple zone, keel-shaped. *Inflorescence*: a spike that can become a leafy panicle.

Leaves: linear to narrowly lanceolate, tiny, opposite, petiole. Prominent mid-vein.

Handlens: two 2-lobed stamens.

Fruit: capsule with 2 chambers, each housing a pair of seeds.

Notes: lovely flowers that are part of the summer flora; favors dry, rocky sites.

WOOLLY TIDESTROMIA (*Tidestromia lanuginosa*)
AMARANTHACEAE (amaranth)

Overview: highly branched, prostrate annual with an overall woolly appearance.

Flowers: yellowish-green to yellowish white; corolla: none; 5 tepals: 2 inner members are shorter than the outer 3. *Inflorescence:* emerge from the axils, subtended by leafy bracts and smaller, bractlets.

Leaves: ovate to circular, gray-green, primarily opposite, petiole to 1".

An interesting botanical oddity: only 1 of the 3 leaves at the node is a true leaf, the other 2 members are involucres (structures derived from leaves).

Stems: reddish with fine, white pubescence.

Fruit: single, red-brown seeded, indehiscent utricle.

Handlens: stellate pubescence on the leaves, 5 stamens and a 2-celled anther. Look for trichomes on the tepals.

Notes: favors sandy and gravelly slopes; summer-flowering amaranth.

HOARY BOWLESIA (*Bowlesia incana*)
APIACEAE (UMBELLIFERAE) (carrot)

Overview: delicate annual with slender, trailing stems. Tiny flowers positioned cryptically within conspicuous foliage.

Flowers: greenish-white to yellowish-green; corolla: 5-9 tiny petals. *Inflorescence*: less than a half dozen flowers in a typical umbel, on a short peduncle, formed from the leaf axils.

Calyx: 5 sepals, tiny, and sharply toothed.

Leaves: cordate to widely lanceolate, palmately lobed (5-7), often opposite, generally entire. Conspicuous, stellate pubescence on the leaves and stem. Slender petiole (0.75-3").

Handlens: 5 stamens.

Notes: favors subdued light; spring is the season for flower formation. Favors open areas and disturbed sites.

Named to recognize William Bowles, an 18th century Irish naturalist. It appears to be an introduced weed that reached our shores through European settlers a few hundred years ago.

SOUTHWESTERN WILD CARROT (RATTLESNAKE WEED)
(Daucus pusillus)
APIACEAE (UMBELLIFERAE) (carrot)

Overview: a sparsely branched annual that can reach 2 ft.

Flowers: white but matures to yellow-brown; corolla: 5 independent and clawed petals. *Inflorescence*: terminal umbels. Central umbel is not distinctively colored; smooth and leafless peduncle can reach 1.5 ft. Whorl of leaves surround the umbel.

Leaves: triangular to ovate, pinnately divided, entire, bristly and pubescent, clasps the stem; elongated petiole (2-6").

Involucre: whorled, located at the tip of the peduncle. Bracts pinnately divided into linear or lanceolate segments.

Handlens: 5 stamens.

Notes: favors disturbed sites and sandy slopes; juvenile, tender, shoots and root consumed by desert dwellers.

Rattlesnake weed, a reoccurring common name, brings to mind one of the few birds that is capable fully of holding its own against this venomous serpent—the roadrunner (*Geococcyx californianus*).

One authority described it as: "Because of its lightening quickness, the roadrunner is one of the few animals that prey upon rattlesnakes. Using its wings like a matador's cape, it snaps up a coiled rattlesnake by the tail, cracks it like a whip and repeatedly slams its head against the ground till dead." A little gruesome, but highly effective, especially when dealing with such a formidable reptile. \

SOUTHWESTERN PIPEVINE *(Aristolochia watsonii)*
ARISTOLOCHIACEAE (aristolochia)

Overview: a creeping or twinning perennial with a pipe-like flower that once seen is never forgotten.

Flowers: green to dark purple-brown; corolla: irregular and tubular. *Inferior ovary*.

The peduncle is protected by bract-like structures

Calyx: tubular and curved, 3 petal-like segments, expands around the style while constricted at its throat.

Leaves: markedly sagittate.

Fruit: dehiscent, multi-valved capsule.

Handlens: 3- to 6-celled ovary; 6 stamens are fused to the style.

Notes: distinct odor to the foliage; flower produces a musky, fetid odor. Sought for its beneficial effects during parturition—reportedly by accelerating fetal emer-gence. Used medically as a treatment for snake bites.

Aristolochia watsonii is pollinated by ceratopogonid flies—small, blood sucking flies of mammals. Its flower produces volatile substances that create a musky, foul odor which these flies relish. The design of the calyx enables the plant to entrap attracted visitors overnight when they are covered with pollen. With their escape in the morning, these released prisoners are ready to pollinate responsive flowers.

This southwestern pipevine produces harmful phytochemicals; pipevine swallowtails *(Battus philenor)* seek out this plant in order to sequester these toxins for their own chemical defense. An identical survival strategy has been adopted by the monarch butterfly who stored toxic cardenolides obtained from various members of the milkweed family.

This survival strategy benefits from the fact that the hording insect does not have to expand energy and resources in the manufacture of the poisons that renders it unpalatable or otherwise unsuitable to potential predators. Instead, it simply steals them from the plant. There are other insects that mimic this swallowtail; they derive its protective benefit without any resource investment.

ANTELOPE HORNS (SPIDER MILKWEED)
(*Asclepias asperula*)
ASCLEPIADACEAE (milkweed)

Overview: herbaceous perennial with several dominate and erect stems.

Flowers: greenish-white; corolla: 5 encircling and joined lobes and 5 purplish and *united* hoods. *Inflorescence*: solitary and terminal, multiple-flowered umbel.

Leaves: lanceolate, narrow to a short petiole, scabrous, and continuous up the stem.

Fruit: wrinkled follicle. Silk-bearing seeds arranged spirally around a central core—looks somewhat like an unopened pine cone.

Notes: derives its common name from the shape of the paired follicles (p.67). Its Latin name was created by Linnaeus to honor Asclepius, the highly acclaimed Greek physician. Found in sunny, rocky habitats. Not a commonly occurring milkweed.

The paired follicles of this milkweed are reminiscent of the horns of an antelope.

The monarch butterfly *(Danaus plexippus)* is a specialist feeder on various members of the *Asclepias*. It feeds on antelope horns foliage and sequesters a toxic phytochemical (cardenolide) which protests it from a variety of predators that are repelled by this compound. This butterfly does not invest any resources in cardenolide production since it derives all that it needs from its food source.

RUSH MILKWEED (AJAMETE) (*Asclepias subulata*)
ASCLEPIADACEAE (milkweed)

Overview: many, essentially leafless stems emerging from a common basal region. Open, reed- or rush-like appearance. Complexed floral structure.

Flowers: pale greenish to yellowish; corolla: 5 reflexed petals and 5 hoods with horns. *Inflorescence*: complex grouping of 5-15 members (panicle) borne on thin elongated pedicles supported by a similarly sized peduncle.

Leaves: spartan in number, linear, ephemeral, sessile, and opposite.

Stems: numerous, erect, gray-green, smooth, extrudes a milky sap.

Fruit: large, green follicle; seeds with silky, white hairs.

Notes: a food favorite of a milkweed bug (*Oncopeltus sanguineolentus),* the tarantula hawk wasp (*Pepsis formosa),* and an occasional monarch butterfly (*Danaus plexippus).*

Its sap is an excellent source of latex (rubber). Greatly favored in desert landscaping due to its marked drought resistance. Its floral hood is actually a nectar sack; the bundled pollen is located between the hoods.

Of the many interactions between desert plants and animals, few are as vital to the plant as their association with insects. These invertebrates have become the premier means for dispersing pollen. Insects not only gather pollen efficiently, but generally, they limit their foraging to specific plants or groups of plants—thereby increasing successful pollination. In turn, plants provide sugary materials and other rewards. This milkweed bug was caught inserting its proboscis into the emerging flower of *A. subulata*. Hordes of *O. sanguineolentus* swarmed over this host plant continuously during the summer. The gravid females lay their eggs on the stem, and the plant sustains the newly emerged larvae. This early interaction between insect and plant (*imprinting*) forages a perennial association between these organisms.

Another insect that utilizes this plant is the tarantula hawk wasp. This animal seeks out and disables, using her potent venom, the far more massive tarantula spider. She can emerge victorious because the spider has to bite the wasp to prevail, it lacks potent venom. The stinger of this wasp can reach 1/3".

The vanquished prey is dragged into a suitable burrow where it is infected with a single egg.

The paralyzed arachnid provides food for the newly emerged wasp larva in a protracted feeding ritual that is quite grotesque. Interactions between insects and other organisms truly display the complexity and intricacy of evolution to its fullest.

A long-lived arachnid, females can attain 20 years, the tarantula spider (*Aphonopelma chalcodes*), maintains the same burrow for years. While appearing formidable, it is generally a gentle and shy creature; however, it can be provoked to bite.

When the young emerge, they appear physically to be female; but true sexual differentiation has not yet occurred.

SPEARLEAF (*Matelea parvifolia*)
ASCLEPIADACEAE (milkweed)

Overview: slender, twinning, and perennial vine and sub-shrub.

Flowers: greenish (purplish cast), tiny (4-5 mm); corolla: 5 stellate elements. *Inflorescence*: 1 or 2 flowers, on a short pedicel, are borne in the leaf axils.

Calyx: 5 glandular sepals (2-3 mm).

Leaves: cordate to sagittate; small, opposite, and bearing a petiole (3/8").

Fruit: grooved and tapering follicle.

Handlens: filaments fused into a tube.

Notes: rocky, open areas.

AMBROSIA BURSAGE (CANYON RAGWEED)
(*Ambrosia ambrosioides*)
ASTERACEAE (sunflower)

Overview: a sprawling perennial subshrub.

Flowers: green; disk flowers only. Basal flowers are pistillate and are borne in small grouping on a spike-like raceme that emerges from the node. Upper portions of the stem yield only staminate flowers.

Staminate: supported by a 7- to 12-lobed involucre.

Pistillate: inflorescence bears 3-5 flowers.

Leaves: triangular, coarsely serrated, and covered in a fine pubescence.

Twig: reddish brown with white pubescence, brittle.

Fruit: a large, conspicuous bur with slender, hooked spines protects a single-seeded achene.

Notes; abundant in washes and disturbed sites. An early-spring flowering plant.

Burs facilitate attachment to passing animals who disperse the ripen seeds. The wind-dispersed pollen is another major source of allergic materials.

Interesting point: the bur is formed by the fusion of three flowers.

TRIANGLE BURSAGE (TRIANGLE LEAF BURSAGE)
(*Ambrosia deltoidea*)
ASTERACEAE (sunflower)

Overview: a subshrub perennial, generally 1-3 ft. in stature, which can reach shrub size.

Flowers: green; *inflorescence*: borne on panicles or racemes found at the apex of the branch.

Staminate: large, packed with numerous stamens which develop at the upper portions of the plant.

Pistillate: located at the base of the spike, much smaller, multiple pistils.

Calyx: fused into a cup-like structure, with triangular lobes, that encloses 20 or more flowers.

Leaves: triangular, coarsely serrated to nearly lobed; far more whitish pubescence on the underside of the blade than above.

Stem: resinous and sticky, white when young.

Fruit: round and glandular bur (1/2") with numerous slender spines.

Handlens: short filaments support anthers that product huge quantities of pollen; yellow stamens.

Notes: under severe moisture stress, the leaves are truly minute, but they attain a far greater size when rainfall is plentiful; this difference in leaf size can be ten-fold or more.

Highly successful competitor that has become truly widespread throughout the Upland Subdivision of the Sonoran Desert; particularly partial to dry (xeric) sites. Pollen is wind dispersed—thereby adding to the suffering from its allergenic pollen.

The dense growth habit of this small shrub facilitates the accumulation of wind-blown debris; it also retains its own fallen foliage. The resulting mass creates a physical barrier against herbivory that protects a variety of young seedlings developing beneath its canopy.

WHITE BURSAGE (*Ambrosia dumosa*)
ASTERACEAE (sunflower)

Overview: erect, highly branched perennial subshrub with a stem supporting soft white pubescence.

Flower: yellowish-green; *inflorescence*: clustered, terminal spike.

Staminate: many members supported by a 5- to 8-lobed involucre.

Pistillate: inflorescence bears 2 flowers which lack a calyx.

Leaves: pinnately divided (1-3 units), sessile, entire, borne throughout the stem. Upper surface: deep green; lower: gray-green, pubescent.

Fruit: burs with many flattened and sharp spines.

Notes: favors washes, roadsides and open areas; another allergenic ragweed.

Can form extensive communities that flower in the summer months; prevalent in the Lower Colorado River Valley.

CUDWEED SAGEWORT (*Artemisia ludoviciana*)
ASTERACEAE (sunflower)

Overview: slender, multiple-branched, and aromatic herb, with silvery-green foliage that reaches 3 ft.

Flowers: white with pale yellow stamens; corolla: tubular. *Inflorescence*: borne as a compact panicle. Head is campanulate and can be nodding.

Ray: 5-12; white and woolly, pistillate.

Disk: 6-2; perfect.

Leaves: linear to lanceolate to elliptical (highly variable); lobed to pinnately divided, entire to dentate. Covered with a dense, white pubescence. Lower: lobed or coarsely tooth; upper: entire. Sessile or minute petiole.

Involucre: oblong to ovate, conspicuously pubescent with overlapping bracts in 2 series (7-13); dry and imbricate.

Stem: dense, whitish, pubescent.

Fruit: smooth achene without a pappus.

Notes: flowers late summer to early fall; over winters via a rhizome. Consumed by many desert dwellers.

DESERT PINCUSHION *(Chaenactis stevioides)*
ASTERACEAE (sunflower)

Overview: pubescent annual with open branching and a pincushion-like flower head (1").

Flowers: white; corolla: tiny (3/16"); *Inflorescence*: positioned at the tip of a short and slender peduncle.

Ray: none.

Disk: white to pinkish.

Calyx: single series of blunt-tipped, equally sized, and pubescent sepals.

Leaves: pinnately lobed (lobes are further segmented), pubescent, tips can be curved.

Involucre: 6-9 uniformly sized, narrowly tipped, and heavily pubescent bracts; covers about three-quarters of the base of the flower.

Fruit: achene with a pappus of 4-5 units.

Notes: a small, white, attractive sunflower that is part of the panoply of early spring plants. The yellow, central core is created by immature disk flowers. The outer, matured flowers resemble ray flowers.

Named for P.J. Esteve, a 16th century Spanish botanist.

Used as a mosquito repellant; a weak infusion was given for stomachache and menstrual disorders.

This *Echinopsis* hybrid produces massive and intricately structured flowers. Their production represents a significant investment in metabolic resources. One would think, therefore, that the flower would remain open for an extended period to maximize opportunities for pollination. In fact, the flower is remarkably short-lived, fading and closing within a single day. This intriguing finding is but one of the many provocative fascinations of desert life.

WOOLLY DAISY (WHITE EASTERBONNETS)
(*Eriophyllum lanosum*) (*Antheropeas lanosum*)
ASTERACEAE (sunflower)

Overview: multiple-branched annual with a slender, woolly stem.

Flowers: white with occasional red venation or tint. *Inflorescence*: solitary at the tip of a peduncle that can reach 2".

Ray: 8-10; ligules to 1/4"; tip can be notched.

Disk: yellow, small and numerous.

Calyx: a green cup formed from 5 sepals.

Leaves: linear, entire, or lobed at the apex, fine pubescence.

Involucre: single whorl, lanceolate, and campanulate.

Fruit: 4-5 angled achene.

Notes: a cryptic plant that is often missed due to its diminutive size; member of the spring flora that is found frequently on gravelly soils.

WHITEDAISY TIDYTIPS (WHITE LAYIA) (*Layia glandulosa*)
ASTERACEAE (sunflower)

Overview: erect, glandular annual with a spicy odor.

Flowers: *Inflorescence*: borne at the end of the flower stalk (3"). Series of bracts separate the ray and disk flowers.

Ray: 3-14; pure white to yellow, 3-lobed ligules that can reach 1" and fade to a rose-purple. Pistillate, fertile, and lack a pappus,

Disk: dozens of yellow flowers compacted in the center of the head. Perfect, with an achene having a pappus that supports 10, white bristles.

Leaves: thin, finely pubescent, and sessile. Upper: dentated and pinnately divided; lower: entire, variously lobed.

Involucre: base of the bracts connected by cobweb-like pubescence, glandular, and uniform.

Notes: honors George T. Lay, a botanist on the ship Blossom that left England in 1825 under Captain Beechey.

PLAINS BLACKFOOT DAISY (*Melampodium leucanthum*)
ASTERACEAE (sunflower)

Overview: perennial herb to subshrub.

Flowers: many flowers emanate from a common area at the base of the plant, but each unit is solitary on a leafless, elongated, and light-brown peduncle (to 4").

Ray: 8-10; white with conspicuous purple venation (underside), and a 2-lobed edge.

Disk: far more numerous; yellow, concentrated in a *small, c*entral space.

Calyx: broad, pubescent sepals having a prominent mid-vein.

Leaves: narrow to oblong, dark green, opposite, prominent midvein, entire.

Involucre: outer whorl of 5 fused, pubescent, and ovate phyllaries.

Fruit: club-shaped achene that lacks a pappus.

Notes: highly drought-resistant, produces many flowers even in unusually dry years. Common name may result from dark zone, at the base of the disk flowers, due to old stigmas and achenes; others say it is derived from the dark, foot-shaped bracts of the ray flowers. Commonly cultivated in the Tucson area.

DAISY DESERTSTAR (*Monoptilon bellidiforme*)
ASTERACEAE (sunflower)

Overview: small annual hav-ing a multi-branched stem, elongated (white) pubescence, and robust flower production.

Flowers:

Ray:12-20; white to purplish-blue, ligule: narrow and tiny with an entire to 3-lobed tip.

Disk: 26-45; yellow.

Calyx: multiple sepals.

Leaves: oblanceolate, entire, petiole.

Involucre: 10-15 in a single, equal series; linear and densely pubescent.

Pappus: single, feathery bristle.

Notes: the tiny grouping of disk flowers is seemingly lost in the center of the flower head. Flowers are displayed throughout the spring.

DESERT ROCKDAISY (*Perityle emoryi*)
ASTERACEAE (sunflower)

Overview: stout, glandular, and sparsely pubescent annual with brittle branches.

Flowers: *Inflorescence*: solitary.

Ray: 10-13; white, bi-lobed, small ligules (0.25") bearing stiff hairs.

Disk: numerous; yellow, *fills much of the flower head.*

Leaves: triangular to ovate (to 4"), petiole, markedly serrate to pinnately lobed, pubescent, and brittle.

Involucre: 2 whorls, lanceolate, glandular, pubescent, ciliated, and campanulate.

Stem: deep green, notched.

Fruit: pappus composed of many, small scales with a single awn.

Notes: favors crevices and rocky habitats; late winter to early spring flowers. Can form an extensive local grouping. Honors Major William H. Emory, Director of the Mexican Boundary Survey.

DESERT CHICORY (*Rafinesquia neomexicana*)
WHITE TACKSTEM (*Calycoseris wrightii*)
ASTERACEAE (sunflower)

Overview: annual with a single to several highly elongated and hollow stems.

Flowers: *Inflorescence*: solitary or clustered in a panicle.

Ray: 8-12; lustrous white to cream with multiple, *purple streaking on the underside of the ligule.* Ligule: straight edged, 5-lobed.

Disk: lacking.

Leaves: oblong to elliptical, sessile; basal: pinnately divided; upper: clasp the stem.

Involucre: outer: sharply pointed, short; inner: longer.

Stem: hollow.

Fruit: achene that tapers to a point; pappus with feathery, brownish bristles.

Notes: desert chicory is another member of the early spring flora. The name recognizes Constantine S. Rafinesque, a scholarly recluse who traveled throughout California in the early 19th century.

Desert chicory is very similar in its appearance to white tackstem, *Calycoseris wrightii*; however, the desert chicory flower stalk lacks tiny, tack-shaped glands that cover the flower stalk of white tackstem.

COCKELBUR (*Xanthium strumarium*)
ASTERACEAE (sunflower)

Overview: large, woody annual with stout and pubescent stems that grows to 2 ft.
Flowers: white to green; *inflorescence:* borne as terminal or axillary racemes.
   Staminate: small, multiple members group as a cluster at the apex. Located below the pistillate flowers.
   Pistillate: form in the node; the involucre of the pistillate flower gives rise to the bur that protects the 2 florets (no corolla), each with pistils that extended through the beak.
   Leaves: cordate to triangular, 3-lobed, coarsely serrated, glandular, and elongated petiole.
   Involucre: 1-3 series of independent bracts.
   Fruit: each barrel-shaped, indurate bur (0.5-1.0") contains 2 seeds that are covered with many stout spines and terminal hooks.
   Handlens: filaments are fused into a tube.
   Notes: favors disturbed sites; a single grouping can contain dozens of plants. Summer-flowering sunflower.
   Toxic to livestock and native dwellers causing rapid loss in blood sugar (hypoglycemia) and hepatic damage.

DESERT ZINNIA (WHITE ZINNIA) (*Zinnia acerosa)*
ASTERACEAE (sunflower)

Overview: perennial subshrub with slender, woolly pubescent stems to grow to about a foot.

Flowers: flower head (1") at stem tips; petals appear to curve downward.

  Rays: 3-6; white, *petal-like.*

  Disk: yellow, much smaller.

Involucre: bracts elliptical and over-lapping with blunt edges.

Leaves: linear, grayish-green, opposite, and ending in a sharp point.

Notes: a spring-flowering sunflower, but it responses well to summer monsoons with an additional burst of flowering.

NARROWLEAF CRYPTANTHA (*Cryptantha angustifolia*)
ARIZONA POPCORNFLOWER (*Plagiobothrys arizonicus*)
BORAGINACEAE (borage)

Overview: annual with dense, slender, and bristly hairs that cover a diffusely branched plant.

Flowers: white with a yellow-colored central cavity; corolla: petals are primarily independent, but fused at their base. Covered with prickly pubescence.

Inflorescence: cyme (often scorpioid) borne solitary at the apex; new flowers emerge as the head uncurls.

Stamens and pistils are cryptically hidden inside the central cavity.

Calyx: yellowish-green, spreading, and bristly.

Leaves: linear to oblong (3/8-11/4"), prominent midvein, bristle-like pustules at the base of the leaf hairs.

Involucre: tiny (1/16"), spreading and bristly.

Fruit: 4 nutlets.

Handlens: anthers: yellow, huge in comparison to the flower as a whole, fused to the corolla wall.

Notes: local *Cryptantha* are very difficult to tell apart without having access to the fruit—one must rely upon intricate variations in the nutlets.

Another abundant plant of the early spring assemblage is the Arizona popcorn flower, *Plagiobothrys arizonicus*, which has much larger leaves than *Cryptantha*.

Handling this plant can leave a red stain on your hands.

EUROPEAN HELIOTROPE (*Heliotropium europaeum*)
BORAGINACEAE (borage)

Overview: annual herb with a finely pubescent stem that can exceed 12".

Flowers: white; corolla: 5 lobes fused basally and about as long as the tube; *Inflorescence*: branched scorpioid cymes without bracts.

Leaves: ovate to elliptical, prominent venation and an elongated petiole.

Fruit: 4 nutlets.

Handlens: small style and conical stigma.

Notes: flowers in the summer months, introduced from Europe. This may be the earliest report of this taxon from Arizona.

The common name is derived from the Greek word *helios* which refers to the sun and *tropaios* from turning back. This is one of a group of plants that track the movement of the sun across the heavens as a means of obtaining additional warmth.

ARCHNUT COMBBUR (*Pectocarya recurvata*)
BORAGINACEAE (borage)

Overview: slender-stemmed and spreading annual with slender leaves and inconspicuous flowers.

Flowers: white; corolla: 5 petals but so tiny as to need magnification to be seen in detail.

Calyx: 5 sepals.

Leaves: linear, narrow, elongated; covered with stiff pubescence.

Nutlet: similar-appearing nutlets, occurring in 2 pairs, are sharply curved downward, margins highly indented with elongated teeth. Each tooth terminates with a sharply hooked hair that is as large as or larger than the tooth.

HAIRYLEAF COMBBUR (*Pectocarya heterocarpa*)
Nutlet: cauline nutlets: 2 nutlets with pronounced teeth that terminate in hooked hairs, the final pair have indistinct margins but bear a tuft of hooked hairs; basal nutlets: 4 nutlets with indistinct margins, reflexed.

BROADNUT COMBBUR (*Pectocarya platycarpa*)
Nutlet: either in 2s or 4s but not paired, similar in appearance to *P recurvata* but the nutlets are flat or only slightly recurved. Teeth on the margin as wide as long, united basally.

This is a very difficult genus of plants to differentiate without having a handlens to view the tiny flowers and fruit. Once again, the fruit, a nutlet, is critical in differentiation at the species level.

Pectocarya are amongst the earliest annuals to usher in the flowering season, capable of covering large areas and creating a virtual carpet of tiny, white specks—as drops of paint from a brush. In spite of the similarity of these plants, they do not readily hybridize. This results from their *cleistogamous* flowers; flowers that do not open for fertilization, and thus are not accessible for cross-pollination.

CALIFORNIA SHIELDPOD (SPECTACLEPOD)
(*Dithyrea californica*)
BRASSICACEAE (mustard)

Overview: multiple-stemmed annual with a basal, leafy rosette and gentle, grayish pubescence.

Flowers: white with a lavender tinge to lavender; corolla: 4, clawed petals that are fused basally; have a cross-like form.

Calyx: covers the fused portion of the corolla.

Leaves: lower: oblanceolate to obo-vate, serrated, bearing a petiole; cauline: ovate to oblong, sessile.

Fruit: paired silique notched at both ends; 2 seeds in each cell.

Notes: derives one of its common names from the resemblance of the paired siliques to spectacles. Favors washes and other sandy sites.

Well-developed fruit form quickly, occurring while there are emerging flowers.

PEPPER GRASS (VIRGINIA PEPPERWEED)
(*Lepidium virginicum*)
BRASSICACEAE (mustard)

Overview: annual to biennial with a single stem that is branched along its upper portion.

Flowers: white; corolla: 4 tiny (<2 mm) and clawed petals. *Inflorescence*: a raceme with pedicels that are slender, tiny, and 4-sided.

Calyx: 4 sepals with light margins.

Leaves: basal: obovate, pinnately lobed to divided, lyrate; cauline: reduced and entire.

Fruit: green silicle (1/8" diameter) that is slightly notched at its apex.

Handlens: 2-4 stamens with white filaments that support yellow anthers; inconspicuous style.

Notes: silicles form at the base of the flower head while new flowers are forming at its apex. Edible and desired for its peppery taste. Early spring flowering that favors disturbed sites.

LACEPOD MUSTARD (*Thysanocarpus curvipes*)
BRASSICACEAE (mustard)

Overview: erect herb with widely spaced branches and highly elongated racemes that are packed with fruit.

Flowers: white with purple splash; corolla: 4 petals. *Inflorescence*: elongated and greenish raceme. Exserted stamens.

Calyx: 4 sepals that are purplish with white margins; equal in length to the corolla.

Leaves: lower cauline: dentate to somewhat lobed, can have a petiole; middle to upper cauline: sessile, entire to dentate, clasping. Basal leaves form a rosette.

Stem: thin, erect, with few branches.

Fruit: flattened and translucent silicle (1/8") on a pedicel that is bent backward; margin is generally perforated.

Handlens: thin, white filament with purple anthers.

Notes: the unusual form of the fruit makes this a visually interesting plant. The peduncle can be a foot long and support dozens of silicles that seem huge, when compared to the tiny flowers which make their appearance in the spring.

CLAMMYWEED (*Polanisia dodecandra*)
CAPPARACEAE (caper)

Overview: erect, highly pubescent, annual herb with a strong, peppery odor. It is glandular and viscid—creating a plant that is truly clammy to the touch.

Flowers: white and purple; corolla: 4 petals, notched lobe, highly exserted. *Inflorescence*: about 2 dozen flowers borne in a raceme. Unequally sized stamens (10-20) are a prominent part of the flower head.

Leaves: palmately compound (3 units), lanceolate, petiole (to 1"). Glandular and pubescent margins.

Stem: glandular with a lacy pubescence.

Fruit: capsule (1-2") with many dark seeds.

Notes: has the distinction of being one of a number of plants originally described by Carl von Linne (Linnaeus), the father of modern plant taxonomy.

Found typically in open areas, along washes and other sandy soils; summer flowering plant.

ONYX FLOWER (COOPER FROSTMAT)
(*Achyronychia cooperi*)
CARYOPHYLLACEAE (pink)

Overview: prostrate annual with many stems radiating from a common point.

Flowers: white; corolla: none. *Inflorescence*: clustered (20-60) cymes that emerge from the axils.

Calyx: 5 oval sepals with a green base, and a whitish upper zone.

Leaves: spatulate, brilliantly green; stipules at the axil.

Fruit: utricle.

Handlens: 10-15 stamens, many are infertile and positioned conspicuously *above* the ovary.

Notes: most abundant in sandy washes. Flowers, produced in the spring, are densely bunched and tiny. It can form a mat which appears to be covered with ice crystals.

Named for Dr. J.G. Cooper, a geologist for the Geological Survey of California who collected plants during his travels.

DESERT SANDWORT (*Minuartia douglasii*)
CARYOPHYLLACEAE (pink)

Overview: slender-branched annual with glandular and pubescent stems.
Flowers: white; corolla: 5 obovate petals that are as long as or longer than the sepals.
Calyx: 5 sepals with rough margins.
Leaves: linear, sessile, lack stipules.
Fruit: capsule that split longitudinally along several planes
Handlens: 10 stamen and 3 pistils.
Notes: favors sandy and rocky soils. Displays its flowers in the spring; flowers often droop, especially if the sky is cloudy.

RUSSIAN THISTLE (TUMBLEWEED)
(*Salsola tragus*) (*S. kali*)
CHENOPODIACEAE (goosefoot)

Overview: open, multi-branched annual that dries to a hard and prickly plant.

Flowers: whitish to greenish to pinkish; no petals. Bracts project from the base of the flower. *Inflorescence*: borne solitary in the leaf axils.

Calyx: tiny, 5 sepals, papery, persistent, bearing 2 spike-like bracts.

Leaves: linear (tiny), bract-like; indurate, terminal spine.

Stem: robust, inter-twining branches produce an overall spherical appearance— often with a reddish coloration.

Involucre: spiny.

Fruit: protected by enlarged sepals, each with a fan-shaped, strongly veined wing.

Handlens: 5 stamens and a single pistil with 2 styles.

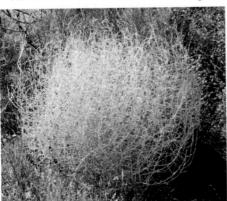

Notes: with up to a million seeds per plant, this is truly a prolific reproducer. Native to Eurasia; currently found in all of the contiguous states except Florida.

Interesting fact: a Hopi Indian name for this plant translates as white man's plant

The aged and dry aboveground portions of the stem break at the soil surface, creating the tumbling tumbleweed of Western lore.

PYGMY WEED (*Crassula connata*)
CRASSULACEAE (stonecrop)

Overview: small, erect, and succulent annual.
Flowers: greenish white with splashes of red; corolla: 4 petals. *Inflorescence*: tiny, small clusters (3-10) spring from the leaf axils.
Calyx: 4 sepals, narrow, typically larger than the petals.
Leaves: ovate to oblong, opposite, united at their base.
Stem: small, erect, reddish tint.
Fruit: follicle with 1-2 elliptical seeds.
Handlens: 4 stamens.
Notes: young members are green but quickly turn red with age. Favors open areas and moist sites. This stonecrop can rival a cactus for its water-holding ability.

RAGGED ROCKFLOWER (BIGELOW CROSSOSOMA)
(*Crossosoma bigelovii*)
CROSSOSOMATACEAE (crossosoma)

Overview: open, straggly-branched, and shrub-like, perennial; typically found growing from the crack or crevice of a rock face.
Flowers: white with a splash of violet; corolla: 5 irregular petals that bear a distinctive claw. *Inflorescence*: solitary from the axils.
Calyx: 5 clustered sepals.
Leaves: lanceolate to elliptical, bluish-green, thick, smooth margin.
Fruit: follicle with 2-5 seeds.
Handlens: numerous stamens which are conspicuous and showy; multiple pistils (2-5) borne on a disk.
Notes: the branches, bearing thorny branchlets, are elongated and pendent, curving in graceful arches from the rock face. Flowers, appearing in the early spring, are as beautiful and pleasantly fragrant as any that grace the desert landscape.

WILD CUCUMBER (*Marah gilensis*)
CUCURBITACEAE (gourd)

Overview: a rapidly growing perennial vine with delicate tendrils.

Flower*:* white to green, stellate; *inflorescence:* staminate: raceme or panicle; pistillate: solitary.

Calyx: 5 sepals.

Leaves: 3 segments—top segment: sharply pointed; bottom segments: notched. Light green, and covered with trichomes. Petiole to 1.5".

Fruit: small, green, globose fruit with sharply pointed projections—much like the head of a mace.

Handlens: 3 sharply angled stamens; prickle-bearing ovary.

Notes: supports a large subterranean tuber. *One source claims the finding of a tuber weighing in excess of 200 lbs.*

Marah, taken from Hebrew, means bitter.

This gourd is an aggressive invader that can cover completely the plant used initially for support as well as a host of unfortunate neighbors.

NARROWLEAF DITAXIS *(Ditaxis lanceolata)*
NEW MEXICO DITAXIS *(Ditaxis neomexicana)*
SAWTOOTH DITAXIS *(Ditaxis serrata)*
EUPHORBIACEAE (spurge)

Overview: a multi-branched perennial with erect and brittle stems.

Flowers: white; *inflorescence*: emerge in groups along the upper portions of the plant.

Staminate: sepals slightly larger than petals, both floral elements are pubescent.

Pistillate: sepals and petals equally sized.

Leaves: linear to lanceolate, pubescent, entire, and sessile; tiny petiole. Solitary leaves emerge from the stem at a 45 degree angle.

Calyx: 5 sepals.

Fruit: pubescent, 3-lobed pod.

Handlens: dense hairs pressing against the pistil; 3-lobed ovary and 10 stamens in 2 whorls.

Notes: complex flower typical of this family; entire plant has a silvery sheen.

For the Advanced Reader: In *D. lanceolata*, the petals of the *staminate flowers* are fused to the filaments; the stigma is flattened. In *D. neomexicana (left)*, the petal are free of the fila-ments; the stigma is club-shaped. There are white-margined sepals in the pistillate flowers.

In *D. serrata*, the back of the petal is exserted and coarsely pubescent, while in *D. neomexicana*, these hairs are short and project from the petal margin. The leaves are not pubescent and the margin is entire to slightly dentated in *D. neomexicana*, while densely pubescent with a dentated margin and coarsely tooth apex in *D. serrata*.

RATTLESNAKE WEED (*Euphorbia albomarginata*)

(*Chamaesyce albomarginata*)
EUPHORBIACEAE (spurge)

Cyathium: this plant produces an unusually complex flower. What appears to be the white petals of a flower are not. Rather, they are petaloid appendages at the rim of a structure known as a cyathium (a cup-like involucre). It houses one pistillate and 15-30 staminate flowers. The apex of the cup-shaped cyathium has 4, white, petal-like appendages with attached reddish and oval glands.

A single stamen is found in the sta-minate flower while the pistillate flower has a green ovary with 3 styles. When fertilized, the central pistillate flower swells, and its ovary (forming a capsule) extends beyond the cyathium. If present, a yellow appendix on one side of the cyathium is a nectar cup.

A commonly occurring example of *Chamaesyce* is the rattlesnake weed (*C. albomarginata*), a plant with tiny, round to oblong, hairy, and opposite leaves with tiny petioles. Other noteworthy features include its milky sap; thin, lacy, red stems; and fused stipules that form papery scales.

This plant obtained its common name from its use in treating rattlesnake bites.

My personal encounter with this western diamondback rattlesnake (*Crotalus atrox*) is one I shall never forget. Upon being disturbed, it rattled ominously while tenaciously holding its ground, fearlessly raised its head, and never took its penetrating gaze from me during its grateful retreat.

An ambush predator, it houses heat-sensing pits within its face that enables it to detect and locate its warm-blooded, mammalian prey.

Another individual, living near my home, is about 5 ft. long. I have seen it venenate an adult rabbit, swallow it completely—creating a massive bugle in its body. The serpent slowly meandered to a shrub for shade and to rest and digest its hapless victim; such a meal can provide sufficient food for the better part of a year.

HALFMOON MILKVETCH (*Astragalus allochrous*)
FABACEAE (legume)

Overview: perennial herb that is prostrate when young, but becomes more erect when matured.

Flowers: white; *Inflorescence*: borne in clusters of 4-8 heads. Banner petal is curved downward.

Leaves: pinnately compound with 11-19 pinnae.

Fruit: bladdery, papery, green pod exhibiting a crescent moon shape.

Notes: many *Astragalus* members are toxic to range animals. This legume is no exception; it stores a poisonous alkaloid that causes an erratic gait. Staggering and loss of muscular control led to the term "loco" to describe the infected animal. Unfortunately, this resulted in the term "locoweed" to describe many members of this genus. Denied these plants, animal recovery is probable.

HOREHOUND (*Marrubium vulgare*)
LAMIACEAE (mint)

Overview: perennial herb with several erect stems; conspicuous white and woolly pubescence.

Flowers: whitish; corolla: bilabiate—upper: 2-clefted; lower: 3-clefted. *Inflorescence*: borne from the axils in whorls.

Calyx: 5-10 sepals.

Leaves: ovate, crenate, highly wrinkled, petiole, covered with white pubescence.

Fruit: nutlet.

Handlens: 4 stamens, one pair shorter than the other pair.

Notes: part of the summer-flowering flora, a frequently uncounted roadside weed.

There is a distinct herbal but hard-to-define odor to the plant. Consumed by humankind for 1,000s of years. Its name may be derived from the Hebrew *marrob* for its bitter juice. Used as a bitter herb in the Feast of Passover. Enjoyed by many as horehound drops; sought after for coughs and sore throats for its expectorant properties. Native to the European continent and Great Britain.

DESERT LILY (*Hesperocallis undulata*)
LILIACEAE (LILY)

Overview: perennial with a straight, stout stem to 7 ft.

Flowers: whitish, with a greenish central strip; corolla: 5-6 elliptical petals elongated into a funnel shape; widely spaced along the stem; fragrant. *Inflorescence*: elongated raceme, borne on an elongated pedicle, with 4-15 flowers supported by papery, ovate bracts.

Leaves: basal: to 20"; cauline: much smaller; wavy margins.

Stem: smooth, elongated, not branched.

Fruit: 3-lobed capsule.

Handlens: 6 stamens with golden anthers.

Notes: flowers in the spring and favors flat, sandy sites. Produces an edible, highly prized, and garlic-flavored bulb.

DESERT ROSE-MALLOW (*Hibiscus coulteri*)
MALVACEAE (mallow)

Overview: woody, sparsely branched, perennial that bears stellate pubescence; can become a 3.5 ft. shrub.

Flowers: pale yellow to cream white with a brownish-red base; corolla: bowl-shaped, formed by 5 overlapping petals that display a red splash at the base. *Inflorescence*: solitary at the end of an elongated peduncle.

Calyx: 5-lobed; supported by 10-14 linear bracts that are as long as or longer than the calyx.

Leaves: ovate, serrated, pubescent, and glandular. Upper: 3-lobed; lower: entire and oval. Lower members are longer than those above.

Stem: coarsely pubescent; gray and woody base.

Fruit: supported by a pedicle that breaks at fruit maturation; seeds bear elongated pubescence.

Handlens: fused filaments form a tube surrounding the style. Style adorned with 5 reddish segments.

Note: many desert plant names recognize the special contributions of Thomas Coulter who traveled to Mexico in 1842 to work as a physician. During his time in Mexico and Arizona, he collected more than 50,000 plant specimens.

DESERT WISHBONE (*Mirabilis laevis* var. *villosa*)
NYCTAGINACEAE (4 o'clock)

Overview: large, highly branched, and low perennial with dark green herbage.

Flowers: when young, the flowers, wrapped and enclosed by the calyx, show patches of magenta, but later a white to pale pink flower emerges. *Inflorescence*: borne solitary at the axil, where leaves also tend to bunch. No true petals—calyx is petal-like.

Calyx: 5-lobed, tubular at its base with a multi-lobed top.

Leaves: cordate, opposite; small and pubescent petiole.

Involucres: sticky, triangular lobes with elongated pubescence.

Fruit: small achene.

Handlens: exserted stamens (3-5) consisting of white filaments supporting golden-yellow, exserted filaments.

Notes: the interesting common name is derived from the late afternoon opening of the flower. A wishbone pattern is seen in the stem branching habit. Favors gravelly and rocky soils.

This is a prolific pollen producer that causes much suffering during the allergy season.

SCARLET GAURA (*Gaura coccinea*)
ONAGRACEAE (evening primrose)

Overview: bushy perennial with several erect and slender stems that reach 3 ft.
Flowers: white but fading to pink or red; corolla: 4 petals, clawed and asymmetrical. *Inflorescence*: a spike-like raceme.
Calyx: 4 markedly reflexed sepals.
Leaves: cauline; linear to lanceolate, entire to slighted dentated, sessile
Fruit: thick basal portion, 4-sided, woody, and indehiscent with 1-4 seeds.
Handlens: 8 stamens, deeply 4-lobed stigmas.
Notes: used by Native Americans to treat stomach disorders in children. Flowers open in the evening hours. Can form large communities on disturbed sites.

FRAGRANT EVENING PRIMROSE (*Oenothera caespitosa*)
ONAGRACEAE (evening primrose)

Overview: biennial with a showy, fragrant flower and a rosette of basal foliage.

Flowers: white but turn red with maturity; corolla: 4 cordate petals. *Inflorescence* solitary member, not supported by a peduncle, emerge from the axils.

Leaves: linear to somewhat oval; dentate to lobed; flat, basal rosette. Primary vein and the petiole can be tinted red.

Stem: spreading and sprawling.

Fruit: 2 rows of seeds per chamber; wart-like projects on the wall of the fruit.

Handlens: anthers are attached at their middle.

Notes: favors sandy soils and washes. From spring to fall, the flowers open late in the day and are gone the next day. *Oenothera. caespitosa* has a stem that does not exfoliate, while this occurs in *O. californica*.

CALIFORNIA EVENING PRIMROSE
(*Oenothera californica ssp. avita*)
ONAGRACEAE (evening primrose)

Overview: coarsely stemmed, exfoliating perennial.

Flowers: white but aging to pink; corolla: 4 large, showy, and independent petals, wavy edge. Prominent and exserted stamens. *Inflorescence*: flowers emerge from the upper axils.

Leaves: cauline members are lanceolate, pinnately lobed, and sessile; margin is highly variable

Fruit: a single row of seeds; smooth fruit wall.

Notes: favors sandy soils, one of the evening primroses, so named for their habit of opening the floral elements at evening time. Prefers sandy and gravelly soils.

BIRDCAGE EVENING-PRIMROSE (*Oenothera deltoides*)
ONAGRACEAE (evening primrose)

Overview: annual with a single, dominant and several secondary stems.

Flowers: white but maturing to pinkish with a yellowish central core; corolla: 4 cordate petals that form a cup-like structure. *Inflorescence*: typically solitary, arises from buds in the upper axils that rest pendently prior to opening. Very prominent stamens and pistils.

Calyx: 4 sepals.

Leaves: obovate to lanceolate, primarily form as a basal rosette, weakly dentated. Petiole plus blade can reach 3". Cauline: nearly entire to pinnately lobed.

Stem: exfoliating, lower portion is smooth but the upper region is gently pubescent. Stems grow as a group to form a structure (to 12"), which when it dries looks like a cage for wild birds.

Fruit: woody capsule that can extend to 3", 1 row of seeds per chamber.

Handlens: 8 stamens.

Notes: flowers open in the evening. Has forged an interaction with vespertine bees who are its dependable pollinators. Among its many picturesque common names are: devil's lantern and lion-in-a-cage.

WHITE PRICKLY POPPY (*Argemone pleiacantha*)
PAPAVERACEAE (poppy)

Overview: stout, coarse, and erect perennial with yellow sap that ages to black; armored with formidable prickles.

Flowers: white with a central area filled with yellow stamens; corolla: 6 thin and delicate (tissue-paper fineness) petals that move readily in the wind. *Inflorescence*: solitary and terminal.

Calyx: bears prickle.

Leaves: strongly pinnately divided, prickles on leaves and stem are pronounced—particularly along leaf venation.

Fruit: capsule that opens by an apical valve and bears a pronounced spine at its tip. Milky-white poppy seeds that turn to a brownish black.

Handlens: deep yellow, circular anthers; solitary pistil with a red maroon spiny stigma.

Notes: this massive poppy, which displays its flowers from late spring through autumn, can reach 5 feet with leaves that can extend eight inches. Packed with noxious phytochemicals, including powerful narcotics, it is distasteful to grazing animals; thus, it tends to occupy stressed, overgrazed areas as well as roadsides.

Can be confused with a thistle. Bears the amusing common name of "cowboy fried eggs".

CREAM CUPS *(Platystemon californicus)*
PAPAVERACEAE (poppy)

Overview: annual with numerous, heavily pubescent stems that emanate from a common basal region.

Flowers: creamy white (can have a yellow splash at its tip or base); corolla: 6 independent petals. *Inflorescence*: solitary, borne at the end of an elongated peduncle (to 8").

Calyx: 3 pubescent and persistent sepals.

Leaves: linear to lanceolate; opposite; mostly basal.

Fruit: multi-chambered capsule.

Handlens: numerous stamens that are supported by flat filaments; a single pistil.

Notes: flowers from spring through early summer; favors sandy soils.

DESERT INDIAN WHEAT (*Plantago ovata*)
PLANTAGINACEAE (plantain)

Overview: annual covered in silky, white pubescence.

Flowers: whitish brown; corolla: round to ovate lobes. *Inflorescence*: dense, pubescent spike, which can grow to 10".

Calyx: 4 imbricate sepals.

Leaves: linear, entire, minute.

Fruit: small capsule with numerous seeds.

Notes: covered with conspicuous pubescence. Grown in parts of Europe and the western regions of India as a com-mercial source of psyllium.

Both *P. patagonica* and *P. ovata* contain complex carbohydrates that absorb moisture to form a gelatinous material.

WOOLLY PLANTAIN (*Plantago patagonica*)
PLANTAGINACEAE (plantain)

Overview: highly compacted, small, annual herb with an elongated flower head, basal foliage, and abundant white and woolly pubescence.

Flowers: white to tan; corolla: inconspicuous, petals fused at their base. *Inflorescence*: borne as numerous, green, fuzzy, cylindrical spikes that pack the flower stalk. Peduncle and flower can grow to 4".

Calyx: 4 papery sepals that are fused basally.

Leaves: long and linear, basal members arising as a bundle from the base of the stem.

Fruit: minute, multi-seeded capsule.

Handlens: 4 exserted stamens.

Notes: these small plants are completely covered in white woolly hairs. A medically useful genus of plants; several species are cultivated as a commercial source for psyllium, a source of dietary fiber. Flowers from spring to early summer.

PLUMBAGO (*Plumbago scandens*)
PLUMBAGINACEAE (plumbago)

Overview: perennial and evergreen subshrub.

Flowers: white tinged with blue, corolla: 5 elongated and tubular petals.

Calyx: viscid and pubescent.

Leaves: oblong to lanceolate, simple, entire; juvenile: intensely red; mature: green. Foliage reassumes its red coloration at the end of the growing season.

Fruit: narrow and viscid capsule.

Handlens: 5 stamens, positioned opposite the corolla lobes.

Notes: highly toxic plant; all parts are potentially harmful. Nevertheless, it is a favor food plant for larvae of the common blue butterfly, *Cyclyrius pirithous*. Exhibits a multi-seasonal flowering pattern.

BRITTLE SPINEFLOWER *(Chorizanthe brevicornu)*
POLYGONACEAE (buckwheat)

Overview: a spreading to erect, pubescent annual that is brittle and densely branched.

Flowers: white to greenish-white; tepals: 5 inconspicuous units. Cylindrical with apical bristles; green bracts (2).

Leaves: basal: linear to oblanceolate; cauline: reduced to a bract.

Involucre: 6 segments form a green tube; ribbed at maturity.

Stem: thin, pubescent.

Fruit: lenticular, dark-brown achenes.

Handlens: 3 stamens, attached at the corolla throat; anthers are white to pale yellow.

Notes: dispersal aided by its property of tearing at the brittle, nodal region, and the subsequent attachment of the severed segment to a passerby.

WRIGHT BUCKWHEAT *(Eriogonum wrightii)*
POLYGONACEAE (buckwheat)

Overview: erect, varies from a small perennial herb to a shrub with a profusion of slender branches.

Flowers: white to pinkish to rose with deeper rose in the central core. *Inflorescence*: cyme-like.

Leaves: basal: elliptic, pubes-cence, especially on the underside; tiny petiole, overall silvery sheen.

Stem: young: light gray, velvety pubescent; mature: red-brown and exfoliating. Clear below the inflorescences, but bearing dark red-brown bracts at the nodes.

Notes: late summer to early fall flowering. This plant contains an interesting toxin that is activated by sunlight. Once ingested, it can pass to the calf via its mother's milk. Infected animals have to be protected from further exposure to sunlight.

CURLY DOCKS (*Rumex crispus*)
POLYGONACEAE (buckwheat)

Overview: slender, smooth-stemmed per-ennial.
Flowers: greenish; perianth resembles a 6-membered calyx; *Inflorescence*: emerge in a whorl from the upper branches.
Leaves: lanceolate, curled or crumbled mar-gins, primarily basal, elongated petioles (to 1 ft.).
Fruit: 3-angled achene.
Handlens: 6 stamens and 3 stigmas.
Notes: a native of Eurasia, it is distributed widely; considered a troublesome weed in many locales, but also sought for its medicinal value. Aggressive invader of disturbed sites.

DESERT ANEMONE (*Anemone tuberosa*)
RANUNCULACAEAE (buttercup)

Overview: erect, perennial herb with an elongated stem that can extend to 1.5 ft.
Flowers: atypical, lack a corolla but have a calyx (5-8) that looks like white petals (can be somewhat lavender or pink at their tip). *Inflorescence*: solitary or bunched at apex of an elongated peduncle.
Bear multiple stamens supported by thin filaments and numerous pistils; de-velop into a delicate, woolly fruit that dis-integrates to release the seeds.
Calyx: 8-10 rose-colored sepals.
Leaves: pinnately divided into 3 seg-ments, grooved, basal or whorled in a group of 3 that occur mid-way up the stem. Petiole can reach 2-3".
Fruit: head of many achenes borne on small, persistent, and very showy styles.
Notes: this showy plant is one of the earliest members of the new season's flora; prefers rocky slopes. This buttercup is supported by a pinkish tuber.

TEXAS VIRGIN'S BOWER (*Clematis drummondii*)
RANUNCULACAEAE (buttercup)

Overview: climbing, woody vine that can inundate completely the host.

Flowers: white to creamy; 4 (occasionally 5) white, petal-like sepals. Dioecious (staminate flower shown above). *Inflorescence*: panicles of cymes.

    Staminate: a horde of showy stamens.

    Pistillate: many members.

Leaves: pinnately compound having 5-7 leaflets with 3- to 4-lobed units, elongated petiole, and *opposite*. Leaf pairs dispersed along the stem, emerge at the stem nodes and at/or near the tip of the branches.

Fruit: achene whose seeds bear very showy, white, and silky appendages (5-10) that visually rival the flowers.

Notes: vine-like by means of its petiolule and rachis. The chewed leaf has a pleasant peppery taste *(be certain of your identification before tasting; some members of this genus are <u>poisonous</u>!).*

BEDSTRAW (*Galium aparine*)
RUBIACEAE (madder)

Overview: weak-stemmed, climbing, annual that also spreads over the ground. Dense mat created by hooked prickles.

Flowers: white (can have green); corolla: *tiny,* 4 sharply pointed petals, which are fused at their base, but still widely spaced. *Inflorescence*: borne at the leaf nodes as 1-3 flowered cymes. *Curved-downward pedicle* (to 3/4").

Leaves: whorls of 6-8; lower: circular with a petiole; upper: narrowly oblanceolate and sessile; sticky by virtue of tiny, hooked hairs. *Lateral veins are distinct.*

Stem: weak and brittle, quadrangular.

Fruit: borne as a group of nutlets bearing hooked bristles that aid in their dispersal.

Notes: dried fruit has been used as a coffee substitute. Can be weed-like in its growing habit.

Habitats extend to 8,000 ft, far more than the 3,000 ft elevation maximum for *G. stellatum,* Native to North America and Eurasia.

DESERT BEDSTRAW (*Galium stellatum*)
RUBIACEAE (madder)

Overview: densely packed, subshrub with bristly branches.

Flowers: greenish-yellow; corolla: 4 sharply pointed petals that are fused at the base, yet conspicuously separated. *Inflorescence*: many-flowered panicle. *Erect pedicle* (1/4").

Leaves: lanceolate to elliptical, sharply pointed, whorled in a widely spaced group of 4-5. Midvein: prominent and white; *lateral veins: indistinct.*

Stems: square, stout, a multitude of spreading, intertwining branches.

Fruit: deeply pubescent nutlet, white and elongated.

Notes: common name derived from its use as a packing material, sought also for ts fragrance.

YERBA MANSA (*Anemopsis californica*)
SAURURACEAE (lizard-tail)

Overview: pubescent perennial that forms a dense mat of spreading vegetation.

Flowers: greenish-white, becoming red streaked or spotted with age. *Inflorescence*: cone-like spike with multiple flowers protected by 4-8 petal-like, white involucral bracts. Lacks any perianth elements.

Leaves: upper: ovate, clasping; basal: elliptical, elongated petiole (both to 8") with stipules.

Stem: hollow; new roots can emerge from the stem nodes to form interconnected colonies.

Fruit: fleshy capsule.

Handlens: 6-8 stamens and 3 fused pistils.

Notes: produces vine-like growth from the leaf node; flower head is reminiscent of *Anemone tuberosa*; at maturity, the entire plant is brick red.

Overwinters in moist habitats from reserves in a rhizome; flowers in early summer.

Yerba is from Spanish for herb and mansa translates as calm or tranquil.

This solitary bee, with its densely pubescent body, provides an ideal material for collecting and holding the pollen of a visited flower.

In seeking its floral reward, this insect is covered in pollen, some of which can be transferred successfully to a recipient flower.

Many insects consistently seek members of the same species, thereby enhancing successful pollination. This is the kind of intimate interaction that has characterized so many facets of plant-insect evolutionary co-dependency.

GHOST FLOWER (*Mohavea confertiflora*)
SCROPHULARIACEAE (figwort)

Overview: a viscid and pubescent annual with campanulate flowers.

Flowers: pale yellow to whitish; corolla: bilabiate—upper: splashed with a reddish brown to maroon; lower: similarly colored solid zone; *Inflorescence*: solitary and protected by 4-5 bracts.

Calyx: 5 sepals.

Leaves: linear to lanceolate, short petiole, basal rosette.

Handlens: 5 stamens, bearing basal pubescence, 2 are united above the base while the remaining members are rudimentary and infertile.

Notes: favors sandy and gravelly sites. The corolla is transparent and seemingly "ghostly" to some observers.

Mentzelia involucrata bears a superficial resemblance to *Mohavea confertiflora*. A sexually active male *Xeralictus* bee does not visit *Mohavea confertiflora,* but he will enter a *Mentzelia* for its nectar reward.

In contrast, the female fly enters this *Mohavea* but she only exposes the top of her abdomen during this visitation. *Mohavea confertiflora* has acquired floral markings that mimic the female's abdomen. A passing male therefore eagerly enters the *Mohavea* to seek out the available female. It is the male not the female which is the target of pollen deposition. Once again, the pollination requirements of the plant have been secured without expending resources on nectar production[1].

Based on the research of Hawks, D., and Yanega, D.

DINGY CHAMAESARACHA (HAIRY FIVE EYES)
(*Chamaesaracha sordida*)
SOLANACEAE (nightshade)

Overview: low-growing, glandular, and pubescent perennial herb with highly picturesque flowers.

Flowers: white with purple tinge; corolla: 5 sided, pubescent appendages at the throat. *Inflorescence*: solitary on slender pedicels that emerge from the axils.

Calyx: 5 campanulate sepals.

Leaves: triangular with wavy margins that can become lobed.

Fruit: berry, supported by a pedicle that is curved downward. As with other members of this genus, the calyx provides protection for the fruit.

Handlens: stamens inserted at corolla base.

Notes: the corolla tube has noticeably pubescence between the bases of the filaments. Its common name results from the leaves that hold debris giving it a dingy appearance. Flowers early in the year through spring.

DESERT THORNAPPLE *(Datura discolor)*
SOLANACEAE (nightshade)

Overview: an erect annual to 20".

Flowers: white with a striking purplish (indigo) patch in the throat; corolla: trumpet-shaped, 10-toothed, and 4-6".

Leaves: ovate, coarsely dentated, green,

Stem: gray and pubescent.

Fruit: viscid, pubescent, and bearing stout spines. Black ripened seeds.

Note: favors sandy soils and washes. The most distinctive difference with *D. wrightii* (6-8") is the far smaller size of the corolla (4-6"), its annual life cycle, and greater color intensity at the throat.

SACRED DATURA (SACRED THORNAPPLE)
(Datura wrightii) *(Datura meteloides)*
SOLANACEAE (nightshade)

Overview: an erect, highly branched perennial subshrub.

Flowers: white tinged with lavender; corolla: fused, 5-tooth petals. An easily recognized plant due to its massive, solitary, funnel-shaped flower to 6-8" that typically droops and possesses a large throat. *Inflorescence*: solitary, emerges at the nodes.

Leaves: ovate (to 6"), fine pubescence with prominent veins, and a distinct black-green color.

Stems: can cover an extensive area.

Fruit: not viscid nor pubescent and bearing slender spines. Light brown, ripened seed.

Notes: highly toxic plants containing powerful hallucinogenic alkaloids; many poisoning, occasionally fatal, have occurred. Employed for numerous uses by ancient desert dwellers.

Flower opens at dusk and closes mid-morning of the next day; its fragrant flowers attract hawk moths (many insects carry this common name) and bees who disperse the pollen. Favors sandy flats and arroyos.

DESERT TOBACCO (*Nicotiana obtusifolia*)
(*Nicotiana trigonophylla*)
TREE TOBACCO (*Nicotiana glauca*)
SOLANACEAE (nightshade)

Overview: flowers emerge all along the hairy and glandular stem.

Flowers: cream to green-ish-white; corolla: tubular with 5 flared petals.

Calyx: less than one-half the length of the corolla; 5 lobes, fused at their base, pointed tip.

Leaves: lanceolate, pubescent, sessile, entire, and sticky to the touch with a prominent mid-vein. Often, a leaf emerges at the node directly opposite the flower.

Handlens: 5 unequal stamens (4+1) with filaments attached at the base of the floral tube. Green anthers (2 conical segments) with white streaking.

Notes: desert tobacco produces a new crop of flowers in response to additional rainfall creating the appearance of persistent flowering.

Storing significant levels of nicotine (a plant alkaloid), this plant was sought after as a tobacco by a host of early desert dwellers. Both nicotine and anabasine were applied as early natural insecticides, particularly in controlling loses due to sucking aphids. Named for Jean Nicot, French Ambassor to Portugal, who introduced tobacco into France in the mid 16th century.

The Yuma and Havasupai planted the seeds in the ashes of mesquite trees as a means of cultivating this plant.

A related plant, a native of South America, is the tree tobacco, *Nicotiana glauca*, with yellow, tubular flowers that are 5-lobed and emerge at the apex as panicles. The leaves are ovate and covered in a powdery dust. Its leaf blade is supported by a petiole that can run from 1-3". An important nectar source for hummingbirds.

Tree tobacco also synthesizes a strong alkaloid stimulant which is not nicotine; instead, it makes anabasine which accounts for nearly all of the stimulatory activity.

WHITE GROUNDCHERRY *(Physalis acutifolia)*
SOLANACEAE (nightshade)

Overview: erect annual to 3.5 ft with angular, multi-branched stems.

Flowers: white to light yellow; corolla: 5 petals; green central core with radiating purple streaks.

Calyx: 5 sepals, pubescent, basally fused, campanulate with triangular lobes. Produces a 10-angled structure that protects the fruit.

Leaves: lanceolate, deeply tooth, basal portion markedly constricted. Prominent venation and fine pubescence on the margin. Petiole to 2".

Stem: angular, substantial.

Handlens: golden-yellow (5) stamens formed as a solid structure surrounding the pistil. Anthers: green, elongated and supported by equally long filaments. Pistil: exserted, basal portion finely pubescent.

Notes: found in open areas such as roadsides; summer-flowering nightshade. Often viewed as a weed in agricultural areas.

BROADLEAF CATTAIL *(Typha latifolia)*
TYPHACEAE (cat-tail)

Overview: elongated perennial with a dis-tinct flowering head.

Flowers: dark brown, cylindrical spike. The upper male spike is contiguous with the lower, female spike—there is no separating interval.

Staminate: grouped into a club-shaped spadix; whitish bracts.

Pistillate: pale green when immature but aging to a brownish tint; thickened above, lacks bracts.

Leaves: greatly elongated; flat, thick and spongy; basal: about a dozen arise from the shoot.

Stems: submerged at their base, cylindrical and lacking joints.

Notes: requires free standing water. Overwinters from a starchy rhizome.

YELLOW

Sunflowers with yellow ray and disk flowers are placed in this section. Sunflowers with white ray and yellow disk flowers are included in the white & green section.

Desert Marigold, *Baileya multiradiata*

SAN FELIPE DYSSODIA (*Adenophyllum porophylloides*)
COOPER DYSSODIA (*Adenophyllum cooperi*)
ASTERACEAE (sunflower)

Overview: shrubby perennial with slender and erect stems supported by a woody base.

Flowers: cylindrically shaped.

Ray: 8-12; yellow to red-orange that can turn purple.

Disk: numerous yellow-orange flowers.

Leaves: pinnately divided (3-5 lobes), linear, *entire*, with a distinct yellow gland at the leaf axil. Basal leaves: opposite higher: alternate.

Involucre: upper: 12-16, each supporting several glands, linear, pointed tip lower: lanceolate, fused at base; exserted.

Elliptical glands dispersed throughout the bract, more circularly shaped glands form a ring at the apex, red patches at the tip of the phyllaries create a conspicuous purple ring.

Stems: multiple, smooth and highly branched, form a rounded bush.

Notes: noteworthy for its strong, peppery-like odor that is highly persistent—remaining long after the plant is handled. Drought deciduous.

Caution: San felipe dyssodia is similar to *A. cooperi* (Cooper dyssodia, *right*); the leaves of the latter plant are shallowly lobed and bear serrated margins.

DESERT MARIGOLD *(Baileya multiradiata)*
ASTERACEAE (sunflower)

Overview: an abundant herbaceous biennial or perennial with a stem that is leafy only at its base.

Flowers: *Inflorescence*: heads (2") solitary at stem tip; flowers supported on long, bractless peduncles located well above the basal leaves.

Ray: 25-50; ligules: 3/8-5/8"; lemon yellow with 3 lobes.

Disk: numbering in the dozens.

Leaves: mostly basal rosette, pinnately divided (deep lobes), and finely pubescent. Gray-green, silvery sheen, winged petioles.

Involucre: several green, uniform, and woolly pubescent whorls.

Notes: a favorite site is disturbed areas such as roadsides, thrives in sandy soils; fierce competitor that benefits from its ability to tolerate even severe drought conditions. All parts of the plant are potentially toxic; nevertheless, sheep apparently relish the flowers and seed heads—suggesting they have an effective detoxification mechanism.

WAXFLOWER *(Baileya pauciradiata)*
ASTERACEAE (sunflower)

Overview: highly branched annual bearing woolly pubescence.

Flowers: *Inflorescence*: cyme-like or solitary from an elongated peduncle (1-2"); 2-3 units in a flower head.

Ray: 5-7; 3-lobed apex; lemony yellow but turning papery with age. The spatulate corolla is open and spreading, but soon becomes pressed against the head.

Disk: 10-20.

Leaves: basal: linear to oblanceolate, can be pinnately (or bi-pinnately) lobed; cauline: linear, infrequently lobed.

Involucre: 8-10 campanulate and pubescent bracts.

Fruit: lacks a pappus.

Notes: this plant can be highly toxic by virtue of a group of harmful phytochemicals (sesquiterpene lactones). Its name recognizes the achievements of the American microscopist, Jacob W. Bailey.

SWEETBUSH (CHUCKWALLA'S DELIGHT)
(*Bebbia juncea*)
ASTERACEAE (sunflower)

Overview: perennial subshru with an intricate, dense, multipl branching pattern that is create by intertwining slender stems.

Flowers: cylindrically shape (1/2-2/3"), emerge at the tip c the stalk. *Inflorescence*: solitar cyme.

Ray: none.
Disk: 20-39; yellow.

Leaves: linear, sparse, tiny rough, and pubescent.

Involucre: multiple bracts, i 3 groupings, with pointed tips extend 2/3 the length of th flower head. Basal portior green and brown; upper: stra colored, thin, and elongatec Outer members can turn red.

Fruit: achenes, pappus of 15 20 white, feather-like bristles.

Notes: favors arroyos and moister sites. Foliage lost with onset of drie conditions; experiences heavy episodic flowering, even during time of water stress.

Interesting fact: Wright metalmark larvae (*Calephelis wrighti*) do not feed on th leaves. Instead, this butterfly con- sumes the epidermis of the stem.

The chuckwalla *(Sauromalus ater)*, a rock-dwelling, desert lizard, is primarily a vegetarian but it will include insects on its daily menu. It relishes this sunflower which bears its name.

It responses to danger by scurrying into a crevice in the rock, and inflating its body cavity with air until it fills the void.

Native inhabitants used a long pole with a hooked end to deflate the body to enable its removal.

CHOCOLATE FLOWER (*Berlandiera lyrata*)
ASTERACEAE (sunflower)

Overview: erect, perennial herb with a distinct odor.

Flowers: solitary on an elongated and pubescent peduncle (to 2 ft.); *Inflorescence*: a solitary cyme.

Ray: light yellow, fertile, 2-lobed ligules (usually 8) with maroon streaking on the underside.

Disk: maroon, sterile.

Involucres: 3 series.

Leaves: can be lyrate, light green and pubescent.

Handlens: chocolate-colored stamens.

Notes: favors roadsides and other disturbed sites. Spring to fall flowering sunflower. Removal of the ligules produces a pungent chocolate odor, but this smell can permeate the air around an intact plant—especially in the morning and during sunny periods.

COULTER BRICKELLBUSH (*Brickellia coulteri*)
ASTERACEAE (sunflower)

Overview: large, bushy plant with distinctly shaped foliage that turns red at the end of the growing season.

Flowers: *Inflorescence*: multiple flowers (about 17), in a panicle-like inflorescence, borne on a slender peduncle. Unopened flower: lightly scarlet-red.

Ray: none.

Disk: yellow or green-white with large, prominent patches of reddish-purple.

Leaves: deltoid to hastate with 1-3 sharp teeth; *opposite.*

Involucre: numerous (20), uniform, markedly elongated, pointed and red tinged. Outer bracts generally smaller than the inner members.

Stem: brittle, yellow-gray pubescence.
Pappus: silky bristles.
Comment: viscid to the touch. Favors desert washes and open areas. *Flower head with no more than 2 dozen individuals (typically 17).*

WOOLLY BRICKELLBUSH (*Brickellia incana*)

ASTERACEAE (sunflower)

Overview: can reach shrub size; a sunflower member with a cylindrical flower.

Flower: light yellow but deeply scarlet-red tinged corolla: (about 0.5"); slender, cylindrical ligules. *Inflorescence*: solitary flower head on a 1-2" peduncle.

Leaves: ovate, *alternate*, sessile, or small petiole, entire to minutely dentated, pubescent.

Involucre: gray, overlapping, multiple whorls (40), green to purple, campanulate. Outer phyllaries: ovate, can be far longer than the inner members; inner: linear.

Stems: dense, white pubessence.

Fruit: pappus with white bristles.

Notes: enjoys the same habitat as *B. coulteri*. *Flower head with many more than 17 individuals—the typical number for* B. couteri.

MALTESE STAR THISTLE (TOCALOTE)
(Centaurea melitensis)
ASTERACEAE (sunflower)

Overview: annual or biennial, with multiple branches, covered with grayish pubescence.

Flowers: yellow; corolla: glandular. *Inflorescence*: solitary or in groups of 2-3. Supported by highly pubescent (reminiscent of a cobweb) bracts.

Leaves: lower: entire to pinnately lobed (lyrate); upper: elongated and narrow, entire.

Glandular, cobweb like pubescence develops on matured members.

Involucre: bracts, tipped with purplish spines, have a reddish base (3/16-3/8"); smaller spinelets (< 3/16").

Fruit: achene with a white pappus; bristles bear rows of tiny barbs.

Notes: *Centaurea solstitalis*, a related plant, has longer, stouter, straw colored spines (to 1"). In some locales, tocalote has become an aggressive "weed". Introduced to the US in the 1500s.

Interesting botanical note—the outer circle of flowers are sterile while the interior members are fertile.

YELLOW STARTHISTLE (*Centaurea solstitialis*)
ASTERACEAE (sunflower)

Overview: annual, with cottony pubescence and branches that arise from the base of the stem.

Flowers: constricted zone between the phyllaries and the flower head.

Ray: none.

Disk: yellow, numerous.

Leaves: basal: pinnately divided into pronounced lobes, bristly to the touch, clasp the stem; cauline: much longer blade.

Involucre: lower: 3-pronged spines (larger than 3/8"); middle: simple spine, upper: spineless; far more massive than the flower head.

Notes: contains a toxicant that affects the brain of horse impeding their fine-movement ability, favors disturbed sites.

Native to the Mediterranean region, this is another invasive "weed" that threatens native plants. This is truly a noxious weed plant that one authority states has come to dominate nearly 20 million acres within the continental U.S.

DESERT COREOPSIS (*Coreopsis bigelovii*)
ASTERACEAE (sunflower)

Overview: erect annual that can reach 3 ft.

Flowers: emerge as a solitary member from a scape.

Ray: 5-10; yellow, to 1".

Disk: 20-50; yellow.

Leaves: pinnately divided (can be twice divided) into linear lobes; primarily basal.

Involucre: outer: 4-7, linear; inner: 6-8, ovate with scarious margins.

Stem: one or more, erect.

Fruit: ray achenes without a pappus; disk achenes with ciliated margins and chaffy scales at its base.

Notes: favors gravelly soils; generic name from the Greek for the resemblance of the achene to a bed bug.

BRITTLEBUSH, (INCIENSO) (*Encelia farinosa*)
ASTERACEAE (sunflower)

Overview: globose perennial subshrub with numerous brittle stems that emanate from a common woody stem.

Flowers: emerge as a *panicle* in groups (3-9) that protrude well above the leafy portion of the plant supported by a smooth peduncle.

Ray: 11-21; bright orange-yellow, 3- lobed.

Disk: yellow, a distinctly green patch can occur centrally.

Leaves: during time of abundant rainfall, the ovate to lanceolate, densely pubescent leaves assume a silvery sheen, but this dulls with the onset of drier weather. Clustered near the stem tips.

Involucre: 3 to 4 series of imbricate bracts.

Notes: a plant greatly favored in home and commercial landscaping. Injured stem secretes a golden-yellow, resinous material that is burnt as incense or used as an adhesive. On occasion, a rarer variant with a lemony yellow corolla is observed.

There is evidence that this plant produces a substance (allelochemical), which is released into the ground and inhibits the growth of other plants.

This ability helps to explain why brittlebush is among the most abundant of the desert perennials, and such an exceptionally successful competitor.

Often one finds brittlebush dominating overwhelmingly a given area; this can also be true of triangle bursage.

RAYLESS ENCELIA (*Encelia frutescens*)
ASTERACEAE (sunflower)

Overview: highly branched, rounded, subshrub with grayish stems that contrasts sharply with its dark green foliage.

Flowers: discoid head (1/2-1") at tip of an elongated and leafless pe-duncle, *solitary*.

Ray: none.

Disk: yellowish orange.

Leaves: ovate to oblong, dark green, petiole, entire, and sparse below the flower head. Pubescence on the margin and underside of the leaf.

Involucre: 2-3 overlapping series, pubescent, glandular, and lanceolate.

Pappus: lacking or inconspicuous.

Handlens: thick hairs, with a basal pustule, cover the blade.

Notes: lacks the woolly pubescence of *E. farinosa*; rather, a softer, white pubescent on the herbage. Colonizer of disturbed sites.

TURPENTINE BUSH (*Ericameria laricifolia*)
ASTERACEAE (sunflower)

Overview: an abundant perennial subshrub that is packed densely with branches.

Flowers: *Inflorescence:* heads in leafy, terminal cymes.

Ray: 3-11; golden yellow.

Disk:10-18; much larger than the phyllaries.

Leaves: linear, delicately curved, small, abound at the branch apex; can surround the stem.

Involucre: lanceolate, 3-4 series, glandular; small.

Notes: glands in the leaf store compounds that impart a pungent, turpentine-like odor and are viscid to the touch. By spring, its seeds (achenes) have dispersed, but it continues to produce light-green, lacy foliage free of flowers. *Tiny* yellow flowers appear late in the summer, and can persist well into winter.

NARROWLEAF GOLDENBUSH *(Ericameria linearifolia)*
ASTERACEAE (sunflower)

Overview: small, dense shrub-like perennial with multiple branches growing from a common point.

Flowers: radiant head, solitary on a leaf-free peduncle that emerges from the leaf axils; monoecious. Persistent floral elements.

Ray: 12-18; yellow (3/8-3/4").

Disk: numerous (3/16-3/8").

Involucre: multiple whorls; lanceolate, large, and conspicuous with a pointed tip, glandular.

Leaves: linear, viscid, sessile (almost clasping), entire, pronounced midvein, covered with pubescence—particularly at the margins.

Fruit: fluffy achene with elongated, fine bristles.

Comment: crushed leaves have a marked odor; stem often supports dead branches. Spring-flowering flora.

DESERT SUNFLOWER *(Geraea canescens)*
ASTERACEAE (sunflower)

Overview: slender annual (can top 3 ft.) that is glandular with white pubescence

Flowers: *Inflorescence:* borne solitary or in a panicle-like formation; head: 2-3".

Ray: 10-21; golden yellow, 2- to 3-lobed.

Disk: numerous; yellow.

Involucre: several whorls (2-3) that are white and densely ciliated.

Leaves: lanceolate to broadly ovate, gray-green dentation, narrows to a petiole that can reach 3".

Fruit: pappus of small awns.

Notes: can form large communities. Gained its generic name from the Greek term for an elderly man in response to the white pubescence of the fruit.

PERENNIAL SNAKEWEED (*Gutierrezia sarothrae*)
ASTERACEAE (sunflower)

Overview: wispy, densely branched subshrub, open and lacy over-all form; bright green upper stems.

Flowers: small (1/4"), bright-yellow ligules (1/8").

    Ray: 3-8.

    Disk: 3-8.

Leaves: linear, resin-coated surface; somewhat sparse—thereby enhancing the open appearance of the plant.

Involucre: 8-21 phyllaries in several whorls.

Stems: thin, delicate and lacy; brown at its base, but green to tan at the upper sections.

Fruit: pubescent, elongated achene with white bristles.

Notes: this late-summer blooming, toxic plant can cause cattle mortality; it has also become a serious rangeland weed. It can be abundant along roadsides and other open areas.

Interesting uses: smoke from incinerated plant was believed effective in fumigating a newborn and mother or for a women suffering pain-riddled menstruation.

Perennial snakeweed and turpentine bush are late summer, flowering plants that can display their flowers for many months. If the summer monsoons are plentiful, they will continue to flower well into late fall to early winter.

COMMON SUNFLOWER (*Helianthus annuus*)
ASTERACEAE (sunflower)

Overview: openly branched annual with a stout stem; scabrous, pubescent leaves and stems.

Flowers: raised, lighter colored flowers at the center of the head.

Ray: more than 15; bright yellow (ligule-1"), prominent venation.

Disk: purple to maroon (1-3").

Leaves: lanceolate to ovate, serrate, elongated petiole. Prominent venation and fine pubescence at the margin.

Involucre: hairy, ovate bracts that narrow at their tip. Highly scabrous and pubescent.

Stem: coarsely pubescent.

Comment: favors disturbed sites and especially desert washes where it has can be abundant.

CAMPHORWEED *(Heterotheca subaxillaris)*
ASTERACEAE (sunflower)

Overview: coarse, viscid, and woody annual; exhibits an open appearance with numerous branches.

Flowers:
  Ray: 20-30; ligules (1/8-3/8").
  Disk: numerous (1/8"); orange; project from the center of the flower head.

Leaves: lower: lobed and clasping; middle: sessile and ovate; all may be finely serrated with a deeply groove mid-vein. *Very viscid to the touch.*

Involucre: bracts separate and distinct in 4-6 series, lanceolate, pointed, covers about two-thirds of the ray flowers.

Stem: finely grooved, thick, solid (0.25"), highly pubescent.

Fruit: ray achenes: smooth, lacking a pappus; disk achenes: densely pubescent.

Notes: a distinct *camphor* odor is released, when the foliage is crushed. Camphorweed is a common member of the late summer to early fall flora and can form large communities. Frequently found along roadsides and disturbed sites.

SEAMLESS BITTERWEED *(Hymenoxys aculis)*
ASTERACEAE (sunflower)

Overview: pubescent perennial with stems to 12".

Flowers: arise from a common, basal point; *inflorescence:* borne solitary at the apex of a leafless structure known as a *scape.*
  Ray: 8-13; bright yellow when young, but becoming cream and reclined at maturity.
  Disk: yellow, small, and 3-lobed.

Leaves: linear, *entirely basal*, softly pubescent, opposite, entire, small glands.

Involucre: independent and densely pubescent bracts, nearly equal in length.

Fruit: pappus with entire to awn-tippled scales.

Note: prefers rocky habitat.

POISON RUBBERWEED (BITTERWEED)
(*Hymenoxys odorata*)
ASTERACEAE (sunflower)

Overview: an erect, odorous annual that can reac
2 ft.

Flowers: heads set in a cyme.

Ray: 6-13; golden-yellow slowly fade to crean
persistent. Fine, green venation throughout th
ligule, which is 3-lobed with open space between th
units, and very narrow at its base.

Disk: numerous.

Involucre: bracts fused at the base, about 8 oute
members.

Leaves: basal, elongated,; pinnately divided int
multiple, linear units. Woolly pubescence on th
under surface.

Stems: purplish base.

Notes: bitter taste, its toxicity is expressed in man
range animals due to a sesquiterpene lacton
(hymenoxon). During times of drought, consumptio
of as little as 0.5% of its body weight can be fatal.

Poison rubberweed has gained in abundance from overgrazing and loss of natur
grasses.

RAYLESS GOLDENROD (JIMMYWEED)
(*Isocoma wrightii*) (*Isocoma pluriflora*)
ASTERACEAE (sunflower)

Overview: subshrub with many erect stems.

Flowers: golden yellow, tiny; *Inflorescence*
terminally clustered (flat-topped) at tip of stem.

Ray: none.

Disk: 7-15, ¼"

Leaves: highly elongated, much nar-rower a
its base, viscid, sessile, borne directly on straw
colored stems.

Involucre: several independent whorls, ti
more conspicuous than basal part.

Fruit: pappus with fine bristles.

Notes: favors disturbed sites, open areas
Aggressive competitor that some view as
noxious weed. Rayless goldenrod can poiso
all livestock; its toxic principle (tremetone) ca
be passed to humans who drink milk obtained from affected animals.

PRICKLY LETTUCE (*Lactura serriola*)
ASTERACEAE (sunflower)

Overview: a tall, erect annual or biennial with prickly basal leaves.

Flowers: pale-yellow but drying to purple.

Ray: 5 teeth or lobed, 14-20 ligules.

Disk: none.

Leaves: oblanceolate; pinnately divided into large, deep lobes; clasp the stem and twist sideways. Become progressively smaller at the upper portions of the stem.

Very pronounced midvein; prickly and bristly appearance to the midvein of the underside and margin of the blade (2-14"). Emit milky sap when cut.

Stem: adorned with prickles and bristles. Erect and hollow, also exudes a milky sap when cut.

Fruit: a single-seeded achene.

Notes: favors disturbed sites. The garden-variety lettuce is *L. sativa*. Careful—bears a resemblance to the sowthistles (*Sonchus*). Found throughout the world in temperate climates.

NEEDLE GOLDFIELDS (*Lasthenia gracilis*)
ASTERACEAE (sunflower)

Overview: typically a low, slender and small, unbranched annual, but under optimal conditions, it can reach 10".

Flowers: supported by 4-12 lanceolate and pubescent bracts.

Ray: 8-13; bright yellow, oval ligule.

Disk: numerous; perfect. Slender, glandular tube with an expansive throat.

Leaves: opposite, linear, pubescent; 2 or more are clustered at the axil.

Involucre: bracts can be numerous, lanceolate, and pubescent along the margins.

Notes: a communal plant, it can cover a broad expanse of desert terrain with hundreds of flowers while successfully excluding other species. The achenes of this and other sunflowers were ground by Native Americans into edible flour.

Lasthenia is named for a student of Plato—she is reputed to have dressed as a man.

LACY TANSYASTER (SPINY GOLDENWEED)

(Machaeranthera pinnatifida)
ASTERACEAE (sunflower)

Overview: perennial to subshrul with an erect and glandular stem.

Flowers: solitary at the tip of th peduncle, supported by multipl series of overlapping, pointe bracts.

Ray: 30-45; yellow, ligules 1/4-3/8".

Disk: numerous; yellow.

Leaves: linear, tiny, sessile, bas pressed against the stem, *silvery green*, and opposite. Pinnatel lobed, lobes bristle tipped. Upper smaller and entire.

Involucre: several whorls: free uniform, narrowly lanceolate. Hemi spheric, glandular and, bristle-tipped.

Pappus: multiple, unequal bristles.

Notes: marked variability occurs in flower size, presence of bristled lobes, and lea form. Carries multiple common names; has undergone numerous changes ii taxonomic classification.

SMOOTH DESERT DANDELION *(Malacothrix glabrata)*
ASTERACEAE (sunflower)

Overview: sparsely branched annual tha produces a pronounced rosette of basal foliage

Flowers: *Inflorescence*: borne at the head c a solitary peduncle.

Rays: 5-lobed, pale yellow when open bu deeper yellow when enclosed.

Disk: none.

Calyx: lanceolate, sharply tipped, oute members shorter than internal segments.

Leaves: basal: oblanceolate, pinnatel divided into lobes; cauline: more linear.

Involucre: bearing white pubescence.

Fruit: pappus: 1-5 bristles.

Notes: blooms in the spring and can be locally abundant; juvenile flowers have a red center.

PINEAPPLE WEED *(Matricaria discoidea)*
ASTERACEAE (sunflower)

Overview: heavily branched, bush-like annual.

Flowers: corolla: yellowish-green,
Ray: none.
Disk: 4 small lobes at the apex of the flower.

Leaves: pinnately divided (1-3 times) into linear segments.

Involucre: small in comparison to the flower head, colorless margin.

Fruit: achenes that lack bristles or awns.

Notes: pineapple-like aroma when the leaves or flowers are crushed; used in herbal medicine and as an herbal tea. Favors open areas such as roadsides; part of the summer-flowering flora.

OAK CREEK RAGWORT *(Packera quercetorum)*
(Senecio quercetorum)

ASTERACEAE (sunflower)

Overview: an erect perennial bearing conspicuous basal foliage.

Flowers:
Ray: light yellow; 8-13.
Disk: darker yellow; 60-70.

Leaves: obovate to pinnately lobed, can be lyrate; margins are crenate to lobed.

Involucre: more than a dozen with a yellow tip.

Stem: one to several purple-tinged members.

Notes: late spring to early summer flowering ragwort.

TURTLEBACK (*Psathyrotes ramosissima*)
ASTERACEAE (sunflower)

Overview: prostrate, aromatic and herbaceous perennial having an overall flattened appearance scaly and pubescent.

Flowers: yellow to somewhat purplish; rayless. *Inflorescence* solitary with a head that is filled with flowers and emerges from a sea of foliage.

Leaves: ovate to kidney-shaped, thick, velvety, and distinc-tively serrated. Silvery-green with prominent venation over the entire surface.

Phyllaries: outer: 5 broad, sparse members; inner: abundant, not broad.

Fruit: pappus that is richly endowed with bristles.

Notes: highly reflective leaves due to the presence of dry trichomes that cover both the upper and lower surfaces. Distinct turpentine-like odor to the herbage.

Primarily a spring flowering plant but responds well to summer rain. Named from the Greek: *psathurotes,* after its brittle stems.

This stunningly detailed image of an unknown orthopteran was selected to represent the countless myriad of insects which are part of the Sonoran Desert invertebrate fauna. (Linda Covey)

WRIGHT CUDWEED *(Pseudognaphalium canescens)*
ASTERACEAE (sunflower)

Overview: multi-branched annual that exceeds 12", and displays an overall silvery-blue appearance.

Flowers: pale yellow; *inflorescence*: clustered at the end of the pedicles. Many are imperfect (pistillate); perfect flowers are also formed.

Leaves: primarily lanceolate with an elongated basal portion, sessile; edges curve inward, prominent midvein. Lower surface: woolly pubescence; upper surface: green, less pubescence.

Involucre: 3-4 series, green base with a silvery tip (translucent); bracts end in a sharp point.

Note: prefers open areas and rocky slopes.

WHITESTEM PAPERFLOWER *(Psilostrophe cooperi)*
ASTERACEAE (sunflower)

Overview: subshrub perennial that tends to assume a spherical shape.

Flowers: borne solitary on an elongated peduncle, the upper portion of which is free of foliage.

Ray: 4-8; 3-lobed, can be angled downward relative to the disk flowers. 5 golden yellow and 3-lobed ligules.

Disk: 5-25; dry to a papery cream color, project well above the ray flowers.

Leaves: linear, entire, and sessile.

Involucre: bracts (10-20), covered with a dense, soft, whitish pubescence, in 2 groups. Outer: lanceolate; inner: shorter and thin.

Stems: whitish, densely packed with hairs.

Fruit: pappus has 4-6 transparent scales.

Notes: this commonly occurring shrub has a long blooming season; responds rapidly to summer monsoon rains with a new flush of flowers. The ray flowers dry and turn a papery white, but they persistent well beyond flowering. Favor open areas such as roadsides and other disturbed sites.

CUTLEAF CONEFLOWER (*Rudbeckia laciniata*)
ASTERACEAE (sunflower)

Overview: erect, perennial herb that can tower to 10 ft and bears one or multiple stems.

Flowers: *Inflorescence*: cymose arrangement on a leafless pedicle.

Ray: yellow; 6-16; markedly drooping.

Disk: yellow; dense cluster that assumes a pyramidal shape.

Involucres: 1 or 2 unequal series.

Leaves: lower: deeply pinnately divided; serrated petiole (to 4").

Fruit: chaffy achene.

Handlens: 5 stamens fused to the base of the corolla, purple anthers.

Notes: favors moist site and flowers in mid summer; pollinated by bees and hoverflies.

The generic name honors a father and son who held the Professorship of Botany, a position that was acquired subsequently by Linnaeus.

THREADLEAF GROUNDSEL
(*Senecio flaccidus* var. *flaccidus*)
ASTERACEAE (sunflower)

Overview: perennial with gray pubescence on the leaves and stems.

Flowers: terminal clusters are cyme like and supported by a slender peduncle.

Ray: 8-13; pale yellow, open space between the ligules.

Disk: numerous; yellow.

Leaves: linear, pinnately divided into 5-9 needle-like units; pubescent under side.

Involucre: campanulate, similarly sized, thin, and pointy, multiple series consisting typically of 21 segments Thin, elongated, basal bract-like structure.

Stem: pubescent with soft tissues above while woody basally.

Fruit: pappus: soft, white bristles.

Notes: favors sandy soils and open areas.

GREEN GROUNDSEL *(Senecio flaccidus* var. *monoensis)*
ASTERACEAE (sunflower)

Overview: perennial with smooth leaves and a stem that can grow to 4 ft.

Flowers: borne at the tip of pedicles that are largely leafless (or greatly reduced) in groups of 2 or 3 (occasionally solitary, 3-4"). Basal bracts exserted and recurved. Bract tips are lightly colored

Ray: 13 or 21; lemon yellow, flowers are sterile.

Disk: orange-yellow, achenes produced only by the disk flowers.

Leaves: pinnately divided into linear portions that look like a hair comb, deep green, sessile, entire.

Involucre: typically 21 segments but can be only 13.

Notes: noteworthy for its toxicity that accounts for its avoidance by range animals (source of potent pyrrolizidine alkaloids). *Senecio* is derived from the Latin *senix,* which refers to an old man. Names so for the white pubescence on many members of this genus.

Early spring thorough early summer flowering.

Interesting use: Navajos, preparing for ceremonial singing, consumed a tea made by boiling the intact plant; it was believed to enhance their musical performance.

LEMMON RAGWORT *(Senecio lemmoni)*
ASTERACEAE (sunflower)

Overview: open, suffrutescent shrub with tiny, white tufts of hairs in the axils of the leaves.

Flowers: borne on largely leafless peduncles.

Ray: 8-10; yellow.

Disk: numerous; orange-yellow.

Leaves: lanceolate, dark green, slightly to markedly serrate (particularly the lower portion of the blade); clasp the stem.

Involucre: lower whorl: widely spaced, curved; upper whorl: uniformly sized, tapered point, little overlap between segments.

Notes: this native plant grows on dry hillsides and rocky slopes.

PRICKLY SOWTHISTLE *(Sonchus asper)*
ASTERACEAE (sunflower)

Overview: erect, herbaceous plant that can grow to 3 ft.

Flower: much like that of *S. oleraceus. Inflorescence*: terminal cluster that is corymb-like and supported by an elongated peduncle that bears scabrous bracts.

Leaves: lower: pinnately divided, lobes almost reach the mid-vein; upper: not lobed or divided. Deep purple, central zone that is much broader than in *S oleraceus. Multiple leaves from a node.*

Markedly and sharply bristle-tipped over the entire margin. *The portion of the lea that surrounds the stem is rounded.*

Involucre: several whorls, markedly bulging base; yellow-tipped trichomes.

Stem: hollow, thick (>1.5"), reddish-purple banding, smooth throughout.

Fruit: small, white with a pronounced translucent margin, white bristles. Its achene is not transversely wrinkled.

Notes: another abundant, aggressive European weed that has become a serious competitor of the native flora.

COMMON SOWTHISTLE *(Sonchus oleraceus)*
ASTERACEAE (sunflower)

Overview: erect, herbaceous plant with a stout stem.

Flowers: *inflorescence:* ligulate heads set in a cyme.

   Ray: yellow.

   Disk: none.

Leaves: upper: sessile, unlobed, apex narrows to an abrupt tip, clasp the stem; lower: lobed, arrowhead-shaped terminal lobe. Minute bristles project from the margins. *Solitary member emerges from the node.*

The portion of the leaf that surrounds the stem is sharply pointed, and the midvein is thick and purple.

Involucre: several whorls, bulging base, supporting yellow-tipped trichomes.

Stem: hollow, thick (>1"), reddish-purple banding; young: pubescent; older: smooth. Milky sap exudes when stem is perforated.

Fruit: pale brown, fissured, broadest in the center, copious white bristles.

Notes: abundant, aggressive European weed with a milky sap. The young foliage of *Sonchus* was consumed as a salad green.

Favors disturbed sites; is found in all of the contiguous states and Hawaii.

LEMMON MARIGOLD (*Tagetes lemmoni*)
ASTERACEAE (sunflower)

Overview: woody perennial that can reach shrub size.

Flowers:

Ray: golden yellow, 6-8 ligules divided into 3-4 units.

Disk: orange-yellow numerous, centrally concentrated.

Leaves: segmented, 3-7 lanceolate sections, serrated, opposite, covered in oily glands. Unusual petiole in that it is serrated.

Involucre: single campanulate series; glandular, tiny lobes.

Notes: once smelled, never forgotten; the lightest touch releases oily materials whose odor is highly persistent. Arizona plant grown in the spectacular San Francisco Public Gardens.

The desert kangaroo rat (*Dipodomys deserti*) feeds primarily on seeds, foliage and insects. It conserves water by producing urine which is many times more concentrated than that of a human. In addition, it can obtain all of the water it requires by metabolism of its foodstuffs; it does not need to drink.

A female can have mul-tiple litters in a single year; the gestation period is about a month. To deal with the desert heat, these nocturnal creatures dig deep burrows with multiple openings that are blocked during the day. They have extraordinary hearing, vital in their survival from such skilled predators as owls and rattlesnakes.

FIVE-NEEDLE PRICKLYLEAF (COMMON DOGWEED)

Thymophylla pentachaeta)
ASTERACEAE (sunflower)

Overview: short, perennial subshrub with numerous slender and leafy stems.

Flowers: *inflorescence* borne solitary on a smooth and elongated peduncles (1-2").

    Ray: 8-13; bright yellow.

    Disk: numerous; yellow.

Involucre: outer: 3-5 small and triangular segments; inner: 13 members, in 2 series, are united at their edges.

Leaves: pinnately divided into 5-11 lobes that are prickled; opposite, and glandular.

Fruit: pappus has 10 scales—inner half divided into 3 awns.

Notes: prefers rocky slopes, arid habitats, and calcareous soils.

TRIXIS (*Trixis californica*)
ASTERACEAE (sunflower)

Overview: highly branched, subshrub with brittle, whitish stems.

Flowers: corolla: bilabiate—large lobe: 3-petals (ligule-like); small lobe: tightly coiled backwards; conspicuous, exserted anthers. Protected by 5-7 bracts *inflorescence*: densely packed panicles.

    Ray: none.

    Disk: 11-27; bright yellow.

Leaves: linear to lanceolate, dark green, sessile to short petiole; margins are frequently rolled under, and entire or gently tooth. Conspicuous mid-vein and glands on the underside of the blade.

Involucre: multiple whorls, largely uniform in length, lanceolate with a pointed tip pubescent. Lower whorls: 2 series; upper whorl: independent, 8-10 members.

Fruit: pappus: white, elongated bristles.

Notes: responds well to the summer monsoon rains with formation of new flowers drought resistant. Prefers dry, rocky exposures; often found growing under the shelter of a tree. Native Americans smoked the leaves; a root infusion was consumed to hasten childbirth.

LINDLEY SILVERPUFFS (*Uropappus lindleyi*)
Microseris lindleyi)
ASTERACEAE (sunflower)

Overview: annual that reaches 2 ft.

Flowers: borne on an elongated flower peduncle that is free of foliage except primarily for a group of basal, rosette-like leave.

    Ray: *light* yellow.

    Disk: none.

Involucre: bracts extend above two-thirds the way to the ligules; on occasion, these sharply pointed structures extend well beyond the ligules.

Leaves: linear; pinnately lobed and highly elongated; dark green, sparse, and basal.

Fruit: ovary matures to a distinctive silvery, lacey seed head composed of a black achene which is dispensed readily by wind currents via a 5-pointed, silver-winged pappus.

Notes: milky sap exudes when the stem is broken. Favors rocky sites, disturbed areas, and roadsides. Can be very abundant during the early days of the spring floral display.

PARISH GOLDENEYE (*Bahiopsis parishii*) (*Vaguiera parishii*)
ASTERACEAE (sunflower)

Overview: globose, shrub-like perennial with multi-branched stems that are covered in stiff pubescence.

Flowers: *inflorescence*: borne solitary at the end of elongated peduncles (to 6") or occasionally in a small cyme.

Ray: 7-15; brownish yellow.

Disk: light yellow and bi-lobed.

Involucre: two series of dissimilar bracts with a tip that narrows abruptly; covered with a fine, whitish pubescence.

Leaves: triangular to cordate, 3 veins project from the base of the blade, wrinkled and *scabrous*. Upper: alternate; lower: opposite.

Fruit: pappus with 2 scales bearing an appendage, and a final pair with lanceolate scales.

Handlens: the hairs on the leaves (upper face) arise from pustules.

Notes: this sunflower member is an abundant desert perennial. A drought-resistant plant that retains its green color and even flowers through much of the arid summer months; strong growth response to monsoon rains. Capable of filling the desert floor with a carpet of color.

A very widely distributed genus who members inhabit a variety of habitats.

TRUMPETBUSH(*Tecoma stans*)
BIGNONIACEAE (bignonia)

Overview: highly branched, perennial shrub with shiny, deep green foliage.

Flowers: bright yellow; corolla: elongated, trumpet-shaped. Bilabiate—2 upper and 3 lower members. *Inflorescence*: either terminal or axillary raceme.

Calyx: tubular, ovate lobes.

Leaves: lanceolate, pinnately compound with 3-9 (typically: 5-7) pinnae, pinna: gently serrated with a pointed tip; opposite. Bright green with a distinct shiny sheen; supported by a slender rachis and petiole (to 2").

Handlens: 4 stamens (2 unequally sized pairs) inserted at the lower half of the throat.

Fruit: elongated capsule, much like desert willow.

Notes: yellow trumpet has two principal varieties: var. *angustata* is native to Texas and New Mexico while var. *stans* is tropical in origin.

Pharmacologically active, it has been used in the treatment of syphilis and adult-onset, insulin-resistant diabetes.

FIDDLENECK (*Amsinckia menziesii* var. *intermedia*)
BORAGINACEAE (borage)

Overview: densely pubescent annual, single to many branches.

Flowers: pale yellow to orange yellow; corolla: tubular. 5 petals each can be marked with reddish-orange splashes of color.

Calyx: 5 deep green sepals covered with elongated, imposing white bristles; deeply pubescent at its edges.

Leaves: narrow and linear *bristling with leafy hairs that also project from the margin*. (The coarse pubescence explains why one of many common names for this plant is *devil's lettuce*). Hairs along the peduncle are even more formi-dable.

Fruit: 4 nutlets, gray to black.

Handlens: stamens and pistils are buried deep within the flower; yellow anthers are supported by tiny filaments that are fused at the top of the floral tube.

Notes: one of the most abundant spring-flowering plants. Often found in large groupings, especially on disturbed sites, but can also occur as a solitary plant.

Some authorities view *A. menziesii* and *A. intermedia* as distinct taxa in which the former has its corolla contained within the calyx while exserted for the latter.

Early in the flowering season, the unopened flower head, covered in a thick, white pubescence is folded inward—bearing a resemblance to the head of a fiddle (*right*).

Over time, the flower head expands to expose younger flowers to pollination. This is a strategy common to many plants which produce a scorpioid raceme or cyme.

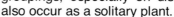

KEY TO LOCAL GENERA OF THE BRASSICACEAE[1]

A. Fruit: silicle
    1B. Fruit: Indehiscent
        1C. Fruit: lacks a septum..........................*Thysanocarpus*[2]
        2C. Fruit: bears a septum................................*Dithyrea*
    2B. Fruit: Dehiscent, 2 or more chambers
        1C. Seed chamber: single seed...........................*Lepidium*[3]
        2C. Seed chamber: 2 or more seeds...............*Lesquerella*
2A. Fruit: silique
    1B. Fruit: 4-sided or nearly so
        1C. Pubescence: stellate...............................*Descurainia*
        2C. Pubescence: not stellate ....*Caulanthus*[4]
    2B. Fruit: not 4-sided
        1C. Fruit:beaked ....*Brassica*[5]
        2C. Fruit: lacks a beak
            1D. Pubescence: simple
                1E. Stamens: unequal............. *Sisymbrium*[6]
                2E. Stamens: equally sized.........*Stanleya*
            2D. Pubescence: forked or stellate
                1E.Leaves:simple............................*Arabis*
                2E.Leaves:pinnatelydivided......*Descurainia*[7]

Six conspicuous stamens (4 large while the final pair is smaller), flowers in terminal racemes or corymbs, 4 petals (commonly clawed) and 4 sepals are features common to plants of this family
White flowers, winged margin around the fruit.
Flattened silique.
Leaves: basal rosette; cauline: linear to obovate, clasping.
Basal leaves do not form a rosette; fruit: 1 row of seeds/cell.
Style: none or inconspicuous, silique: 1-4", petal clawed.
Seeds: 1-2 rows/chamber.[2] White flowers, winged margin around the fruit.

BLACK MUSTARD (*Brassica nigra*)
BRASSICACEAE (mustard)

Overview: single to multi-branched annual to can top out at 8 ft.

Flowers: yellow; corolla: small and clawed petals (less than 1/3"). *Inflorescence* terminal raceme on a tiny pedicle.

Calyx: 4 sepals.

Leaves: oblong to obovate, pinnately divided and lyrate. Upper members no clasping and may be pendant.

Stem: base can be pubescent.

Fruit: silique (less than 1") with a 4-sided to conical, generally ascending beak.

Handlens: 6 erect stamens bearing yellow anthers.

Notes: favors disturbed or open sites; found through the continental US. Originally from the Mediterranean area where it has been cultivated as a spice fo millennia.

Interesting point: one authority muses that this may be the plant that is referred to by Jesus in Matthew 13:31-32.

SAHARA MUSTARD (ASIAN MUSTARD)

Brassica tournefortii)
BRASSICACEAE (mustard)

Overview: annual with massive basal foliage and tiny, yellow flowers.

Flowers: dull yellow; corolla: 4 petals (<1/4"); elongated and tapered base. *Inflorescence*: raceme of 6-20 floral elements.

Calyx: 4 green sepals with reddish-brown streaks, linear but tapered at its tip.

Leaves: pinnately divided, basal rosette, terminal lobe is the largest segment (lyrate) of the dark-green and massive leaf, dentate to serrate, petiole.

Basal: conspicuous mid-vein and secondary venation.

Handlens: 5 stamens with golden-yellow anthers are supported by light green filaments; pistil extends beyond the stamens.

Stem: coarsely pubescent at its base, but smooth at the upper portions.

Fruit: indehiscent silique. The ovary develops rapidly; open flowers at stem tip lower over a series of ever-increasingly long (to 3") fruit as one moves basally. Distinct pedicel (3/8-3/4") support the fruit at a 45° from the stem; *flattened or conical beak.* 2 cells with 7-15 red seeds/cell

Notes: invasive Mediterranean weed that is a prolific, fast-growing seed produce; competes aggressively with the native flora. Favors open, disturbed sites.

GREEN TANSYMUSTARD *(Descurainia pinnata)*
BRASSICACEAE (mustard)

Overview: herbaceous annual with glandular and pubescent herbage.

Flowers: yellow; corolla: 4 tiny petals. *Inflorescence:* terminal raceme that can reach 1 ft.

Leaves: lanceolate to ovate; lower: bi-pinnately; upper: pinnately divided (1- or 2 times), sessile.

Stem: multiple units that branch at their upper portion.

Handlens: a must for viewing internal structures; 6 stamen (4 +2).

Fruit: thin silique (about ½") supported by a pedicle that projects from the stem.

Notes: favors disturbed sites and other open areas; summer-flowering mustard that is bitter tasting but edible

Generic name honors Francois Descourain, a French pharmacist and botanist.

GORDON BLADDERPOD (*Lesquerella gordonii*)
BRASSICACEAE (mustard)

Overview: annual with many slender, elongated, and densely pubescent stems.

Flowers: bright yellow (becomes reddish with age); corolla: 4 independent and spatulate petals.

Leaves: upper: lanceolate and serrated; basal: lyrate. Leaf pubescence can produce a silvery sheen.

Fruit: silicle (1/8") supported on an S-shaped, stout pedicle.

Handlens: sagittate anthers; 4 elongated and 2 shorter members.

Notes: in the early spring, this mustard can dominate large areas with a sea of yellow flowers. As with many mustard plants, developing fruits are mixed with many opened flowers. Favors gravelly and sandy soils and roadbeds; can form an extensive community.

LONDON ROCKET (*Sisymbrium irio*)
BRASSICACEAE (mustard)

Overview: large annual with open, slender stems that branch from their base; it can exceed 3 ft.

Flowers: pale yellow; corolla: multiple petals, *small* (1/16-3/16"). *Inflorescence*: clustered at the top of a thin, green (turns reddish purple) peduncle.

Leaves: upper: spartan, linear, and highly elongated (3-4"); basal: broader, lanceolate to pinnately divided (pinnately divided section near the node).

Handlens solitary, green stigma, style is tiny or absent. 6 yellow anthers.

Fruit: thin, green, cylindrical (*no beak*) siliques. The fruit develop so rapidly that flowers with a noticeably expanding ovary are part of the young, racemic head. *Pedicles are thinner than the fruit.*

Notes: aggressive competitor that some consider a weed. One of the early members of the spring flora. Upper section, appearing to support linear leaves, is devoid of leaves; these structures are the siliques. Another plant that has arrived from Europe.

ORIENTAL HEDGEMUSTARD (*Sisymbrium orientale*)
BRASSICACEAE (mustard)

Overview: erect, branched, and grayish annual to biennial.

Flowers: yellow; corolla: 4 petals (1/4-3/8"). *Inflorescence*: terminal raceme.

Leaves: lower: pinnately divided, arrowhead-shaped terminal lobe; upper: lanceolate, 2-lobed, entire to gently toothed.

Fruit: linear silique (3-4"), *pedicles are as thick as the fruit.* Single row of smooth, brown seeds.

Notes: favors disturbed sites and open areas.

DESERT PRINCESPLUME (*Stanleya pinnata* var. *pinnata)*
BRASSICACEAE (mustard)

Overview: many-stem-med perennial whose branches emanate from a common point.

Flowers: lemon yellow; corolla: 4 segments, dense, clawed, wavy pubescence within the throat. *Inflorescence*: an elongated, terminal raceme that can reach 3 ft.

Calyx: 4 sepals.

Leaves: lower: oblong, markedly pinnately lobed; upper: linear to lanceolate and entire.

Fruit: 1-3" silique with a pedicle that can reach 1". Tiny, brown seeds.

Notes: toxic by virtue of its selenium accumulation. Dominant vegetation on high selenium-containing soils.

SELENIUM POISONING

A number of desert legumes are toxic to livestock and humans because they accumulate vast quantities of selenium from the soil. Selenium is a toxic, metallic element that resembles chemically sulfur. This mimetic property creates problems for the consuming animal since selenium replaces sulfur in essential compounds—these seleno-compounds do not function properly.

Unless the consuming animal possesses a significant level of selenium tolerance, it can be highly toxic, leading to a condition known as blind staggers. The symptoms include perspiration, blindness, abdominal pain, colic, diarrhea, increased heart and respiration rates, and lethargy. Death can occur quickly.

YELLOW BEEPLANT (YELLOW SPIDERFLOWER)
(*Cleome lutea*)
CAPPARIDACEAE (caper)

Overview: unpleasantl odorous annual with stou branches that arise primaril along the upper portions of th stem.

Flowers: light yellow; co olla: 4 obovate to oblong petals *Inflorescence*: short stalk.

Calyx: yellow, minutely tooth fused basally.

Leaves: lanceolate, pa mately compound, 3-7 bu usually 5 segments; primaril basal.

Fruit: elongated capsule (t 2.5") with a joint in its centra section.

Handlens: stamens: 6 c more, exserted, yellow; fila ments elongated (3/8-5/8").

Notes: the pod is dehiscer releasing rough, globose seed during the summer months.

One of the largest of thi country's toads (up to 7"), th Sonoran Desert toad (*Buf alvarius*) is olive green t brown. It is amply defended b toxic secretions from its glands one of the active principles, a derivative of tryptamine, i hallucinogenic.

The tadpoles develop i about 2 month; the adults fee upon an assortment of insects, primarily beetles, but they have been known to ea other toads.

FINGERLEAF GOURD (COYOTE MELON)
Cucurbita digitata)
CUCURBITACEAE (gourd)

Overview: prostrate to climbing perennial, tendril-bearing plant with distinctly shaped foliage.

Flowers: orange-yellow; corolla: campanulate, 5 petals (1-2").

Leaves: overall cordate shape with 5 linear to lanceolate units that project like the fingers of a hand; lobes can be serrated.

Fruit: globose dark-green gourd, bearing yellowish streaking, ages to a straw color.

Notes: can grow a massive tuber; flowers open before dawn and close before noon. Dioecious; the pistillate flowers bear the much sought after gourds. Javalinas favor the starchy tuber and other animals relish the gourd's seeds.

Late spring to early fall flowering. Certain male bees sleep overnight within the flower and wait for a feeding female.

The pulp is astringent to humans and can be markedly toxic. It contains cucurbitacin, a highly bitter triterpenoid glycoside that was used by Native Americans to wean their babies. On the other hand, it is called "coyote melon" for their love of the fruit.

This desert gourd extends in all directions from the parent plant, moving up, over and blanketing neighboring plants—advancing like a horde of army ants.

MARICOPA (FRECKLED) MILKVETCH
(*Astragalus lentiginosus* var. *maricopae*)
FABACEAE (legume)

Overview: stout erect stems with an open, sprawling appearance.

Flowers: light yellow; corolla appearing as if in 2 parts but actually consisting of banner, wing and keel petals. *Inflorescence* flowers positioned on an elongated raceme (15-20 floral units).

Calyx: reddish-purple, bearing white and/or black pubescence.

Leaves: pinnately compound with 5-9 pairs of pinnae; pinna linear to ovate, entire, and smooth

Stem: substantial and smooth

Fruit: sessile pod is bladdery and papery with 2 flat chambers; often freckled (purple-spotted), lanced late and tapering to a point. Curve upwards, often the end touches the stem.

Notes: a host of recognize varieties, many are pink, or whitish pink, to purple— expect marked variation. Favor open areas, disturbed sites, and roadways.

Desert soils are generally limited i nitrogen, but many legumes are able t convert atmospheric nitrogen into form usable for making foodstuffs. Thi unusual ability, rare among flowerin plants, is an important reason for the hardiness and competitive success.

This *Astragalus* enjoys healthy an deeply green foliage, even after tw months of extreme summer hea devoid of rain. Its robustness is due i large measure to this ability to make its own nitrogen-rich fertilizer.

HOG POTATO (PIGNUT) (*Hoffmanseggia glauca*)
FABACEAE (legume)

Overview: an herbaceous perennial that can reach 12".

Flowers: yellow with red spotting; corolla: spreading petals. *Inflorescence*: bears stalked glands.

Calyx: stalked glands.

Leaves: twice-pinnately compound, 5-11 pinnulae with 10-20 compound leaflets; primarily basal.

Stems: slender, reddish, stalked glands.

Fruit: glandular pod with a short stalk.

Notes: mid-spring through summer flowering regime; this legume is sustained by a tuber that is sought actively by hogs.

Has acquired noxious weed status in many locales

FOOTHILL DEERVETCH (*Lotus humistratus*)
FABACEAE (legume)

Overview: low-growing, heavily pubescent annual that forms a dense mat.

Flowers: yellow (turns red with age); wing and keel petals are equal in length. *Inflorescence*: solitary, sessile flowers that emerge at the nodes.

Calyx: 1-2 lobes, spiked, about equal to or larger than the corolla.

Leaves: pinnately com-pound (mostly 3-5 pinnae), but they can appear to be palmately compound; pinna: elliptical to oval.

Fruit: dehiscent, long (0.25-0.5"), and thin; bears stiff, elongated pubescence and an elongated or curved beak. **Notes** flowers in the spring, can form extended colony. Favors roadsides, sandy or gravelly soils and disturbed sites.

SHRUBBY DEERVETCH (*Lotus rigidus*)
WRIGHT DEERVETCH (*Lotus wrightii*)
GREENE BIRDSFOOT TREFOIL (*Lotus greenei*)
FABACEAE legume)

Overview: subshrub with rigid, erect and ascending stems that assume an overall globose shape.

Flowers: bright yellow banner and wing petals look similar. Banner petal underside has a reddish zone.

Inflorescence: flower head (1-3) forms as a cluster that is borne on a thin, highly elongated peduncle (up to 5.0" that can be leafless. Small, leafy brac can occur at the base of the flower.

Calyx: purple, pubescent, sharply tooth; largest segments are those that support the banner petal.

Leaves: pinnately compound with 3-5 pinnae (terminal member is often the largest); dense, soft, pubescence petiole; reddish-brown stipule. Dis-tance between the leaf nodes is much longer than the length of the leaflet.

Stem: circular, smooth, bright green. Nodes are broadly spaced.

Fruit: soon after the flower opens, the fertilized ovary has grown sufficiently to create a straw-colored, elongated, and pointed seedpod that grows to more than 1".

Notes: one of the earliest perennial plants to flower. Its resistance to drought and its ability to fix nitrogen aid in making this a common sight along roadsides and other open areas.

Lotus greenei has a distinct rachis and a peduncle that is longer than the compound leaf. In contrast, *L. wright.* (*left.*) supports a peduncle that is no longer than the com-pound leaf, lacks a rachis, but has compound leaves They are clustered at the apex of the petiole, and emerge like the digits of the hand. At maturity, the fruit bears stiff pub-escence.

Lotus greenei is also similar to *L. rigidus* but the latter is erect rather than prostrate. Brown pubescence covers much of *L. greenei* while in *L. rigidus* the pubescence is white.

ANNUAL YELLOW SWEETCLOVER (*Melilotus indicus*)
YELLOW SWEETCLOVER (*Melilotus officinalis*)
FABACEAE (legume)

Overview: erect (to 3.5') annual legume with tiny flowers.

Flowers: yellow; corolla: tiny petals. *Inflorescence*: borne as a spike-like, terminal raceme (1-4") that projects from the leaf node and is supported by a green and pubescent peduncle.

Calyx: 5 largely independent and highly tapered sepals.

Leaves: pinnately compound with 3 pinnae; sharply dentate, red midvein, petioles to 1". Pubescent and glanded midvein.

Stem: erect, stout and highly branched.

Fruit: one-seeded pod with bumps.

Notes: the yellow corolla of *M. indicus* (annual) does not exceed 1/8" while that of *M. officinalis* (biennial) reaches 1/4". *Melilotus officinalis* can grow to 6 ft.

Yellow sweet clover, *Melilotus officinalis,* (*right*) contains the phytochemical coumarin that is responsible for its fragrance, which some people find obnoxious. Both *Melilotus* were introduced to Arizona from Eurasia.

DESERT SENNA (*Senna covesii*)
FABACEAE (legume)

Overview: perennial subshrub that can reach 2 ft.

Flowers: bright yellow; corolla: 5 separate and prominently veined petals *Inflorescence*: terminal panicle that is clustered at the axils.

Calyx: strongly veined, thin, highly pubescent.

Leaves: elliptical pinnae (2-3 pair) bearing fine, white, velvety pubescence; yellow band at the margin and midvein. Elongated petiole with a pointed gland at its base (1-1.5"); rachis is as long as or longer than the petiole.

Stem: green with dark streaking.

Fruit: oblong, straight and erect, less than 1", finely pubescent, brownish-green and persistent. Pod terminates with a tiny, sharp projection; dark brown inner wall Dried state: 2 segmented, V-shaped, lighter coloration at the pod edges.

Handlens: orange anthers.

Notes: flowers visited by carpenter bees and bumblebees that dislodge the pollen by rapid oscillation of their wings. Carpenter bees have a hair on the thorax that holds effectively the pollen while it is transported to a recipient flower.

Enjoys a long flowering season, particularly if summer rains are plentiful. Favors sandy soils, open and disturbed areas. Can occur locally in large numbers.

WHISPERING BELLS (*Emmenanthe penduliflora*)
HYDROPHYLLACEAE (waterleaf)

Overview: erect and multi-branched annual that is heavily scented, glandular, and viscid.

Flowers: pale yellow; corolla: bell-shaped, 5-lobed and nodding (pendulous). *Inflorescence*: cyme; borne on thin, often curved pedicles.

Calyx: 5 ovate and largely independent sepals; elongated pubescence, especially at the margin.

Leaves: pinnately divided, serrated margins. Basal: short petiole; higher: sessile to clasping.

Fruit: many-seeded capsule.

Handlens: two-segmented, curved stigma; thin, white filaments.

Notes: flowers are borne tightly coiled, but unravel with time. Corolla dries on the plant, becoming papery and generating lovely, whispering sounds in the wind.

GOLDEN BLAZINGSTAR (DWARF BLAZINGSTAR)

(*Mentzelia pumila*)
ADONIS BLAZINGSTAR (*Mentzelia multiflora*)
LOASACEAE (stick leaf)

Overview: biennial, spindly subshrub.

Flowers: golden-yellow; corolla: star-shaped petals (10). *Inflorescence*: terminal cyme that emerges at the leaf nodes; some flowers lack a pedicle.

Calyx: 5 narrow, sharply pointed sepals, massive and highly scabrous. Bracts (1-2) at its base.

Leaves: linear to narrowly lanceolate, deeply and irregularly serrated, lightly colored, highly prominent midvein. *Extremely abrasive texture* (scabrous), sessile.

Stem: whitish-brown, light coloration contrasts sharply with deep green foliage. Stout, scabrous, pubescent.

Fruit: capsule, single seed, pointed base.

Handlens: multiple whorls (3-4) of stamens consisting of 60-100 members; outer members are the broadest. Distinct trichomes (see next page) cover the leaf surface.

Notes: ovary rests well below the corolla. Favors disturbed sites. Heavily barbed plant parts aid significantly in dispersion of the plant. Flowers make their appearance late in the day.

TRICHOMES

Mentzelia pumila and other desert plants produce herbage guarded by a covering of hooked trichomes (*right*). While affording effective defense to the plant, these surface structures also impale beneficial insects such as bees (*left*).

Like many organic pesticides, this protective mechanism lacks specificity; the protective benefit accrued to the plant does not come without cost[1].

SLENDER JANUSIA (DESERT VINE)
(*Janusia gracilis*) *(Cottsia gracilis)*
MALPIGHIACEAE (malpighia)

Overview: delicate, vine-like, twinning perennial with slender stems that can extend 8-10 ft. from ground level.

Flowers: yellow; corolla: 5 petals that are paddle-like in shape with a delicate handle. *Inflorescence*: clustered at the axils or solitary.

Calyx: 5 sepals, glandular at its base, persistent.

Leaves: linear to lanceolate, opposite, small, entire. Upper surface of the blade is covered with a distinct pubescence.

Fruit: red, 3-segmented samara with a green base; thin and hairy with conspicuous venation on the segment.

Handlens: stout filaments united at their base.

Notes: bees harvest oil from paired glands on the underside of the sepal.

---

[1] Based on the research of Dr. T. Eisner, who provided the digital images.

INDIAN MALLOW (*Abutilon incanum*)
MALVACEAE (mallow)

Overview: perennia covered in a velvety pub escence.

Flowers: yellowish orange to orange; corolla: 5 petals with a deep red patch at the base that radiates outward.; petals ben downward. *Inflorescence* borne in a panicle.

Leaves: ovate with a cordate basal portion; soft velvety pubescence; crenulate; prominent petiole.

Fruit: multi-chambered (not more than 5) capsule.

Notes: excellent source of strong fibers suitable for producing rope. A favorite of pollinating bees Favors gravelly soils and rocky outcroppings.

Subspecies *pringlei* can also occur; look for deep orange petals with maroon spotting.

The ferruginous pygmy owl (*Glacidium brasilianum*) hunts at dawn and twilight, when the desert is relatively cool, for various birds, invertebrates, reptiles, and mammals. They will attack successfully a dove many times their body mass.

The females produce a clutch of 3-5 eggs, after a gestation period of 4 weeks. Young owlets are on their own after only a month of parental care.

These non-migratory birds have suf-fered severe loss of habitat—their numbers are in rapid decline throughout their natural habitat. While they favor riparian habitats, a young female perched in a neighbor's small ebony tree for about 3 weeks; much to our regret, she disappeared as silently as she came.

DEVIL'S CLAW (*Proboscidea althaefolia*)
MARTYNIACEAE (unicorn plant)

Overview: prostrate, viscid, and pubescent perennial with a strikingly beautiful flower.

Flowers: golden yellow; corolla: 5 lobed, deep throat that bears splashes and streaks of red. *Inflorescence*: raceme.

Calyx: 5 sepals.

Leaves: oval, scalloped lobes, entire, pronounced venation and petioled. Lower: primarily opposite.

Fruit: a curved and elongated capsule. At maturity, part of the fruit wall splits to create 2 curved pieces forming the "devil's claw"; once seen—never forgotten. When the claw splits open, dozens of black, edible seeds are released (see p.189).

Handlens: 4 stamens as 2 pairs (didynamous).

Notes: a prostrate creeping plant of the summer flora. Bumblebees and carpenter bees are active pollinators of the flower.

Native people cultivated this plant for its fruit as a source of fibers for basket weaving. The cultivated plants produce enlarged "claws", the fiber source (see p. 189).

ROUGH MENODORA (*Menodora scabra*)
OLEACEAE (olive)

Overview: perennial herb that can be a subshrub.

  Flowers: pale yellow; corolla: 5 or 6 ovate petals fused at their base. *Inflor escence*: bears leaf-like bracts.

Calyx: 8-11 sepals; narrow, *sharply pointed* pubescent, red-tipped, and scabrous.

Leaves: oblong to ovate, sparse, and entire. The alternate, upper members are smaller and wider than the lower and opposite foliage.

Fruit: 2-lobed, translucent capsule that opens by a horizontal slit; top of the capsule falls off, but leaves a persistent, lower portion (*left.*).

Handlens: 2 stamens, with conspicuous anthers and a green style with a globose stigma, project above the petals.

Notes: another desert inhabitant that responses to summer monsoon rain with a fresh flush of foliage and prolific flowering.

  Later in the season, the herbage turns a distinct red while adorned with the creamy white remnants of the

fruit.

ЗOLDEN CUP (*Camissonia brevipes*)
ONAGRACEAE (evening primrose)

Overview: annual with conspicuously pubescence stems that are branched only ear their base.

Flowers: bright lemony-yellow (drying green); corolla: 4 ovate petals, campanu- ate and nodding. Typically lack (but may be present) the red spots of *C. californica*. *nflorescence*: a nodding raceme. A reddish caste to the flower indicates its ertilization.

Calyx: pubescent.

Leaves: when young, form as a basal rosette. Linear to lanceolate with a notable nidrib (red) and red areas at the leaf apex. *Petiole is roughly equal in length to the lade.*

Fruit: 2 rows of seeds within the chamber.

Handlens: look for a club-shaped stigma—*all* Camissonia *share a similarly haped stigma.* 8 yellow, globose stamens, pubescent anthers, and pistils as long as he stamens.

Notes: leaves are much broader than *C. californica.* Flower opens in the evening nd remains so throughout the following day.

CALIFORNIA SUNCUP *(Camissonia californica)*
ONAGRACEAE (evening primrose)

Overview: erect and spindly with prominently thickened and coars stem; supports small, linear leaves an flowers at its nodes.

Flowers: lemony-yellow; corolla: separate petals that project back wards. Numerous red spots pepper th area around the base of the pistils an stamens; these reproductive structure are exserted, almost reaching the edg of the corolla.

Leaves: basal rosette, lanceolat deeply pinnately lobed but becomin more linear progressively up the stem.

Fruit: sessile, linear, and *pointe downward.* One row of seeds (purpl spotted) in its chamber.

Handlens: 8 stamens divided into 2 groups equal in number but unequal in size Elongated style with a globose stigma.

Note: the flower stalk is thick and substantial thereby creating a rigid, erec appearance to the plant.

HEARTLEAF SUNCUP *(Camissonia cardiophylla)*
ONAGRACEAE (evening primrose)

Overview: ranges from a simpl herbaceous annual to a perenni subshrub.

Flowers: yellow but becoming red wit maturity; corolla: 4 petals. As the flowe matures, its ovary elongates to create tubular structure that supports the rem nants of the perianth. *Inflorescence* dense, terminal racemes.

Leaves: cordate, irregular den-tatio petioles can be as long as the blade Distributed throughout the stem; thick glandular and pubescent.

Fruit: capsule supported by a shor pedicle.

Handlens: unequal stamens.

Notes: named *cardiophylla* for it heart-shaped leaves.

MINIATURE SUNCUP (*Camissonia micrantha*)
Oenothera micrantha)
ONAGRACEAE (evening primrose)

Overview: prostrate to spreading, densely pubescent with pronounced basal leaves.

Flowers: yellow; corolla: 4 petals, occasional red spot(s) at the base; unopened flowers are red. *Inflorescence*: emerge from leaf axils throughout the plant.

Calyx: 4 sepals, highly pubescent.

Leaves: basal rosette: linear to lanceolate, entire, narrow at the petiole (can be as long as the blade, 1-4"). Upper: much more diminutive, ses-sile; basal: pronounced midvein.

Stem: basal portions are red, can be exfoliating.

Handlens: 8 uneven stamens; 4 short while the remaining members are much longer.

Fruit: 4-sided capsule that can curve and project at a 90° angle from the stem.

Notes: favors sandy soils and disturbed sites.

YELLOW LINANTHUS (*Linanthus aureus*)
POLEMONIACEAE (phlox)

Overview: erect or ascending, slender-stemmed annual.

Flower: golden-yellow with a bright orange throat; corolla: 5 rounded lobes, funnel-shaped. *Inflorescence*: open cyme on a short peduncle (to 3/8"). Stamens form a conspicuous circle around the corolla throat.

Calyx: as large as the corolla, can obscure the petals; deeply clefted lobes.

Leaves: palmately divided into 3-7 tiny lobes; opposite, project as a ringed group at intervals along the stalk.

Stem: slender, elongated, can be glandular.

Handlens: exserted pistil; sta-mens attached at the corolla throat—the latter upports a ring of pubescence.

Notes: early spring bloomer, favors sandy sites.

DESERT TRUMPET (*Eriogonum inflatum*)
POLYGONACEAE (buckwheat)

Overview: open, sparsely stemmed annual c biennial herb with basal foliage, and an inflated stem.

Flowers: pale yellow to reddish; corolla: tiny (1/16" petals are narrowly ovate. *Inflorescence*: bunched a the end of a delicate flower stalk (cyme-like) an supported by 3 scale-like bracts.

Calyx: 5-pointed, pubescent.

Leaves: oval to cordate, all basal, coarsel pubescent, curved inward and wrinkled.

Stem: gray-green, swollen immediately below fir branch point. Multiple branches emanate from ju above the swollen stem section.

Fruit: light brown and smooth achenes.

Tidy Larder: tiny female wasps, belonging to th genus *Onyerus*, bore a small hole in the inflated ster section, and fill the base with small pebbles. Larval materials are added nex followed by her eggs, and finally it is covered again with additional pebbles. Th newly emerged larvae are thereby provided adequate food to complete the development within the protective confines of this ingeniously constructed larder.

Some believe that the swollen stem is due to the feeding activity of thes hymenopterans that irritate the woody tissues. Field studies have established tha this is not so. Moisture is far more important, the degree of stem inflation is relate to water availability. *Eriogonum deflexum* lacks this expanded or "inflated" stem.

PURSLANE (*Portulaca oleracea*)
PORTULACACEAE

Overview: annual with succulent, prostrate stem.

Flowers: yellow; corolla: 4-6 petals with lobe margins; *Inflorescence*: borne solitary or in clusters (2-5 at the apex. Individual units open for a limited time in th morning of sunny days.

Calyx: 2 sepals united at their base directly sup-po the petals and stamens.

Leaves: oblanceolate to obovate, tiny petiole to ses sile, succulent, and flat.

Stems: greenish with a reddish tinge, succulent.

Fruit: capsule with numerous seeds.

Handlens: 5-20 stamens; elongated, smooth, an yellow filaments; 4- to 6-lobed styles.

Notes: edible plant that has been consumed b humans for centuries; an outstanding source of omega 3-fatty acids. Native to India and the Middle East.

YELLOW COLUMBINE (*Aquilegia chrysantha*)
RANUNCULACEAE (buttercup)

Overview: perennial subshrub whose flowers contain an impressive spur.

Flowers: golden-yellow; corolla: 5 petals, dramatically long spur (to 3") that projects backwards. Large assemblage of stamens that is even longer than the corolla tube (to 4").

Calyx: 5 lanceolate sepals.

Leaves: segmented into several lobes; elongated petiole (2-6").

Handlens: 5 independent pistils.

Fruit: follicle.

Notes: favors moist sites; truly an extraordinarily picturesque flower; not surprisingly, a popular plant in desert gardens. Found in moist sites such as the river banks where it can form an extensive and visually striking community.

SNAPDRAGON PENSTEMON (*Keckiella antirrhinoides*)
SCROPHULARIACEA (figwort)

Overview: spreading to an erect, woody perennial that can grow to 8 ft.

Flowers: yellow; corolla: tubular with a wide throat; bilabiate—upper: large lip with 2 lobes that form a hood; lower: 3 lobes. Darkens as it dries.

Leaves: oblanceolate to obovate, opposite, entire, petiole; older members: clus-te at the leaf nodes. Drought-deciduous.

Stem: woody, brown, gently pubescent; can spread to a length of 8 ft.

Handlens: yellow, densely pubescent, exserted staminode accompanies 4 fertil stamens.

Notes: before the flower opens, the floral parts display 5 red cleavage zones Gains its name from its resemblance to a snapdragon, but its stem is far woodie than that of a snapdragon.

One author described the flower rather humorously: "The corolla is 2-lipped. Th upper lip forms a hood and the lower one opens like a hungry mouth with 2 saggin jowls."

COMMON MONKEYFLOWER (*Mimulus guttatus*)
SCROPHULARIACEA (figwort)

Overview: a small annual plant, but under favorable conditions acquires a perennial life cycle.

Flowers: yellow; bilabiate—upper lip: tube-like, double lobed; lower: 3-lobed, throat area speckled with red spots. Pubescence on the petal folds. Pubescence around the throat appears to seal the opening. *Inflorescence*: racemes, supported on elongated peduncles (1-3"), emerge at the nodes.

Calyx: fused sepals with purple streaks; about half as long as the corolla tube. Five lobed—one is larger than the remaining members are.

Leaves: ovate, dentate to irregularly lobed, blade is twice as long as wide. Upper: sessile; lower: petiole. Form at the node as an oppositely positioned pair.

Stem: hollow, smooth, green; roots develop from the nodes of the stem; conspicuous clear zones between the nodes.

Handlens: stigma notched, flattened; pistil elongated but not exserted.

Notes: highly toxic to grazing cattle; hummingbirds, however, relish the flowers. Favors wet sites such as creeks and streams where it can be locally abundant.

WOOLLY MULLEIN *(Verbascum thapsus)*
SCROPHULARIACEA (figwort)

Overview: biennial with a massive stem and a rosette of basal leaves.

Flowers: yellow; corolla: 5 petals, united at their base. *Inflorescence*: highly elongated spike (6-7') that can be half the total length of the plant.

Calyx: 5 lanceolate sepals.

Leaves: oblanceolate; basal entire, petiole, rosette, velvet pubescence; cauline: clasping Combined with the petiole, the basal leaf can exceed 16".

Handlens: upper 3 filaments white to yellow, pubescent; lower 2 filaments: sparsely pubescent.

Notes: an invasive weed of disturbed sites, native to Europe and northern Africa and Europe, which threatens local flora.

Favored in herbal medicine for its emollient and astringent properties.

IVYLEAF GROUND CHERRY *(Physalis hederifolia)*
SOLANACEAE (nightshade)

Overview: perennial with highly glandular stems that are branched diffusely from the basal region.

Flowers: yellow to green-ish yellow; corolla: 5 bell-shaped segments; 5 splashes of purple brown at the central core *Inflorescence*: solitary flowers borne on lateral, nodding peduncles. Pedicels shorter than the flowers.

Calyx: 10 green veins, campanulate, viscid, and recurved Lobes are 3/4 the length of the tube.

Leaves: cordate to oval, entire to serrated margins, petioles to 1.5"

Fruit: green berry housed within an enlarged calyx.

Notes: plant typically spreads along the ground but can be erect; favors gravelly soils and rocky slopes. Overwinters via a rhizome.

THICKLEAF GROUNDCHERRY (YELLOW NIGHTSHADE)
(Physalis crassifolia)
SOLANACEAE (nightshade)

Overview: compacted, intricately branched perennial.

Flowers: dull yellow; corolla: 5 fused and campanulate petals; 5 pubescent zones encircle the base of the lobes.

Pedicle (0.6-1.2") at least as long as the corolla.

Calyx grows and expands to create a 10-ribbed bladder that houses the seed.

Leaves: ovate to deltoid to subcordate, fleshy, entire to wavy; petiole as long as the blade.

Stem: angle of the stem changes abruptly.

Handlens: yellow stamens, conspicuous and mostly exserted.

Fruit: greenish berry protected by a papery calyx.

Notes *P. crassifolia* can take the form of a shrub while *P. hederifolia* is herbaceous.

Favors dry sites, gravelly and sandy soils. Drought-tolerant. Name after the Greek word *physalis* (a bladder), which refers to the inflated, mature calyx.

These ground cherries can be confused. *Physalis crassifolia* has a pedicle that is longer than the flower; the lobes of the calyx are more than 2/3 the length of the corolla tube. *In P. hederifolia*, the pedicle is smaller than the flower and the calyx lobes are no more than 1/2 the length of the corolla tube. *P. hederifolia* has 2 varieties: var. *fendleri* which is not glanded while var. *palmeri* bears glands

Pinnacle Peak Park, Scottsdale, Arizona. A wonderful place to hike, view spring flowers, and expand your botanical knowledge.

RED, PINK, MAGENTA & PURPLE

Many of the plants of this colored group are actively sought by bees and hummingbirds, agents that effectively disperse their pollen.

New Mexico Thistle, *Cirsium neomexicanum*

ARIZONA FOLDWING (*Dicliptera resupinata*)
ACANTHACEAE (acanthus)

Overview: annual or perennial, densely branched, and supporting highly picturesque flowers.

Flowers: purplish-violet to magenta: corolla: small, tubular, projects above a pair of cordate bractlets. Bilabiate—upper petals: elliptical, white patch with purple splashes; lower petals: triangular, solid color. *Inflorescence*: large peduncle supporting a cyme or solitary from the axil.

Calyx: 5 overlapping sepals bearing a white margin.

Involucre: flat, cordate and smooth.

Handlens: two stamens with unequal anthers and magenta filaments.

Notes: petals emerged from a sheath that will serve to protect the seeds. Monoecious, staminate flowers can be scarce.

FRINGED AMARANTH (*Amaranthus fimbriatus*)
AMARANTHACEAE (amaranthus)

Overview: monoecious annual with long, erect branches and red herbage.

Flowers: no corolla; *inflorescence*: *long*, terminal, spike-like clusters.

Pistillate: 5 tepals, clawed, somewhat spatulate.

Staminate: 5 tepals and 2 or 3 stamens.

Calyx: fan-shaped, edges bear slender, elongated projections (ciliated).

Leaves: linear to narrowly lanceolate, elongated (1-4"), petiole (to 1").

Stem: red.

Fruit: utricle.

Handlens: 3 stamens, 3 branches to the style.

Notes: this species is generally monoecious but can be dioecious. Staminate flowers are uncommon.

Late summer flora. Found in sandy washes, disturbed sites, and roadsides; dries to a rust-brown color.

FRINGED TWINEVINE (CLIMBING MILKWEED)
(*Funastrum cynanchoides* var. *hartwigii*)
HAIRY MILKWEED (*Funastrum hirtellum*)
ASCLEPIADACEAE (milkweed)

Overview: a twining plant that covers the host with thin green stems that intertwine like fibers of a rope.

Flowers: wine-red with white borders, ciliated margins, and a central core filled with 5 stamens that have a large, white appendage as well as a 5-segmented ovary. Corolla: 5-lobed and raised petals. *Inflorescence*: umbel borne on short pedicles supported by elongated peduncles (to 2").

Calyx: 5 stellate, green sepals with reddish tips and margins.

Leaves: typically, linear to narrowly lanceolate but can be cordate, opposite, pronounced mid-vein. Clasping or borne on a small petiole.

Fruit: solitary follicle (2-4").

Notes: when the petals are unfolded, flowers are reminiscent of a tiny bird's nest with 5 eggs; has the milky sap found commonly in milkweeds. Favors sandy washes.

Another variety of *F. cynanchoides*, var. *cynanchoides* has broader leaves.

Many authorities still use the generic name—*Sarcostemma*.

A related climber is the hairy milkweed, *F. hirtellum (right)*, with similar flowers but the leaves are pubescent and the corolla is a lightly colored greenish-yellow.

NEW MEXICO THISTLE (*Cirsium neomexicanum*)
ASTERACEAE (sunflower)

Overview: a large, erect, white, and woolly biennial that can reach more than 6 ft. This thistle is covered with dense, gray pubescence, and heavily armored with formidable bristles.

Flowers: *inflorescence*: open, cyme-like clusters.

    Rays: none.

    Disk: pink to magenta, occupy the top third of the flower head (1-3"); central core of the head is whitish while pigment is concentrated at the apex.

Involucre: green, multiple whorls, sharply pointed with a spine that can reach 0.75", densely pubescent. Upper bracts: erect, curved upward; lower: angled downward.

Leaves: oblong to oblong-lanceolate, attached to stem at the nodes, armored and spiny. Dark green, deeply grooved, can exceed 16" in length. Lower: spiny petiole; upper: sessile, gradually reduced in size.

Handlens: look for nectar-bearing appendage between the corolla and the internal organs.

Notes: this thistle is a favorite of a large array of insect pollinators. Stem, foliage, and involucres are covered in pubescence.

SPREADING FLEABANE (*Erigeron divergens*)
ASTERACEAE (sunflower)

Overview: heavily branched, pubescent biennial or perennial that grows to 2 ft.

Flowers: slender peduncle (to 2").

Ray: 75-150 (2-4); light purple to lavender to white, numerous small ligules (3/16").

Disk: yellow. Outer members: pale yellow; inner: deeper yellow and larger throat.

Calyx: uniform sepals form a solid cup that supports the flower head (1").

Leaves: sessile, and covered with fine pubescence. Lower: obovate, entire to lobed to pinnately divide; upper: linear to oblanceolate, entire. Can appear to be clasping. Petiole to 2.

Involucre: lanceolate, equally sized in a single series, pubescent and glandular, continuous (not overlapping), can have a lavender splash.

Pappus: inner: brittle bristles; outer: narrow scales.

Notes: a commonly occurring fleabane that can form a large grouping. Rayless flowers found occasionally; favors open and disturbed areas.

HOARY ASTER (*Dietaria canescens*) (*Machaeranthera canescens*)
ASTERACEAE (sunflower)

Overview: herbaceous perennial that can top 36".

Flowers: *inflorescence*: panicle to cyme-like, located at the tip of long branchlets.

Ray: reddish-purple to magenta to violet (0.5").

Disk yellow, tiny (1/4-5/16").

Leaves: lower: narrowly lanceolate or linear to obovate, entire to serrated and rough; upper: sessile (lower foliage has a short petiole). Groupings of much smaller leaves at or near the axil, which also bears a single, much larger leaf.

Involucre: large and hemispheric, multiple and glandless whorls (3-10) that taper to a point; segments typically bend backward and project outward, reminiscent of a bur.

Fruits: finely pubescent achenes with a pappus of rusty-silvery bristles.

Notes: drought tolerant, responses well to summer monsoons, favors open areas and roadsides. Can form large groupings. Gray-white pubescence on stems.

SPANISH NEDLES (*Palafoxia arida*)
ASTERACEAE (sunflower)

Overview: annual sunflower that can be per-ennial with a cylindrical flower head and erect multi-branched stems.

Flowers: white corolla with exserted, purplish-red style branches. *Inflorescence*: a flat-topped cyme with 10-20 flowers.

Ray: none.

Disk:18-40.

Leaves: lanceolate to linear, entire, glandular, and pubescent.

Involucre: 2-3 uniform series, can be free of glandular spots.

Stems: largely foliage-free, elongated to about 2 ft.

Fruit: four-angled pappus with 4-10 scales.

Notes: flowers bear a resemblance to *Adeno-phyllum*. Part of the summer-flowering flora. Genus is named for Jose de Palafox, a Spanish military commander.

ODORA (*Porophyllum gracile*)
ASTERACEAE (sunflower)

Overview: bushy and small perennial subshrub cylindrical flowers.
Flowers: solitary, arise at the apex of a peduncle (about 1").
　Ray: none.
　Disk: purple or white with deep and distinct purple streaking,
　Leaves: linear, sessile, and entire.
Involucre: cylindrical to campanulate, uniform; occurs as a group of 5, containing numerous glands, purplish splashes—especially at the tip.
　Fruit: pappus: rose-colored, slender bristles.
Notes: particularly odoriferous plant with a *pungent, highly persistent aroma*. Greatly favored as forage by cattle and deer.

Odora is superficially similar to san felipe dyssodia (*right*) but the latter bears yellow disk flowers, many more phyllaries, and has a far more intense and persistent herbal odor (see p. 116).

MOJAVE ASTER (*Xylorhiza tortifolia*)
ASTERACEAE (sunflower)

Overview: perennial that can reach subshrub size with many branched stems that arise from a woody base.

Flowers: *Inflorescence*: solitary flower borne on an elongated peduncle (3-9").

Ray 40-60; light blue to lavender or purple to magenta.

Disk: 70-100; yellow.

Leaves: oblong to linear, sessile, softly pubescent, hairs project from the edge of the serrated margin, glandular. Prominent venation.

Involucre: softly pubescent, glandular, and needle-like tip. Outer: greenish, densely glandular; inner: straw-colored with irregularly indented margins. 4-5 imbricated series.

Stems: branching limited to lower portions.

Fruit: pappus of rigid bristles.

Notes: favors sandy washes and disturbed sites.

PERENNIAL ROCKCRESS (*Boechera perennans*)
(*Arabis perennans*)
BRASSICACEAE (mustard)

Overview: early-flowering, perennial herb with tiny flowers and slender stems that reaches 12".

Flowers: pink to purple; corolla petals: 4, conspicuous venation, clawed and spatula-shaped. *Inflorescence*: raceme; long, slender pedicle bends downward, creating a pendent flower head.

Calyx: erect and pubescent.

Leaves: basal: oblanceolate, dentate, markedly pubescent, petiole; upper: lanceolate (can be sagittate), sessile, and smooth.

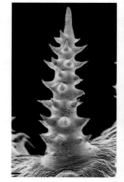

Fruit: silique (1.5-2.5"), seeds stored in a single row.

Notes: mature plants retain older foliage under the new, basal leaves.

Point of Interest: the leaves bear trichomes (epidermal structures), that can contain irritants or toxicants to chemically protect the plant (*right*). Their sharply barbed form also provides physical protection.

SLEEPY CATCHFLY (*Silene antirrhina*)
CARYOPHYLLACEAE (pink)

Overview: annual having an erect stem with little branching.

Flowers: pink to purple to lavender; corolla: 5 petals, notched, that forms a fused floral tube; independent and spreading. *Inflorescence*: compacted or open cyme, on a thin pedicle (0.5-1.5"), that is supported by a pair of linear bracts.

Calyx: 5 sepals that are fused into a tube. Immature: rapped in a green, lanceolate structure with the colored flower emerging at the tip.   Sticky, triangularly lobed at its ip.

Leaves: lower: oblanceolate to spatulate; upper: linear, smaller; opposite, entire, sessile (or a diminutive petiole). Some pubescence at the blade base.

Stem: slender and generally smooth, but viscid patches form beneath the upper eaf nodes.

Fruit: capsule (3 celled) with 6 short, teeth that curve downward.

Notes: corolla can be white or pink; flowers close at night and open with the new Jay. Found in disturbed sites, favors sandy soils.

TEXAS BINDWEED (*Convolvulus equitans*)
CONVOLVULACEAE

Overview: trailing, vine-like, and pubescent perennial that can extend to 6 ft. or more.

Flowers: white to pink (can have a reddish core); corolla: petal margins are toothed, can be campanulate. *Inflorescence*: typically solitary, but can have 2-3 members on a peduncle that arises from the leaf axil.

Calyx: densely pubescent.

Leaves: hastate, tooth margins, petiole (to 2").

Fruit: spherical capsule with 1-4 black and smooth seeds.

Handlens: 5 stamens and brown anthers; single style with 2 stigmas.

Notes: flowers in the spring, lacks tendrils; favors sandy and gravelly soils.

NUTTALL MILKVETCH (*Astragalus nuttallianus*)
FABACEAE (legume)

Overview: slender, annual legume; stem can reach about 2 ft.

Flowers: large, visually striking; *banner: purple to magenta* with a white zone marked with purple streaking; *wing*: magenta. *Inflorescence*: raceme with 3-4 clustered members or solitary. Elongated peduncle (1-4").

Calyx: lanceolate; tiny (1/16") and broadly campanulate.

Leaves: pinnately compound with 5-17 pinnae (pinna: notched at tip), stipules.

Fruit: linear, 2-celled (0.5-1.0"), curved at its base.

Stem: grows along the ground to markedly ascending,

Notes: named for Thomas Nuttall, a prominent 19th century botanist.

DOWNY PRAIRIE CLOVER (*Dalea neomexicana*)
FABACEAE (legume)

Overview: prostrate perennial with densely pubescent and glandular stems and foliage.

Flowers: red to lavender to whitish; corolla: rounded, glandless *wing* petal. *Inflorescence*: dense, woolly raceme.

Calyx: multiple sepals; elongated, generally longer than the corolla.

Leaves: pinnately compound with 7-13 pinnae, pinna: pubescent, glands regularly spaced along the edge, tip notched, and V-shaped. Rachis: pubescent and glandular.

Notes: young, immature ovary resembles a lima bean; favors sandy soils and open, disturbed areas.

ELEGANT LUPINE (BAJA LUPINE) (*Lupinus concinnus*)
FABACEAAE (legume)

Overview: a typically prostrate, pubescent legume that can reach 12".

Flowers: young petals: purple; older: magenta. *Banner*: off white; *keel*: bear their purple color primarily at the petal edge.

Calyx: similarly sized sepals, upper unit is markedly lobed.

Leaves: palmately compound (6-8 leaflets), densely pubescent, long petiole (can reach 3").

Stem: spreads along the ground to erect.

Fruit: small pod, straight, densely pubescent, 2-4 seeds.

Notes: favors sandy soils and washes; can be abundant along roadsides and other open areas.

ARIZONA CENTAURY (*Centaurium calycosum*)
GENTIANACEAE (gentian)

Overview: an erect annual to biennial.

Flowers: pink, yellow ring at the throat surrounds a greenish patch; corolla: 5 petals form a *pointed* and tubular structure. Pedicle: 0.4-1.5".

Calyx 5 lobes that are equal in length to the sepal tube; thin and largely independent.

Leaves: obovate to elliptical, basal rosette, opposite, entire, succulent, clasping.

Stem: sessile to tiny petiole.

Handlens: large anthers, numerous golden-yellow and exserted stamens; stigma lobes widely parted.

Notes: favors sites with ample moisture; a rare and white variant occurs occasionally.

FILAREE (*Erodium cicutarium*)
GERANIACEAE (geranium)

Overview: one of the earliest blooming annuals.

Flowers: rose to magenta with basal purple streaking; corolla: 5 unfused petals. Highly elongated and persistent style (1-2").

Calyx: bristle-tipped, silvery with purple venation.

Leaves: ovate, pinnately divided (9-13 units), basal rosette. Oldest units can reach 12".

Fruit: sharply angled and pointed capsules develop quickly from the flowers.

Notes: introduced from Eurasia, it has become widespread throughout the US. Analysis of the adobe bricks from Spanish building erected in the 18th century revealed its long-term presence in America.

The ovary wall expands rapidly to create a beak- or needle-like fruit that is well developed before the flowering cycle ends. This is a classical example of rapid fruit development by short-lived, annual plants. The Greek for heron (the bird) is *Erodios*; this is the generic name root taken for the fruit's resemblance to a heron's bill.

TEXAS STORK'S BILL (TEXAS FILAREE)
(*Erodium texanum*)
GERANIACEAE (geranium)

Overview: a low-growing annual or biennial covered in fine pubescence.

Flowers: purple to magenta to lavender; corolla: 5 independent, unequally sized lobes.

Calyx: silvery with purple venation.

Leaves: cordate and pinnately lobed (3 units) with an enlarged middle lobe. Prominent venation, no stipules, and an equally sized petiole.

Stem: often reddish.

Notes: five-segmented fruit has a shape derived from its elongated, erect style. Beak-like pod coils in a manner reminiscent of filaree. Filaree, however, has pinnately divided leaves. This is a native *Erodium*.

MOCK PENNYROYAL (DWARF PENNYROYAL)
(*Hedeoma nana*)
LAMIACEAE (mint)

Overview: diffusely branched, aromatic perennial with a smooth stem.

Flowers: light purple to magenta; corolla: spreading throat; bilabiate—lower: 3 lobes, splash of white; upper: 2 lobes. *Inflorescence*: solitary from the leaf axils.

Leaves: basal: ovate, petiole; upper: much reduced in size, appear as bracts. Entire to slightly dentated.

Fruit: smooth and oblong nutlet.

Handlens: 4 stamens (some may be infertile).

Notes: named from the Greek: *hedus, sweet; osme*, odor.

TEXAS BETONY (SCARLET HEDGENETTLE)
(*Stachys coccinea*)
LAMIACEAE (mint)

Overview: a squared-stem annual that can attain 2 ft.

Flowers: light pink to scarlet; corolla: tubular (about 3/4"). Bilabiate—upper lip: elevated; lower lip: 3-lobed and angled downward. *Inflorescence*: groups of about 6 flowers spread in a whorl around the stem.

Leaves; oval to triangular, grayish-green, opposite, crenulate, with prominent venation. Upper: petiole to 3"; lower: tiny or lacking.

Stem: soft pubescence throughout.

Handlens: 4 stamens project from beneath the upper lip.

Notes: favors rock crevices and moist habitats.

CALIFORNIA LOOSESTRIFE (*Lythrum californicum*)
LYTHRACEAE (loosestrife)

Overview: herbaceous perennial with erect stems that are covered with leaves, and exhibit a shedding, papery bark.

Flowers: reddish purple; corolla: 6 petals. *Inflorescence*: spike-like in appearance but actually a raceme that is either solitary or in pairs from the leaf node, borne on a tiny pedicle.

Calyx: minute and similar in size to the corolla; ribbed (12) with tiny, erect dentation.

Leaves: linear to lanceolate, gradually narrowing at the apex; lower: opposite; upper: alternate and reduced.

Stem: 4-5 angled, exfoliating, and papery bark.

Fruit: capsule: ribbed and cylindrical.

Handlens: 6 stamens at the base of the corolla tube; needle-like style.

Notes: an aggressive plant that has been declared an undesirable "weed" in several states. Favors moist sites, particularly along creeks and streams.

DESERT FIVE-SPOT (*Eremalche rotundifolia*)
MALVACEAE (mallow)

Overview: annual with a stout and erect stem.

Flowers: lilac to mauve; corolla: 5 petals, each with conspicuous reddish-purple "eye spots", form a cup-like structure. Showy internal stamens and pistils.

Leaves: circular to kidney-shaped (basally notched), distinctively crenate margin; solitary member at the end of an elongated petiole.

Stem bearing simple, bristly pubescence; open appearance.

Notes: the flower head maintains its globular shape, hiding the picturesquely spotted corolla that is displayed within its interior.

The desert bobcat, *Felis rufus*, a solitary creature in which males and females live apart, has a litter of only 2 or 3 kittens—born sightless and vulnerable. As with other animals, the male does not contribute to the rearing of the litter. After some 9 months of training, the growing kittens must fend for themselves.

A fierce animal, it can take down a young deer, but various rabbits are the main component of its diet. It is a patient hunter who waits for small prey to come within range, and then attacks—grabbing the fleeing animal with its piercing, retractable claws. Larger prey elicits stalking behavior, and then a final sprint to vanquish the victim.

A striking behavioral adaptation is that the hind feet land in the same spots as that occupied by the forward limbs; this minimizes such noise as the breaking and crushing of materials on the desert floor.

DOUBLE CLAW (*Proboscidea parviflora*) (*Martynia parviflora*)
MARTYNIACEAE (unicorn)

Overview: spreading, sprawling annual with highly viscous foliage and distinct fruit.

Flowers: pinkish purple; corolla: bilabiate—2 upper lobes and 3 lower members, one member with a streak of golden yellow, which functions as a nectar approach.

Leaves: ovate to cordate to variously triangular, entire to somewhat lobed, *highly viscous.*

Calyx: 5 viscid and pubescent sepals.

Fruit: highly elongated and hooked pod-like capsule.

Handlens: 4 stamens (didynamous).

Notes: a late-flowering unicorn; this picture was taken on 21 October. Another *Proboscidea* whose fruit was sought after for their elongated fibers employed in basket weaving.

The fruit wall segments have been opened to expose internal details. The seeds are lodged within the dark, woody structure at the base of the two sharp, hook-like "claws" that are part of the fruit. Some dozen black seeds are housed within the fruit.

DESERT SAND VERBENA (*Abronia villosa*)
NYCTAGINACEAE (four o'clocks)

Overview: annual with highly branched, stout stems that are both viscid and pubescent.

Flowers: purplish to magenta; corolla: divided into 5 fused petals, funnel-like, each 2-lobed. Much lighter central core. *Inflorescence*: 15-35 members in a globose head.

Leaves: circular to lanceolate, petioles to 2", opposite.

Stems: viscid, pubescent, tend to be prostrate and spreading.

Involucre: lanceolate, viscid, and rough.

Handlens: 5 stamens, bound to and located within the corolla tube.

Notes: favors sandy soils and full light. Another member of the spring flora that can be abundant locally.

Obtained its common name from its physical resemblance to verbena; it is not related genetically to this group of plants.

SCARLET SPIDERLING (*Boerhavia coccinea*)
NYCTAGINACEAE (four o'clocks)

Overview: heavily branched perennial with glandular and pubescent stems.

Flowers: scarlet red to purplish red; corolla: campanulate, 5-lobed. *Inflorescence*: cymose with numerous glandular and pubescent peduncles.

Leaves: ovate to circular, upper surface: dark green; lower: much lighter.

Stem: sticky; densely pubescent; overall delicate, lacy appearance.

Fruit: pubescent.

Handlens: 1-3 small but exserted stamens.

Notes: found on gravelly hillsides and washes, summer-flora member.

COULTER SPIDERLING (*Boerhavia coulteri*)
NYCTAGINACEAE (four o'clocks)

Overview: annual that is profusely branched. The leaves are clustered heavily at the base while the upper portions are thin and lacy with much smaller foliage and tiny flower heads.

Flowers: pale pink to white; corolla: tubular, 5-lobed. *Inflorescence*: slender raceme sup-ported by a slender peduncle.

Leaves: lanceolate to ovate; upper surface: dark green; lower: much lighter, opposite.

Leaves (as a group) and flowers emerge from the axils which are widely spaced.

Stem: sticky, yellow zones on the upper portions of the stem; overall delicate, lacy appearance.

Fruit: smooth.

Handlens: 1-2 stamens that are not exserted.

Notes: favors gravelly hillsides and washes, member of the summer flora

COLORADO FOUR O'CLOCK (*Mirabilis multiflora*)
NYCTAGINACEAE (four o'clocks)

Overview: perennial herb to subshrub, with many stems and dark leaves, that can support a spectacular floral display.

Flowers: pink to magenta; no true corolla. *Inflorescence* emerges as a small group (3-6) at the nodes of upper leaves.

Calyx: petal-like, 5-lobed campanulate to funnel-shaped

Leaves: ovate to cordate, viscid, glandular, and opposite small petiole.

Fruit: achene.

Handlens: 5-10 elongated stamens, slightly exserted pistil.

Notes: prefers sandy habitats; flowers in late spring; responds to summer rain with a second burst of flowers. Produces a volatile chemical that attracts hawk moths, its primary pollinating agent.

DESERT BROOMRAPE (*Orobanche cooperi*)
OROBANCHACEAE (broomrape)

Flowers early in the year.

Overview: fleshy parasite that can grow in clusters.

Flowers: dark purple; corolla: bilabiate—upper: 2-lobed, recurved; lower: 3-lobed. Blunt petal tip. *Inflorescence*: borne on an erect, elongated, and conical spike.

Calyx: lobes (4-5) are longer than the tube, triangular.

Leaves: scale-like, purple.

Stems: underground, can form extensive clumps.

Handlens: Four 2-lobed stigmas and pubescent anthers.

Notes: a parasitic flowering plant that gains sustenance from the roots of host plants. This parasite prefers bursages, cheesebush and other members of the Asteraceae, but it is also found on creosote bush. This plant and other member of its genus have become serious pests of American agriculture.

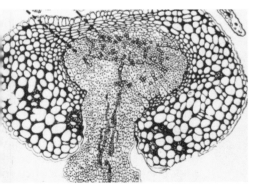

Orobanche cooperi produces tiny seeds that grow into a parasitic plant which produces a *haustorium*—a specialized tissue system that enables it to tap into a living host.

In this generalized representation, the lighter, densely packed tissues of the haustorium have pierced the larger, darker host tissues. This intimate interconnectivity enables the parasite to steal nutrients. The host gains nothing; it is truly a one-sided exchange. In the biological world, the concept of fairness in giving and taking has no relevance.

ARIZONA IPOMOPSIS (ARIZONA SKYROCKET)
(*Ipomopsis arizonica*)
POLEMONIACEAE (phlox)

Overview: perennial with erect stems that project from its base.

Flowers: red to a rosy pink with some yellow splashes; corolla: 5-lobe elongated, and tubular. *Inflorescence*: 5-13 flowers borne on a single-sided spike.

Calyx: sepals are fused partially.

Leaves: pinnately divided (7-11 lobes), basal rosettes, mid-vein bea conspicuous pubescence.

Notes: found above 1,000 m. Favors rocky soils and washes.

The collared peccary (*Peca tajac),* commonly known as th javalina, generally forages as large family group. They empl scent glands in their rump delineate their territory, a identify group members.

They love prickly pear cac especially those that grew in th author's garden. They round o their diet with roots and grasse various invertebrates and sm mammals. Being a shy creatur one only sees the evidence their visitation. Nevertheless, provoked, they are a formidab advisory. Unlike many dese creatures, javalinas cannot co themselves by panting; thus, th wisely find a comfortable and shady place to relax during the heat of the day.

DESERT CALICO (*Loeseliastrum mathewsii*))
POLEMONIACEAE (phlox)

Overview: prostrate annual, with bristles and pubescence, in which the flowers project from within the basal foliage.

Flowers: white to pink; corolla—bilabiate: upper: 3 petals, mix of maroon and white; lower: paired, 3-notched petals. Showy and exserted stamens and styles.

Leaves: linear, pinnately lobed, bristle-tipped lobes.

Notes: can form extensive communities in sandy and gravelly areas. So visually distinct as to require little description. Name honors Washington Matthews, who collected plants in the Owens Valley of California.

QUEEN'S WREATH (CORAL VINE) (*Antigonon leptopus*)
POLYGONACEAE (buckwheat)

Overview: twining, vine-lik perennial that advances vi tendrils that can extend fo dozens of feet.

Flowers: red to light pink corolla: none, 5 tepals *Inflorescence*: raceme born on a sort pedicel (3/8").

Leaves: ovate to cordate dark-green, opposite; pro nounced venation—particu larly on the undersurface.

Fruit: 3-angled achene.

Notes: native to Sonora an Baja California; a favore ornamental. Mid-summer t fall flowering. A white hort cultural variety exists. Ove winters as an edible tuber.

ABERT BUCKWHEAT (*Eriogonum abertianum*)
POLYGONACEAE (buckwheat)

Overview: herbaceou annual.

Flowers: white, be coming a mix of white an red with a yellow centra core; no corolla—tepals *Inflorescence*: cymose; pe duncles can reach 2" an are markedly pubescent.

Involucres: 5-toothe and campanulate seg ments.

Leaves: basal: obovate conspicuously pubescent margins entire to crenulate cauline: linear to lanceolate, sessile.

Fruit: brown, lenticular achenes.

Notes: flowers in the spring, but responds strongly to summer monsoon rains Favors sandy soils and gravelly washes.

FLATTOP BUCKWHEAT (*Eriogonum deflexum*)
POLYGONACEAE (buckwheat)

Overview: open, lacy, multi-branched annual with a flat-top crown. Primary stem supports many secondary branches with few leaves and tiny flowers.

Flowers: whitish-pink to rose; corolla: multiple petals (to 1/8" wide) emerge from a common, 5-lobed, green, cup-like calyx; support by a slender peduncle.

The secondary branches are largely divorced of foliage and bear well-spaced, pendent flowers (size: about that of a rice kernel); often, a solitary flower emerges at the branch node.

Calyx: pale yellow-white but becoming red with maturity.

Leaves: oval to cordate, basal, entire, pubescent, and spartan. Petiole to 2", reddish pubescence; underside covered in woolly pubescence.

Handlens: ruby-red, globose anthers on thin, creamy white filaments.

Notes: concentrated in open areas and disturbed sites, especially along roadbeds. As the plant dries, it assumes a maroon color.

The desert tortoise (*Gopherus agassizii*) actively seeks water and will excavate a depression to gain pooled liquid. It can increase by half its body mass during a single drinking session. It consumes an array of desert annuals and perennials. They burrow into the soil to create a refuge to escape the desert heat and avoid predators. Ravens are a serious predator, but habitat destruction, and illegal collecting have taken a significant toll on their numbers. Seemingly indifferent parents, the newly born babies must fend for themselves; they receive no significant parenting. Long-lived creatures, with a life span of 80 years; century-old specimens have been found. *If you find one, please do not pick it up!*

CALIFORNIA BUCKWHEAT (*Eriogonum fasciculatum*)
POLYGONACEAE (buckwheat)

Overview: densely bushy subshrub resplendent in red and white blossoms that seem to be everywhere.

Flowers: clump at the ends of a cyme. The red is seen best when the flower is closed, but upon opening, it reveals white petals with a central green patch. Conspicuous pubescence within the flower.

Calyx: narrow, sharply pointed, as long as the petal; each segment supports a petal.

Leaves: lanceolate, margins reflexed; basal leaves: diminutive, entire, possess fine pubescence, concentrated at the nodes. Upper surface: gently pubescent, dark green; lower surface: paler, woolly pubescence (*lanate*). Densely clustered at the nodes. A secondary wave of leaves form in the primary leaf nodes.

Fruit: inconspicuous, brown achene.

Handlens: very fine, white filaments support 2-segmented, ruby-red anthers.

Notes: valuable plant that provides nectar for a host of bee species.

This interesting variant of *E. fasciculatum (right)*, with its numerous long stems, is common along roadsides and other open areas.

CANAIGRE (WILD RHUBARB) (*Rumex hymenosepalus*)
POLYGONACEAE (buckwheat)

Overview: massive, coarse, and succulent perennial with a pinkish to bronze-brown flower stalk, and a substantial, erect stem.

Flowers: whorls of 5-20, cordate tepals. *Inflorescence*: large number of flowers combine to form a massive flower stalk—a terminal raceme or panicle or combination; each cluster of flowers, attached by a thin pedicle, to a common, thick and flattened peduncle.

Calyx: 3 outer, scarlet-purple to red lobes protect a group of 3 translucent, inner elements, the latter group cover the fruit.

Leaves: basal: oblong to elliptical with pointed tip and curled margins; stout petiole and prominent mid-vein. Shorter members on the solitary, heavy stem.

Fruit: cordate, winged, a pink-red capsule that is 3-sided and somewhat cordate.

Handlens: large, feathery stigma and massive, yellow anthers.

Notes: multiple tubers and the roots are sources of tannin for tanning hides; the above ground portions have a variety of medicinal uses. Petioles and leaves are consumable as a source of salad greens, but it stores oxalic acid—a plant chem-ical which should be avoided in large amounts.

Sandy washes and brightly illuminated areas, such as an open roadbed, are favored habitats. If moisture is adequate, it can flower over the entire year.

REDMAIDS (*Calandrinia ciliata*)
PORTULACACEAE (purslane)

Overview: small, succulent and prostrate annual.

Flowers: reddish purple corolla: 5 independent petals. *Inflorescence*: raceme. Conspicuous bright orange stamens and streaking on the petal surface.

Calyx: 2 sepals, overlapping, persistent, and pubescent.

Leaves: linear to oblanceolate, red splash at the apex.

Fruit: 3-valved capsule.

Handlens: 3-15 stamens, 3-branched style.

Notes: Native Americans dried the shiny black seeds to prepare an edible, oily meal.

Flowers, forming in the early spring, are only open during the brightly lit time of day. A white-flowered variant occurs.

INDIAN PAINTBRUSH (PURPLE OWL CLOVER)
(*Castilleja exserta*)
SCROPHULARIACEAE (figwort)

Overview: glandular annual with stiff pubescence, and erect flowers that are grouped at the end of the stem.

Flowers: mass of pink-purple to magenta floral bracts. corolla: bilabiate—upper: rose to purple, forms a small beak that is hooked downward; lower: 3-lobed pouch with 3 tiny, terminal teeth and yellow splashes.

Calyx: fused, tubular, lobes multi-colored as above.

Leaves: very thin, pinnately divided into 5-9 lobes, pubescent and glandular.

Handlens: 4 fused stamens within the upper corolla lip.

Notes: a parasite on roots of other flowering plants. Dispersed within this colored mass are the ovary-bearing portions that can be identified by the splash of bright yellow over a scarlet-red base. Capable of forming a large, dominate community.

WOOLLY PAINTBRUSH (*Castilleja lanata*)
SCROPHULARIACEAE (figwort)

Overview: a perennial that ranges from 2 to 3 ft.

Flowers: several flowers enclosed in red, 3-lobed, ciliated bracts; tubular, exserted, glandular. Corolla: tubular, green lobes with a red tip.

Calyx: green, yellow, and red.

Leaves: lower: elongated and linear (2-4"); upper: pinnately lobed, purple, ciliated margins. Pubescent ridges along the veins.

Handlens: 2 yellow, dissimilarly sized anthers borne on a common, green fila-ment. Stigma: red; fertile ovary densely packed with ovules.

Notes: another parasitic plant that derives essential foodstuffs and moisture from host-plant roots. Entire plant is covered in white, woolly hair. Able to flower continuously throughout the year.

TWINING SNAPDRAGON (*Maurandya antirrhiniflora*)
SCROPHULARIACEAE (figwort)

Overview: an herbaceous per-ennial with highly branched, slender stems.

Flowers: magenta to reddish to purple-blue (highly variable); cor-olla: bilabiate—upper: 2- lobed; lower: 3-lobed. Pubescent and tubular throat. Lower lip supports a raised, whitish palette just before the corolla throat.

Calyx: 5 independent sepals.

Leaves: hastate (3-5 units) to sagittate, entire, equally sized petiole,

Fruit: dehiscent capsule with ridges is surrounded by 5 independent and narrowly pointed calyx segments.

Handlens: 4 stamens in 2 pairs (didymous).

Notes: its showy snapdragon-like appearance makes it a favorite for cultivation. Favors crevices and other protected habitats. A red-flowered form occurs in the northern part of its range. Recognizes Dr. Maurandy, Professor of Botany at Carthagena.

CRIMSON MONKEYFLOWER (*Mimulus cardinalis*)
SCROPHULARIACEAE (figwort)

Overview: a viscid perennial with a stem that can exceed 30".

Flowers: scarlet-red; corolla: bilabiate—upper: arched; lower: turned downward. Pedicle is longer than the calyx; stamens are highly exserted.

Calyx: highly elongated, terminates in narrow, sharp segments.

Leaves: obovate, serrate, sessile, and viscid.

Handlens: ciliated anthers.

Notes: favors stream banks and other moist sites. Can form an extensive community.

PENSTEMON

All of the penstemon have opposite foliage; a terminal, showy inflorescence; tubular, generally a bilabiate corolla; a four-sided stem; a deeply lobed calyx with unequal sepals; and 5 stamen—of which one is sterile (staminode) and can be heavily bearded.

EATON PENSTEMON (*Penstemon eatonii*)
SCROPHULARIACEAE (figwort)

Overview: perennial with several erect and smooth stems and pendent flowers.

Flowers: striking red to scarlet; corolla: 5 lobed, tubular, Bilabiate—2 petals longer than the remaining 3 members. *Inflorescence*: clustered (up to 6) along an elongated peduncle emerging from the leaf nodes; attached to peduncle on a red pedicle.

Calyx: 5 pointed sepals, tiny in comparison to the corolla, purple streak at the margin, gentle pubescence and a tip that is recurved.

Leaves: ovate to lanceolate, opposite, thick, entire, leathery. Successive leaf pairs oriented 90° relative to prior pair. Stem appears to pierce center of blade.

Fruit: ovate capsule.

Handlens: filaments bear a touch of red, anther divided into 2 units with red banding. Five stamens: one non-functional (staminode), remaining stamens are fertile and pubescent.

Notes: hummingbirds are attracted to the red flowers; their beaks are adapted to obtain the nectar reward at the base of the long, tubular corolla. Flowers can be concentrated on one side of the stalk rather than mixed (as in *P. subulatus*).

PALMER PENSTEMON (*Penstemon palmeri*)
SCROPHULARIACEAE (figwort)

Overview: an eye-catching perennial that can exceed 4 ft.

Flowers: pale lavender to pale pink; corolla: narrow, expansive terminal portion. Bilabiate—upper lip: 2 erect lobes, reflexed; lower lip: 3 red- to magenta-striped lobes. Elongated, whitish pubescence (sparse) inside the throat.

Leaves: lanceolate, fused around the stem, basally positioned, opposite, serrated, and thick; pairs alternate at 90° angle. Basal leaves can reach 3" and are supported by an equally long petiole.

Handlens: a sterile stamen covered with dense, golden pubescence, and other fer-tile stamens project well away from the corolla.

Notes: a stunningly beautiful, highly fragrant Penstemon in a group of plants beloved for their decorative appearance. Favors washes and roadsides.

PARRY PENSTEMON (*Penstemon parryi*)
SCROPHULARIACEAE (figwort)

Overview: herbaceous perennial with flowers that emerge as multiple groups encircling the stem.

Flowers: *magenta to pink*; corolla: 5 rounded lobes, fused along most of its length. Bilabiate—upper lip: 2-lobed; lower lip: 3-lobed. Each lobe has a distinct central line, and is glandular and pubescent.

Calyx: 5 thin sepals with a red margin.

Leaves: linear to triangular, dentate, blue-green and clasping. Fused together to form a solid ring around the stem.

Handlens: sterile stamen (staminode) with lacey, golden-yellow pubescence; remaining stamens of two types: milky-white, V-shaped, fused units or red and narrow. Filaments are clear at their base, but red at the upper portions.

Notes: large opening at the center of the flower allows easy view of the internal organs. Flowers are a favorite of hummingbirds and many insects.

DESERT PENSTEMON *(Penstemon pseudospectabilis)*

SCROPHULARIACEAE (figwort)

Overview: a typical penstemon with stems that appear to pierce the center of the leaf blade.

Flowers: pink to reddish-pink with maroon streaking inside the throat; corolla: 5 petals that are fused into an elongated throat. Glandulated both within and surrounding the throat.

Leaves: lanceolate to ovate, finely serrate, bluish-gray cast. Paired members emerge at a 90° relative to a prior pair.

Handlens: valves of the anther sac are widely spaced. Staminode: included and smooth.

Notes: there is a bulge on the upper half of the corolla. Favors washes and canyons.

ARIZONA SCARLET-BUGLER
(HACKBERRY BEARDTONGUE) *(Penstemon subulatus)*
SCROPHULARIACEAE (figwort)

Overview: herbaceous perennial with numerous stems.

Flowers: ruby-red; corolla: tubular (1"), 5 equally sized lobes (appearing somewhat bilabiate). *Inflorescence*: borne at the leaf axil on a thin, narrow peduncle.

Calyx: 5 triangular sepals. Base of corolla is green.

Leaves: linear (3-4"), opposite, entire, concentrated at the base of the stem, prominent mid-vein.

Stem: hollow, light green, smooth.

Handlens: 5 elongated stamens, a single member is sterile. Anther: creamy-yellow when young, becomes orange with a white central core.

Notes: an important source of nectar for foraging hummingbirds, presents its flowers in the spring.

ORANGE & APRICOT

Only a small number of desert flowers display these agreeable colors.

Rush Milkweed, *Asclepias subulata*

DESERT HONEYSUCKLE (*Anisacanthus thurberi*)
ACANTHACEAE (acanthus)

Overview: perennial plant that can reach shrub size.

Flowers: reddish-orange to red; corolla narrow, elongated (to 2") and tubular Bilabiate—lower: 3 petals that can be tightly coiled; upper: final, fourth segment.

Calyx: 5 sepals, fused at their base, highly glandular, narrowing to a slender tip.

Leaves: lanceolate, entire, opposite, highly clumped along the stem.

Handlens: elongated, red filaments. Anthers V-shaped with a yellow central core and crimson edges. Exserted stamens (2) and a white pistil.

Stem: woody, exfoliating.

Fruit: elongated, 5-segmented, and flattened capsule. Each segment houses 2 seeds.

Notes: primarily part of the late-spring flowering plants; prefers arroyo banks.
The red to orange color, the elongated floral tube, the turned-backed petals, and abundant nectar production are all signs of adaptation to favor hummingbird visitation.

DESERT MARIPOSA LILY (*Calochortus kennedyi*)
LILIACEAE (lily)

Overview: showy, sparsely branched perennial with a dazzling flower.

Flowers: orange to vermilion with a brown purple basal zone; corolla: 3 petals, elongated hairs line the throat *Inflorescence*: umbel-like with 6-8 flowers. Pronounced stamens and 3 pistils.

Leaves: linear, gray-green, margins reflexed.

Stems: erect and solitary.

Fruit: 3-angled capsule.

Handlens: 6 conspicuous purplish anthers.

Notes: prefers washes and other open area where it can form extensive communities that carpet the desert floor. Stores food reserves in a bulb.

PALMER INDIAN MALLOW (*Abutilon palmeri*)
MALVACEAE (mallow)

Overview: large and woody, perennial.

Flowers: yellowish-orange to orange; corolla: 4 or 5 petals that are often closed, campanulate, and may have a pointed tip.

Inflorescence: borne solitary from the leaf axils on thin peduncles.

Calyx: 4 sharply pointed and symmetrical sepals.

Leaves: cordate, thick, velvety pubescence. Slightly dentate margin, conspicu-ous venation on the underside of the blade.

Elongated petiole attached to the blade where the veins converge. Green petiole and stem streaked with red.

Fruit: multi-chambered (7-10 units) capsule, soft pubescence.

Handlens: multiple, green styles (upper section: reddish) supporting red stigmas. Numerous large yellow anthers (2-units) adorn a thin, golden-yellow filament.

Notes: favors open areas and disturbed sites[1].

The great blue heron, *Ardea herodias*, is truly an imposing avian when it takes flight, spreads open its massive wings, and swoops down onto the water's surface—so gracefully that it hardly makes a ripple.

Active mostly at dawn and dusk, they are adroit fishing birds who use their elongated beaks as a spear. They will dine on various reptiles, amphibians, insects and other arthropods. An interesting observation: if they miscalculate the size of their prey, since they swallow it whole, they can choke.

Both sexes are active in the birthing process, taking turns keeping the nest warm and cozy. After about 2 months, the young chicks can live on their own; within 2 years, they are sufficiently matured to raise their own family.

---

[1] Indian Mallow, *Abutilon incana*, can be more orange than yellow (see p. 162)

BLADDERMALLOW (*Herissantia crispa*)
MALVACEAE (mallow)

Overview: multi-branched an-nual o perennial subshrub that can attain 2 ft.

Flowers: *pale* yellow with a conspicuous orange core; corolla: 5 petals. *Petals end in a point.* Numerous centrally clustered stamens.

Leaves: cordate, thick, heavily pubescent, conspicuous dentation silvery green, pronounced petiole venation deep and net-like.

Fruit: (8-15 units) *has sufficient mass to bend the stalk at a sharp angle* spherical, papery, pubescent, and ribbed.

Notes: ciliated margins occur on al structures that are part of the fruit. Often found near rock faces and crevices.

Three species of scorpions are found commonly in the Arizona Upland Sub-division of the Sonoran Desert. The most frequently encountered species is the desert hairy scorpion, *Hadrurus arizonenis.* Bearing impressive venom glands and stingers, they readily subdue their prey which consists primarily of small insects and an occasional vertebrate.

These are viviparous arachnids that carry their young (a miniature version of the adult) on their back where they remain secured until they have completed their initial molt. Parental care terminates at that time.

Rarely seen in daylight, they sojourn the day under a rock or similar shelter; they are active at night even though they can tolerate desiccation that causes a 40% loss in body mass. Another ambush predator, they patiently await their prey. While sighted, they none-the-less hunt by their tactile senses. Once stung, the hapless victim is torn apart and consumed. In return, they are suitable food for various birds, bats, large spiders, and lizards.

DESERT GLOBEMALLOW (*Sphaeralcea ambigua*)
EMORY GLOBEMALLOW (*Sphaeralcea emoryi*)
MALVACEAE (mallow)

Overview: perennial subshrub.

Flowers: usually apricot-orange, but can be red or pink; whitish-green internal zone. Corolla: 5 petals overlap to form a shallow, floral cup.

Inflorescence: borne as a raceme or panicle that emerges from the leaf nodes.

Calyx 5 basally fused sepals taper to an abrupt point, and are densely pubescent (stellate).

Leaves: typically divided into 3 units with ruffled edges, markedly wrinkled, deep green foliage contrasts sharply with its chocolate-brown stem. Conspicuously grooved veins on the surface and elevated on the underside.

Stem: light green, thick, and substantial.

Fruit: circular and partitioned into 8-16 chambers. A pubescent seed is housed within each chamber.

Handlens: leaf surface is blanketed with hairy structures that look like stars filling the nighttime void. Numerous, *fused* yellow stamens, on thin, white filaments, surround a group of pistils that rises from green tissues at its base.

Notes: globemallow can dominate an area and number in the tens of thousands. Nectar is an important food resource for honeybees and bee specialists on this plant.

Another common globemallow, *S. emoryi* can be distinguished by its smooth lower leaf surface and leaves that are longer than wide. The leaves are as long as wide in *S. ambigua*. There is also a mauve form: var. *rosace*.

SCARLET GLOBEMALLOW (*Sphaeralcea coccinea*)
MALVACEAE (mallow)

Overview erect, multi-stemmed peren-nial.
Flowers deep orange; corolla: 5 notched petals. *Inflorescence*: borne in dense terminal cluster; supported by a small peduncle (shorter than the calyx). Leaf-like bracts at the base of the flower.
Calyx: 5.
Leaves deeply divided into 3-5 lobes, stellate and coarse pubescence, silvery green.
Stem stellate pubescence.
Fruit: 10 or more chambers.
Notes. flowers in the spring; found on sandy soils and disturbed sites. Can form extensive, localized patches.

Normally part of the northern Arizona flora but it can extend into the Sonoran Desert.

A similar appearing mallow, *Sphaeralcea laxa,* grows in the Tucson area.

SCARLET PIMPERNEL (*Anagallis arvensis*)
MYRSINACEAE (wax-myrtle)

Overview low growing to some-what bushy annual.
Flowers orange-red; corolla: 5 petals fused basally, tubular; supported by an elongated peduncle. *Inflorescence* emerge from the leaf nodes.
Calyx 5-lobed, crenate margins with stalked glands.
Leaves ovate, sessile, and op-posite lower surface: dark purple spots; upper shiny and light green. Can occur as a whorl of 3 members.
Stem 4-angled, can root at the nodes.
Fruit drupe-like nut.
Handlens 5 stamens that are fused at the base of the petals, yellow anthers.
Notes: flowers are thought to close with the onset of inclement weather; this led to the common name of "poor man's weatherglass". Commonly considered a weed and it is highly toxic. Favors open areas and disturbed sites.

MEXICAN GOLDEN POPPY
Eschscholzia californica **var.** *mexicana)*
PAPAVERACEAE (poppy)

Overview: annual to perennial with long stems that droop with age.

Flowers: bearing *four* petals, it can vary in color from smooth yellow with just a touch of centrally located orange, through all mixtures of yellow and orange, to a largely orange blossom. Most flowers, however, are yellow with an orange inner region housing the stamens and pistils.

Inflorescence: arise at the apex of a stalk; all of the petals are joined in a small, green, and cup-like structure formed by fusion of the sepals. Peduncle can reach 6".

Leaves: bluish-green, typically with three deeply grooved and divided parts; primarily basally located.

Fruit: an elongated capsule housing a horde of seeds.

Notes capable of covering an entire mountainside; one of the most aesthetically pleasing spring flowers. A stunning variation with a white corolla occurs occasionally.

Named for Dr. J.F. Eschscholtz, a naturalist with the Russian explorers of our Pacific Coast in the early part of the 19th century.

ARIZONA POPPY (*Kallstroemia grandiflora*)
ZYGOPHYLLACEAE (caltrop)

Overview: prostrate annual with a showy flower, and pinnately compound leaves that can grow to 3 ft.

Flowers: yellowish orange with orange splashing at its core corolla: 5 largely independent petals. Stamens (with their orange anthers) and the pistil are highly conspicuous.

Leaves: pinnately compound (10-18 pinnae) opposite, pubescent stipules.

Fruit: multi-lobed that breaks into many nutlets with 1 seed per chamber.

Notes: favors sandy soils and open areas, late summer flower-ing.

Many desert creatures are not herbivores. From April to July, the gila monster (*Heloderma suspectum*), a highly efficient hunter, seeks bird eggs, baby birds, rabbits, and wood rats. The remaining months of the year, it remains inactive in its burrow during the daylight hours. It is not only the largest of the North American lizards, but also solitary in its life pattern. Its potent venom is injected through a groove in its tooth. While only painful to humans, small mammals succumb by respiratory paralysis.

This lizard feeds most actively when spring flora is most robust and therefore best able to support those plant consumers that will become welcome morsels on the gila's menu. This desert dweller enjoys a rather indolent life, largely free of the need to hunt and fear of predation. *Myth: if it bites you, it will hold on until it's dead.*

BLUE, VIOLET & LAVENDER

Many individuals within this group are recognized easily due to their distinct and highly picturesque appearance. Most dominate the early spring flora.

Some members could have been placed within the red flower group.

Bluedicks, *Dichelostemma capitatum*

PINK PEREZZIA (BROWNFOOT) (*Acourtia wrightii*)
ASTERACEAE (sunflower)

Overview: shrub-like perennial with clasping leaves and colorful, showy flowers.

Flowers: violet-pink to lavender to lavender-purple; corolla: bilabiate—lower lip: 3; upper lip: 2. *Inflorescence*: 8-11 flowers, in a single head (corymb-like) that is clustered at the apex of the peduncle.

Leaves: ovate to oblong-lanceolate, dentate to serrate, wrinkled, sessile, and sagittate or clasping; pronounced midvein on its underside. Highly glandular with trichomes along the margin.

Involucre: at least 3 dissimilarly sized whorls, glandular, ciliated margins.

Stem: flattened, not circular.

Pappus: elongated, numerous, and massive white bristles.

Notes: part of the winter-spring assemblage of flowering plants, but responds strongly to summer monsoon rains with a new flush of light green foliage and flowers. Favors sandy and gravelly sites.

TANSYLEAF ASTER (*Machaeranthera tanacetifolia*)
ASTERACEAE (sunflower)

Overview: one- to multiple-stemmed, glandular, and pubescent annual or biennial.

Flowers: open space between the ligules; borne on a slender peduncle.

Ray: 15-20; purple-blue to blue-violet (can be whitish); ligules: 3/8-3/4".

Disk; numerous; yellow.

Leaves: lower: pinnately divided (sometimes doubly divided); lobes support a small, terminal spine; upper: linear, entire to gently dentated. Pubescent, glandular.

Involucre: multiple whorls (3-5), bracts elongated with a narrow, spreading tip.

Pappus: long, white, silky bristles.

Handlens: minute pubescence and glands on the stem and leaves.

Notes: found in washes, and disturbed sites. Flowers appear in the summer months.

WIRE LETTUCE (*Stephanomeria pauciflora*)
ASTERACEAE (sunflower)

Overview: perennial herb to subshrub with highly branched, multiple stems that can assume a globose, spherical shape. There is an open appearance to the plant since the leaves are narrow and little in number.

Flowers: blue or lavender to pink; *inflorescence*: solitary on a peduncle that emerges from a leaf node.
     Disk: none.

Leaves: basal: lanceolate, abundant; upper: linear, far more spartan in number, much smaller, entire, and somewhat rolled under from the margin.

Involucre: 5 inner bracts and smaller, outer members.

Stems: heavily branched, wiry, bluish-green.

Pappus: brownish-tinged bristles.

Handlens: stamens pronounced, deeply pink to magenta.

Notes: desert straw is a late spring to early summer flower producer, making its appearance when most annuals are dried and withered. Flowers are remarkably drought tolerant and persist through the hottest portions of summer and well into the winter months.

    On occasion, one finds individuals with white petals. Hopi Indians used this plant to stimulate lactation.

MOJAVE ASTER (MOHAVE ASTER) (*Xylorhiza tortifolia*)
ASTERACEAE (sunflower)

Overview: perennial, that can reach small shrub size, with many branched stems that arise from a woody base.

Flowers: *inflorescence*: solitary flower (2") borne on an elongated peduncle (3-9").

Ray: 40-60; light blue to lavender or purple to magenta.

Disk: 70-100; yellow.

Leaves: oblong to linear, sessile, softly pubescent, hairs project from the edge of the serrated margin, glandular. Prominent venation and rough in texture.

Involucre: softly pubescent, glandular, needle-like tip. Outer: greenish, densely glandular; inner: straw-colored with irregularly indented margins.

Stems: branching limited to lower portions.

Notes: favors sandy washes rocky slopes, and disturbed sites. Part of the spring-flowering sunflowers.

DWARF WHITE MILKVETCH (*Astragalus didymocarpus*)
FABACEAE (legume)

Overview: slender, prostrate to ascending annual supporting gray pubescence and a distinctive fruit.

Flowers: light blue to purple to magenta with white splashes; *inflorescence*: raceme of densely packed, tiny flowers (1/4") supported on a slender peduncle (0.5-1.5").

Calyx: campanulate, teeth as long as the remaining portion, black and white pubescence.

Leaves: pinnately compound with 11-17 pinnae (3/16"); pinna: linear to oblanceolate with a notched apex.

Fruit: small (1/4"), coarsely wrinkled, and erect paired pods protect a single seed.

Notes: a pair of pods, bearing sharp, transverse ridges, and its small size (1/8") aid greatly in identification. Part of the early spring flora.

SOFT DALEA *(Dalea mollis)*
FABACEAE (legume)

Overview: perennial with soft pubescence and tiny, flat, and resinous glands.

Flower: *wing*: lavender to whitish, bears a gland at the tip of the notch, broadest at its base. *Inflorescence*: dense spike studded with a silky pubescence.

Calyx: white with purplish tinge, exhibits dense pubescence and lobes that are as long as the sepal tube.

Leaves: pinnately compound (odd) with 9-13 pinnae; glands dispersed along the margins.

Stem: softly pubescent, housing brown glands.

Fruit: tiny (1/4") and pubescent pod.

Notes: flowers found as late as early winter, prefers sandy soils. This legume flowers in its first year; perhaps, related to its short-life span.

The cactus wren (*Camylorhynchus brunneicapillus*), the state bird of Arizona, consumes a variety of insects, but it also makes seeds and fruit part of its diet. It is very partial to *Opuntia* fruit.

This is another desert creature that seldom actively drinks, relying instead upon water extracted from its foodstuffs.

Exhibiting marked fidelity, the pair bond for life. While the female selects the nest site, both parents share the toils of building. Typically, they make their home in a cactus (frequently a cholla) where it is protected, primarily from snakes, by sharp spines. It will also select various leguminous shrubs and trees for nest building.

MOJAVE LUPINE (COULTER LUPINE) (*Lupinus sparsiflorus*)
ARIZONA LUPINE (*Lupinus arizonicus*)
FABACEAE (legume)

Overview: tall and slender annual with a pubescent stem, and a flower head that can reach 8".

Flowers: *banner*: purplish-blue with zones of yellow and white; *wing*: purple, petals curved, conspicuous purple venation; *keel*: cryptic, beak-shaped, encloses the stamens. *Inflorescence*: a raceme.

All petals, except the banner, exhibit attached stamens (about half their length). When the young flower is fertilized, its corolla turns wine-red. Peduncle: densely pubescent and elongated (to 3").

Calyx: lacy, white pubescence; upper: 2 parted; lower: 3 toothed

Leaves: lanceolate, palmately compound (7-11 leaflets), whorled and densely clustered at its base. Petiole to 3".

Handlens: golden-yellow pollen and anthers.

Notes: *Lupinus sparsiflorus* is an aggressive competitor that can occupy large areas, often in conjunction with Mexican golden poppies, creating a spectacular carpet of colors.

Mojave lupine is heliocentric; it alters its orientation in harmony with the movement of the sun across the sky. Scientists believe that this response provides additional internal flower warmth which enhances attraction of insect pollinators.

This lupine is not Arizona lupine, *Lupinus arizonicus* (*left*), which has a magenta flower.

PARRY DALEA (Parry False Prairie Clover)
(*Marina parryi*) (*Dalea parryi*)
FABACEAE (legume)

Overview: subshrub perennial with slender, purplish, and glandular stems.

Flowers: *banner*: violet-blue with a white central core; *keel*: white at the top and violet-blue at the basal and side regions; largest of the petals. *Inflorescence*: terminal spike-like raceme (1-2").

Calyx: silky pubescence, wine-red streaks. The lobe length is equal to that of the tube.

Leaves: pinnate compound with 11-23 pinnae; glandular and opposite.

Stems: gland dotted.

Fruit: tiny (1/8") pods.

Handlens: 10 stamens fused into a common structure.

Notes: favors open area and disturbed sites, sandy soils and gravelly washes. Genus named for Marina, who interpreted for Cortez during his conquest of the New World.

DAINTY DESERT HIDESEED (DESERT EUCRYPTA)
(*Eucrypta micrantha*)
HYDROPHYLLACEAE (waterleaf)

Overview: weak, delicate, slender-stemmed annual that is glandular, and supports prickly pubescence.

Flowers: blue-purple to white with a yellow throat; corolla: 5 lobes, united and campanulate, shallow lobes. *Inflorescence*: terminal or axillary cyme.

Leaves: oblong, pinnately divided (7-9 units); upper: clasping and alternate; lower; opposite. Conspicuously pubescent.

Stems: scented, viscid, pubescent.

Handlens: stamens inserted onto the corolla, bluish anthers.

Notes: early spring flowering plant. Can be cryptic, hiding within other plants or in shallow crevices.

BRISTLY NAMA (PURPLE MAT) *(Nama hispidum)*
HYDROPHYLLACEAE (waterleaf)

Overview: highly pubescent annual that can grow to 12".

Flowers: blue to purple-lavender with a light yellow to green central core and a white perimeter; corolla: 5, campanulate. *Inflorescence*: solitary or several flowers in a cyme borne on a small pedicle.

Calyx: spatulate sepals.

Leaves: linear to narrowly spatulate, velvety pubescence, margins curled downward and entire, minute petiole to sessile.

Stem: can exceed 6", spreading at ground level and then becoming erect.

Fruit: 2-valved capsule with dozens of small, yellow to brown seeds.

Handlens: 2 stigmas (funnelform). Stamens attached just above the base of the corolla are unequal in length, and above one-half the length of the corolla.

Notes: favors rocky and sandy soils; flowers most of the year.

DESERTBELLS (CALIFORNIA BLUEBELLS)
(Phacelia campanularia)
HYDROPHYLLIACEAE (waterleaf)

Overview: a glandular, roughly pubescent annual that can react 2 ft.

Flowers: blue; corolla: 5 fused petals that create a deep, campanulate struc-ture. *Inflorescence*: loose raceme with slender pedicles.

Calyx: small, 5 pointed.

Leaves: cordate, some with red edges, lobes variously toothed, long petiole (to 8"). Prominent venation on the underside of the blade.

Handlens: 5-6 exserted stamens, equally long style.

Notes: all *Phacelia* deposit a nectar reward at the base of the petal that is obstructed by a portion of the stamens. This feature forces a foraging bee to dislodge pollen to secure its nectar reward.

Desertbells, generally a less abundant *Phacelia,* is the most visually striking of the three *Phacelia*. It can form extensive communities, favors disturbed sites.

Its inclusion in seed mixtures used to repopulate barren sites has led to its presence in the southern portion of the Arizona Upland Subdivision.

NOTCH-LEAF SCORPION-WEED (CATERPILLAR WEED)

(*Phacelia crenulata*)
HYDROPHYLLACEAE (waterleaf)

Overview: annual or biennial with green, heavily scented herbage that is pubescent and glandular; can reach 6 ft.

Flowers: light purple-blue to deep violet with a white throat; corolla: 5, campanulate, and pubescent. Blue-purple veins run through the petals. *Inflorescence*: multiple flowers, on a short pedicle, create a terminal panicle.

Calyx: equally sized lobes.

Leaves: oblong to elliptical, *crenate to deeply lobed margins (5-7 units)*, short petiole to sessile. *Solitary* leaves emerge directly from a peduncle that is coarsely pubescent. Odoriferous foliage.

Fruit: capsule with 4 seeds that are grooved along the edge.

Stems: red, pubescent and viscid.

Handlens: 5 exserted stamens (0.5"), equally elongated style (12-15 mm).

Notes: an early spring flowering plant. The flower head is usually coiled; as it unfolds, younger flowers are exposed for pollination. It is this curved appearance that reminds some of a scorpion's tail. Other spring annuals share this manner of exposing newly emerged flowers for pollination.

Favors open areas and rocky terrain; can be a very abundant component of the early spring flora.

DISTANT PHACELIA (WILD HELIOTROPE)
(*Phacelia distans*)

Overview: slender annual with rough-surface texture throughout; upper portions are glandular and bear stiff pubescence. This *Phacelia* can reach 4 ft.

Flowers: light blue; corolla: campanulate.

Calyx: lobes are unequally sized.

Leaves: can be somewhat similar to *P. crenulata*, but typically distant phacelia is far more delicate and lacy, appearing to be pinnately divided.

Stems: weak, straggling and similar to *P. crenulata*.

Fruit: seeds are not grooved along the edge.

Handlens: style is 7-12 mm in length. The basal portion of the filament is white.

Notes: distant heliotrope and notch-leaf scorpion-weed are generally abundant members of the spring flora. In general, *P. distans* has light, sky-blue petals while *P. crenulata* petals are a much deeper blue.

.

DESERT FIESTAFLOWER (*Pholistoma auritum*)
HYDROPHYLLACEAE (waterleaf)

Overview: trailing, weak-stemmed, and straggly annual.

Flowers: pale blue to purple to lavender; corolla: 5, dark spots and scale-like appendages, dropping, campanulate. *Inflorescence*: cyme or terminal, projecting from the node.

Calyx: 10, red edged, alternately bent forward and back, coarsely pubescent.

Leaves: oblong to ovate, deeply lobed (5-13), winged petioles. Base of the blade is cordate, tip pointed; cauline: clasping.

Fruit: bristly capsule.

Handlens: dark anthers contrast against lightly colored petals.

Notes: a spindly plant with 4-sided, very rough stems that can interlock to create a tangled mat of plant parts. This plant, with weak and sprawling stems, is covered in curved hairs.

COMMON HENBIT (HENBIT DEADNETTLE)
(*Lamium amplexicaule*)
LAMIACEAE (mint)

Overview: annual with stems that emerge from a common base.

Flowers: reddish-purple to lavender; corolla: tubular (enlarged throat); bilabiate—upper: densely white, bearded on the backside; lower: 3 tiny, lateral lobes. *Inflorescence*: borne at the leaf nodes in whorls consisting of 1-3 flowers.

Calyx: about as long as the corolla tube, 5 toothed, purple.

Leaves: ovate, coarsely crenate, opposite. Upper: sessile, clasping; lower: petiole.

Stem: 4-sided.

Handlens: 4 stamens borne on white filaments, purple and pubescent anthers. 2 stigma, 4-segmented ovary.

Fruit: brownish nutlet.

Notes: native to Europe, western Asia and northern Africa, it has become a tenacious weed in many parts of the U.S. Found in all contiguous states, nearly all of Canada and even Greenland.

When cut, it grows vigorously from the remnants; it will be difficult to eradicate.

CHIA (*Salvia columbariae*)
LAMIACEAE (mint)

Overview: annual, adorned with a striking floral head, and a square stem.

Flowers: blue to lavender; corolla: bilabiate—upper: 4, fused petals; lower: larger petal with purple spots and streaks on a field of white. *Inflorescence*: flowers emerge from a large head that persists when the flowers are no longer present. Elongated peduncle (scapose) is largely leafless.

Calyx: sharply pointed and exserted.

Leaves: oblong, once or twice pinnately divided; crinkled texture, mostly basal with recessed veins. Crushed plant emanates a pungent odor; prominent midvein and tiny bristles on under surface. Petiole: elongated, flattened, reddish.

Involucre: enlarged, multiple whorls; reddish-purple and sharply pointed bract tips project dramatically from the surface.

Fruit: tan to gray, specked nutlet.

Handlens: stamens are exserted and fused to the inner petal surface.

Notes: this attractive plant has the typical 4-sided, square-shaped stem characteristic of the mints. As the plant ages, the flower head dries and hardens to create material prized for dry flower arrangements.

Chia demonstrates fully the value of a handlens for revealing a wealth of fascinating and absorbing plant details.

BLUEDICKS *(Dichelostemma capitatum)*
LILIACEAE (lily)

Overview: perennial with a long, largely leafless, solitary stalk (scape) that supports flowers with 6 perianth parts.

Flower: bluish-violet to bluish-purple; corolla: constricted throat. *Inflorescence*: multiple flowers (2-15) emerge as an umbel protected by purple, lanceolate bracts.

Leaves: linear to ovate, ephemeral, basal members reach 16".

Handlens: 6 bright yellow stamens: inner members are fused to the wall of the perianth; membranous appendages surround the anthers. Three, purple segments at the base of the ovary.

Involucre: large and ovate, whitish to dark purple.

Fruit: capsule.

Notes: this plant often occurs as a solitary, single member, but it can also form extensive communities.

A perennial, subterranean corm (a food storage organ) sustains blue dicks Cormlets, produced by the mother corm are attached by stolons; these smaller units are responsible for most of the vegetative reproduction. A host of animals disperses the cormlets while consuming the corms.

BLUE FLAX (*Linum lewisii*)
LINACEAE (flax)

Overview: perennial subshrub with gentle arching and smooth stems.

Flowers: sky blue to lavender (can be white) with darker streaking and a yellowish central core; corolla: 5 independent petals. *Inflorescence*: terminally positioned on an elongated, slender pedicel (1").

Calyx: 5 sepals, more persistent than the corolla.

Leaves: linear to lanceolate, spirally arranged, sessile, and single veined.

Fruit: 10-celled, dehiscent capsule with 2 seeds per cell.

Handlens: 2-5 styles that are much longer than the stamens. Five stamens fused basally and forming a tube-like structure.

Notes: a close relative, *L. usitatissimum,* the source of linseed oil and fibers for making linen. *Linum lewisii* honors Captain Meriwether Lewis. Typically found at elevations higher than 1,100 m.

A similar flax, *Linum pretense*, is found at elevations below 3,600 ft.

The cottontail rabbit (*Sylvilagus audubonii*), is named for its fluffy white tail. These herbivores are sustained primarily by grasses. However, in the winter, they rely upon bark and twigs. Most interestingly, they are *coprophagic*, which means they consume their feces. This eating behavior permits the cottontail to extract the last vestiges of nutrition from its food, since it passes through the digestive system for a second time.

Their sizeable ears are not only critical in their survival from predators, but also are filled with surface blood vessels that facilitate release of body heat.

These rabbits can bred before they are 3 months old; they can produce 20-30 off springs in a single year. Moreover, the female can mate immediately after giving birth. Such fecundity is essential, as they are a stable food of numerous predators; a factor that accounts largely for their 2-year life span.

MINIATURE WOOLSTAR (*Eriastrum diffusum*)
POLEMONIACEAE (phlox)

Overview: tall, wiry, open, and diffusely branched annual.

Flowers: blue with an internal yellow core; corolla: 5-lobed, tubular. *Floral lobes shorter than the tubular section.* Cottony deposits at the leaf axils and flower bracts. *Inflorescence*: 3-20 flowers in a terminal cluster with a pubescent head.

Leaves: linear to pinnately divided (3-5 lobes), terminate in a sharp tip.

Involucre: 3-lobed bracts.

Fruit: capsule.

Handlens: 5 tiny (1/16") and unequally sized stamens are attached to the upper corolla throat.

Notes: gains its common name from the clumps of woolly pubescence at the leaf nodes and the base of the flowers. Typically, the flower is regular in symmetry which means it can be divided into 2 sections along multiple planes. A member of the spring-flowering flora.

DESERT WOOLSTAR (*Eriastrum eremicum*)
POLEMONIACEAE (phlox)

Overview: annual with flowers grouped into hemispheric heads that are covered with a cottony pubescence. Multiple branches from a common base.

Flowers: bluish; corolla: irregular (0.6-1.0"), *floral lobes equal in length to the tubular section.* Woolly pubescence.

Calyx: unequal, sharply tipped.

Leaves: narrow, pinnately divided into 3-7 lobes.

Involucre: 3 bracts are bent backwards; 5- to 9-lobed.

Fruit: ovate to oblong capsule.

Handlens: violet stamens, sagittate anthers. Stamens: not equal, set at the base of the throat and bent toward the lower throat; bearing a 0.5-1" anther. Both the pistil and stamens can be markedly exserted.

Notes: the flower can be divided into 2 sections only along one plane. There is a bilabiate quality to the flower with the upper 2 petals being distinct from the lower 3. Flowers from spring into early summer; favors sandy sites.

LESSER YELLOWTHROAT GILIA
(*Gilia flavocincta ssp. flavocincta*)

BROADLEAF GILIA (*Gilia latifolia*)
POLEMONIACEAE (phlox)

Overview: annual with a thin, overall delicate appearance, and numerous slender stems.

Flowers: lavender, yellow to white throat; corolla: 5 basally fused lobes with blue spots at the base. *Inflorescence*: panicle supported by an elongated stalk (to 1").

Calyx: small, green, pointed with purple streaks.

Leaves: lower: pinnately (or twice-) divided; upper: less indented.

Handlens: exserted stamens, with colorless filaments, support blue-green anthers; 3-celled ovary. Stamens are attached to the upper portion of the corolla throat.

Fruit: capsule.

Notes: favors sandy site.

Another member of this genus: *G. latifolia,* (*right*) is an abundant component of the early spring flora.

Advanced Readers: this is an excellent plant in which to study floral inflorescence. The flower head is a cymose panicle. Start by determining the panicle nature of the floral inflorescence. Remember, this is a complex raceme. Next, note how the individual flowers emanate from different points on the peduncle to form a flat-topped structure (cyme) with the youngest members at the extremities of the inflorescence.

BARESTEM LARKSPUR (*Delphinium scaposum*)
RANUNCULACEAE (buttercup)

Overview: perennial herb with palmately divided leaves, and a conspicuous floral spur.

Flowers: a complex flower with 4 showy petals and 5 deep or royal blue to purple (with a white or blue-tinged upper zone) sepals. One sepal supports a conspicuous spur. Emerge along the stem on an ascending pedicle.

Leaves: obovate to somewhat spatulate, limited to basal members that are palmately divided (3-5 units). Margins: entire to rounded or clefted lobes.

Stems: reddish base, smooth and elongated (8-20") with few branches.

Fruit: 3-segmented follicle.

Notes: a visually striking plant that flowers in the spring. The floral spur is a nectar repository; while securing their nectar reward, foraging bees are covered with pollen.

Produces alkaloids that are toxic to cattle, horses, and sheep. Hopi Indians ground the flowers with corn to make an effective emetic.

WATER SPEEDWELL (*Veronica anagallis-aquatica*)
SCROPULARIACEAE (figwort)

Overview: aquatic perennial bearing its fibrous roots from nodes at the lower portions of the stem.

Flowers: lavender to blue with violet streaking; corolla: 4-lobed (<0.5") with a splash of violet. There are 3 equally sized lobes while the final member is smaller and lacks streaking.

Inflorescence: many-flowered racemes emerging at the axils and supported by a curved pedicel.

Calyx: 4 smooth sepals. Each member positioned between the petals.

Leaves: ovate to elliptical, *bright green*, clasping, *opposite,* entire to serrate, sessile (lowest leaves may be supported by a small petiole). Typically emerge as a pair that is spaced widely along the stem.

Fruit: capsule.

Handlens: 2 stamens (expanded at their mid-section) and a stigma.

Notes: restricted to riparian habitats. Overwinters by a rhizome. Native to Europe.

SILVERLEAF NIGHTSHADE (*Solanum elaeagnifolium*)
SOLANACEAE (nightshade)

Overview: perennial herb that is covered with dense stellate and silvery pubescence.

Flowers: purple to violet to blue-violet or white; corolla: 5 pointed and deltoid lobes with 5 conspicuous, exserted, and bright yellow stamens. Unequally sized anthers are highly conspicuous

Calyx: rigid, yellow spines.

Leaves: silvery, linear to lanceolate, wavy margin, yellowish spines on underside of leaf and stem.

Stems: slender, yellow spines.

Fruit: green berry that turns yellow.

Notes: both the seeds and foliage at all stages of development are highly toxic. Produces a protein-degrading enzyme (similar to papain) that has been used to curdle milk for cheese production.

This beautiful *Solanum* is an aggressive weed that has taken over desert habi-tats. It is nurtured, during adverse times, by an underground rhizome. It stores a toxic alkaloid—solanine that is also produced by other solanaceous plants. Pernicious alkaloids are commonplace in this family of plants, which accounts, in large measure, for their documented toxicity.

GOODDING VERBENA (DESERT VERVAIN)
(Glandularia gooddingii) (*Verbena arizonica*)
VERBENACEAE (vervain)

Overview glandular and pubescent annual or perennial with several stems.

Flowers: pink through purple-blue; corolla: 5 double-notched lobes attached basally, tubular. Form as a cluster.

Calyx: a mixture of independent and united segments (3-5); whitish pubescence between the fused sepals.

Leaves: ovate to lanceolate, opposite, highly pubescent, variously divided (3-5 lobes) and serrated. Upper: surface covered in bristly, white pubescence; lower: similar pubescence on the surface of the veins. Petiole to 5/8".

Stems: square.

Fruit: nutlets.

Handlens: short, white pubescence at the tip of the throat; stamens attached to the inner walls of the corolla; solitary, green pistil.

Notes: early spring flowering vervain, which can flower much of the year. Goodding verbena has become widely planted as an ornamental.

The coyote (*Canis latrans*) is the quintessential consumer—it never encounters a food item it does not relish. Rabbits support the overwhelming bulk of their diet, but this canid can handle anything it can swallow from a scorpion to dry desert grasses.

One day, while walking along a local golf course, I encountered a group of 6 coyotes (it is a productive place to hunt the rabbits that come out to nibble on the succulent turf grasses) far more intent on joyfully frolicking, than any need to chase rabbits. It was a carefree, almost whimsical, moment in their demanding daily hunting routine that is seldom seen.

LARGE SHRUBS & TREES

The division between shrubs and trees is arbitrary. Perennial plants that attained larger size, generally by possessing more woody tissues, have been placed within this section. In general, trees are more massive than large shrubs.

Ironwood, *Olneya tesota,* with Desert Mistletoe, *Phoradendron californicum*

CHUPAROSA (*Justica californica*)
ACANTHACEAE (acanthus)

Overview: grayish-green, perennial shrub whose softly pubescent branches are often without leaves, but seldom without tubular flowers.

Flowers: red to orange-yellow; corolla: 5 fused petals, highly tubular. Bilabiate—upper portion: 2-lobed; lower section: 3-lobed. Fine, white pubescence at petal base. *Inflorescence*: terminal racemic clusters.

Involucres: equally sized segments, broadly spaced, purple, delicate pubescence.

Leaves: ovate to triangular; drooping in appearance; covered with a delicate, silvery pubescence; margins entire to gently dentate; opposite. Most are solitary, but they can bunch at the apex.

Stems: grayish-green, intertwine to create a tangled mass.

Handlens: deep purple stigma, much lighter-colored style; exserted pistil. Stamens pressed against the inner surface of the upper lip; one anther positioned lower along the filament than the other members.

Fruit: two-celled capsule.

Notes: chuparosa displays multiple cycles of flowering which creates the impression that it is in perpetual bloom. The flowers are edible and said to have a cucumber taste. On occasion, a yellow variant is found.

This drought-resistant perennial is an important food source for hummingbirds. Carpenter bees overcome the obstacle of blossom shape by cutting the corolla tube at its base, and gathering nectar without contributing to pollination.

SWEET SUMAC (*Rhus ovata*)
ANACARDIACEAE (amaranthus)

Overview: a dense, leafy, and evergreen shrub to small tree.

Flowers: white to pink; corolla: 5 petals with fine hairs along the lobe margin; either perfect or pistillate. *Inflorescence*: dense panicles.

Calyx: red, ciliated margins.

Leaves: ovate to elliptical, thick, leathery, evergreen, and generally entire. Sheen to the upper surface, fragrant, folded along the mid-vein.

Stem: shaggy bark and thick and reddish stems.

Fruit: red drupe; glandular and pubescent.

Notes: favorite of a variety of birds, drought-resistant. Unlike many sumacs, that can be toxic and allergenic, this plant is grown in ornamental gardens. Flowers from February through May.

SKUNKBUSH SUMAC (*Rhus aromatica*)
ANACARDIACEAE (sumac)

Overview: densely branched shrub whose branches arch downwards.

Flowers: white to yellowish; *Inflorescence*: clustered, sessile spikes.

Calyx: yellowish-green.

Leaves: trifoliate: terminal leaflet is the largest segment; pubescent and crenate to serrate. Terminal lobe is diamond shaped while the lateral members are ovate.

Fruit: bright red and viscid drupe; has a citrus flavor.

Handlens: 5 stamens and 3 styles.

Notes: edible berries that also serve as a mordant in dyeing.

MULE'S FAT (SEEPWILLOW) (*Baccharis salicifolia*)
ASTERACEAE (sunflower)

Overview: erect, woody, and dioecious perennial that can exceed 10 ft.

Flowers: white; *inflorescence*: borne as a cluster from the axil, or terminally as a panicle. *Inflorescence*: terminal clusters.

Staminate: 17-48.

Pistillate: 50-150.

Involucre: bracts in 4-5 whorls (imbricate), upper: tinged in red, irregularly toothed.

Leaves: lanceolate but taper to a narrow strip at the node; entire to dentate, petioles winged. Underside: prominent mid-vein, often with two companion side veins.

Stem: slightly ridged and gray-brown with reddish fissures.

Pappus: white, elongated, feathery bristles.

Notes: favors moist sites, can form dense thickets.

DESERT BROOM (BROOM BACCHARIS)
(*Baccharis sarothroides*)
ASTERACEAE (sunflower)

Overview: large, woody shrub with persistent, elongated, and parallel branches.

Flowers: a dioecious species with a discoidal head. *Inflorescence*: panicle.

Ray: none.

Disk: produce an abundance of white, silky, wind-dispersed seeds that cover the plant in large, cottony masses and drift in the wind like snow.

Staminate flowers: 18-35, 5-toothed corolla.

Pistillate flowers: 14-30, white, tiny; prodigious amounts of capillary bristles.

Involucres: bracts in several overlapping (imbricate) series.

Leaves: linear to lanceolate, light yellow-green, sessile, and entire; primarily borne at the tip of the branchlets. Tiny and ephemeral.

Can be free of foliage through much of the year, but retains its overall green appearance.

Stem: slender, viscid, and bright green. Its stout and woody, erect, and highly branched structure produces its broom-like appearance.

Fruit: achene with a pappus of small, white, and very feathery bristles.

Handlens: green spots at the head of the bracts of the staminate flowers.

Notes: this is an aggressive competitor that often seeks protection by growing from within another plant; abundant in distressed and disturbed sites. Truly qualifies as an obnoxious weed that consumes vast desert acreage while plummeting native species.

Road construction can create an open shoulder that is quickly occupied by this aggressive plant. After a certain level of development, its removal is highly problematic, as it grows woody and develops a tenacious root system

CHEESEWEED BURROBUSH (*Hymenoclea monogyra*)
ASTERACEAE (sunflower)

Overview: woody, bushy, and multiple-stemmed perennial.

Flowers: greenish-white; monoecious.

Staminate: 5 to 6-segmented involucre with ovate lobes.

Pistillate and staminate flowers are not segregated but grouped in the upper branch axils; positioned above an ovate, scale-like bract.

Leaves: filiform (thread-like), entire, short, dark green.

Stem: straw colored, substantial, and woody.

Involucre: *pistillate*: 7-12 segments in a single whorl.

Notes: favors washes and disturbed sites; can become the primary vegetation, forming a thicket when open areas are available for propagation. Cheeseweed burrobush has a more tree-like structure than *H. salsola* with stouter, woodier stems. It is part of the autumn array of flowering plants, and a major contributor to the community of allergic plants.

A powerful wall of water, flooding the Cave Creek water channel, swept away much of the existing plants in the fall of 2005. Nevertheless, the dominance of this sunflower is clearly evident.

BURROBUSH (*Hymenoclea salsola*)
ASTERACEAE (sunflower)

Overview: rounded, straggly subshrub; many thin, light green stems with small leaves.

Flowers: white; corolla: lacking; monoecious. Bears solitary, tiny, and burr-like flowers.

Staminate: discoidal heads emerge at the upper stem tips.

Pistillate: individual flowers, positioned at the lower portions of the inflorescence, are supported by several linear, bract-like structures that are enclosed by silvery-red scales; elongated style. *Inflorescence*: many flowers in spiked clusters.

Leaves: threadlike, pinnately divided, entire, short, dark green. Pungent odor when crushed, woolly pubescence on the underside.

Stem: thin, pale straw, upright, arising from a single base, branched throughout, often arching out and bending down to the ground.

Involucre: staminate: campanulate, 5-7 lobes; pistillate: one or more linear bracts.

Fruit: winged and beaked achene that is attached to a persistent bract.

Notes: another allergenic sunflower; crushed foliage emanates an unpleasant odor reminiscent of cheese. Part of the spring assemblage of flowering sunflowers. Favors sandy soils and washes.

On disturbed sites, this plant can be an aggressive competitor that fills the landscape.

DESERT BARBERRY (*Berberis haematocarpa*)

BERBERIDACEAE (barberry)

Overview: evergreen, upright, and spreading shrub that resembles superficially a holly.

Flowers: yellow; corolla: 6 fragrant petals. *Inflorescence*: 3-7 members in a raceme borne on a slender peduncle (1").

Leaves: ovate to lanceolate; pinnately compound; (3-9 pin-nae); lateral pinnae: 1-3 teeth; terminal pinna: 3-6 teeth. Crenate, thick and rigid.

Stem: erect, lacks spines; grayish-purple, smooth.

Fruit: succulent, reddish-brown, edible berry that is used to make jelly.

Notes: favors hillsides and washes, spring flowering. Excellent food source for birds and small mammals. In the spring, a gauzy puparium, made by the white-winged moth, *Eucaterva variaria*, can hang from its limbs.

DESERT WILLOW (*Chilopsis linearis*)

BIGNONIACEAE (bignonia)

Overview: large shrub to small tree with numerous slender, often drooping branches.

Flowers: pink to lavender with patches of white; corolla: bilabiate— upper: 2-lobed; lower: 3-lobed. Wavy and purple patch on lower lobes, as well as lavender streaks that project into the interior. *Inflorescence*: borne in racemes at branch tips.

Calyx: 2-lobed, light green, fused.

Leaves: linear, simple, entire; generally alternate, but can be opposite or whorled.

Fruit: slender, elongated (to 8"), brownish capsule that splits to form two curved, *highly persistent* pieces. Flat seed with terminal, tufted pubescence.

Handlens: 5 stamens: 4 are 2-lobed; fused to the corolla tube.

Notes: a deciduous tree, it drops its foliage during the winter. Another desert plant that prefers open areas; widely planted as an ornamental which has numerous cultivars including one with reddish flowers. Can be a reliable indicator of subterranean water.

Interesting use: infusion of plant parts employed as an anti-fungal, vaginal douche.

ELEPHANT TREE (*Bursera microphylla*)
BURSERACEAE (torchwood)

Overview: varies from a large shrub to a small tree with thick, semi-succulent limbs.

Flowers: white; corolla: 5 small petals. *Inflorescence*: solitary or in a small cluster. Peduncle to 1", but the pedicle is tiny.

Calyx: 5 ovate sepals.

Leaves: pinnately compound with 10-30 pinnae; dark green, shiny, sessile, and deciduous. Emanate a camphor-like odor when crushed.

Bark: immature: red brown; older: butterscotch yellow, peeling ridges. Highly aromatic, cherry-red branches.

Fruit: 3-angled light purple to bluish drupe housing one yellow to orange-red seed; requires a second season to reach maturation.

Notes: common name derived from the branches that resemble the trunk of an elephant. Gum from this tree was employed in treatment of venereal disease; the red sap is useful in dyeing.

Interesting note: the wood consists of 60-70 percent water, an important adaptation to limited water availability.

Can reach true tree size in Sonora and Baja California where winter climate does not cause a die-back of the cold-sensitive limbs.

BLADDERPOD SPIDERFLOWER
(*Cleome isomeris*) *(Isomeris arborea)*
CAPPARIDACEAE (caper)

Overview: heavily branched, sprawling perennial.

Flowers: deep yellow; corolla: 4 petals. *Inflorescence*: terminal raceme sub-tended by bracts.

Calyx: 4 sepals fused half way up their base.

Leaves: pinnately divided into 3 units, petiole to 1.25", pungent odor.

Stems: stout, gray-green when young, but turning gray with age.

Fruit: conspicuous, pendent capsule (inflated and bag-like); light green, but turning brown.

Handlens: six, exserted and showy stamens.

Notes: an early-part-of-the-year flowering plant. A member of this family is the source of commercial capers. Favors washes and roadsides.

The female Becker white butterfly (*Pieris beckerii*) oviposits her eggs on this plant which serves as a food resource for the larvae. Interestingly, these insects can also feed on a variety of mustards; this suggests an overlap in the phytochemical profiles of these plants.

CRUCIFIXION THORN (*Canotia holacantha*)
CELESTRACEAE (bittersweet)

Overview: forms a shrub-like tree with a small but stocky trunk and thin, spine-tipped branches.

Flowers: white to greenish yellow; corolla: 5 petals. *Inflorescence*: small, axillary racemic clusters.

Calyx: 5 triangular sepals.

Leaves: almost scale-like, spartan foliage.

Stem: bark: light green to light brown, deeply furrowed; branches: highly resin-ous and rush-like, sharp, terminal thorns.

Handlens: five stamens and a 5-celled ovary that is supported by accessory tissues.

Fruit: much of the plant is covered with dark, dried, and persistent, 5-segmented capsules that house dark-brown, winged seeds.

Notes: black, cushion-like structure at the base of twigs and flowers. Food production (via photosynthesis) essentially delegated to the twigs.

REDBERRY JUNIPER (*Juniperus coahuilensis*)
UTAH JUNIPER (*Juniperus osteosperma*)
CUPRESSACEAE (cedar)

Unusual conditions have created viable habitats for at least two species of juniper normally growing at considerably higher altitudes: *Juniperus osteosperma* and *J. coahuilensis*. These conifers have been found in several places in the lower elevations of the Sonoran Desert. While these trees are stunted but reasonably healthy, fruit formation has not been observed, even during years of exceptional rain.

Redberry juniper (*right*) grows as a large shrub to a small tree with a pronounced central stem and spreading and ascending side branches that develop from ground level to produce an open, irregular crown. When present, the fleshy, berry-like cones are important food sources for several songbirds, Gambel quail, coyotes, foxes, raccoons, and rock squirrels.

Utah juniper (*left*), also a large shrub to small tree, has a pronounced central trunk and multiple lower branches, but they arise well above ground level. Native American Indians employed the dried seeds as a material in jewelry making. Sandals as well as digging sticks and other farming implements were constructed from its durable wood.

WHITETHORN ACACIA (*Acacia constricta*)

FABACEAE (legume)

Overview: a small leguminous tree whose branches are armored with very sharp and paired, white spines (to 2") that emerge at the nodes.

Flowers: orange yellow; corolla: 5 petals, fused and tubular; resemble a small, puffball—an effect created by numerous colored stamens.

Stems: young: reddish; mature: brown to gray-brown; furrowed.

Leaves: twice pinnately compound (1" long) with 6-8 pairs of pinnulae (single, terminal pinnula) with 6-12 compound leaflets.

Fruit: light to dark chocolate-brown, thin and narrow (2-4") with constriction between the seeds; papery, dehiscent, single row of small black seeds.

Note: twisted pods are persistent, they remain on the tree well after they have opened and dispensed their seeds.

This legume produces a flower lacking nectar and with little pollen; yet, it is actively visited because its perfume-like odor fools pollinators.

CATCLAW ACACIA (*Acacia greggii*)
FABACEAE (legume)

Overview: shrub to small tree that rarely exceeds 20 ft.

Flowers: cream colored to light yellow; corolla: petals are inconspicuous; it is the elongated stamens that create most of the visible flower. *Inflorescence*: densely packed on a spike (2-2.5") supported by a small peduncle.

Leaves: 3 to 6 pairs of *tiny* pinnulae with 4-6 compound leaflets; the rachis supports a nectary.

Stem: spines: broad at the base, curved backward, and spaced variously along the stem.

Fruit: legume that is typically twisted, curved, and highly constricted; houses about a half dozen brown seeds in a recessed cup-like portion of the pod.

Note: named for the sharp, curved thorns, broad at the base, that cover the plant, and snag tenaciously the passerby. Most drought resistant of the desert *Acacia*. Commonly found in washes and rocky hillsides.

Pods, leaves, and roots were used to prepare infusions. A highly regarded honey is produced from its fragrant flowers.

SWEET ACACIA (*Acacia farnesiana*) (*Acacia smallii*)
FABACEAE (legume)

Overview: small, fragrant, and thorn-laden leguminous tree.

Flowers: yellow; small, globose flower head. *Inflorescence*: numerous, perfect flowers emerge from an axillary head.

Calyx: small, green, sepals fused along most of their length, tiny tip.

Leaves: twice-pinnately compound, 2-8 pinnulae with 8-12 compound leaflets. Can retain its foliage during a warm winter.

Handlens: exserted filaments with their yellow anthers create the globose flower form. Resin gland and small, paired set of very sharp thorns at the leaf node.

Fruit: dark brown to blackish, dehiscent pod; ends pointed. Seeds stacked in two rows. Not constricted.

Notes: favored as an ornamental plant for its attractive, floral appearance and markedly fragrant blossoms that appear in the spring. These blossoms are employed in perfumery.

Acacia Fruit. *Top. Acacia constricta* (top left); *A. greggii* (right), and *A. smallii* (bottom left).

RED BIRD OF PARADISE (DWARF POINCIANA)
(*Caesalpinia pulcherrima*) (*Poinciana pulcherrima*)
FABACEAE (legume)

Overview: multi-stemmed shrub to small tree.

Flowers: small, upper petal is bright yellow, while the larger lower members are yellow with splashes of orange-red; corolla: 5 irregular petals. *Inflorescence*: panicle at the end of elongated peduncles. Very showy and dramatic stamens and pistil.

Leaves: twice-pinnately compound; up to 12 pinnae with as many as 9 compound leaflets.

Stem: supports sharp thorns.

Fruit: brownish pod (to 5") that hangs down from the branch.

Notes: originally from islands in the Caribbean, where it was employed to create living fences.

Native throughout the New World Tropics into central Sonora, it has become a favorite in landscape designs; escaped plants have become part of the desert flora (see p. 288).

FAIRYDUSTER (*Calliandra eriophylla*)
RED FAIRY DUSTER (BAJA FAIRY DUSTER) (*Calliandra californica*)
FABACEAE (legume)

Overview: a small, densely branched, and unarmored subshrub with delicate leaves and a particularly picturesque flower.

Flowers: rose pink to pale-pink; dozens of long, delicate, white, and elongated stamens, colored scarlet at the tip, make up a single "flower puff". The corolla and calyx are minor components.

What looks like an individual flower is actually created by the grouping of multiple units.

Calyx: 5 sepals that are fused basally, red tipped and glandular.

Leaves: twice pinnately compound, 12 to 22 pinnulae with 4 compound leaflets.

Fruit: small (2"), conspicuous ridge on its brown, flat pod, opens explosively to disperse seeds; curled pod is persistent.

Note: one of the more visually appealing plants of the desert due to its puffy, delicate flowers—well deserving of its common name. The red fairy duster, *C. californica*, named for its red stamens (*upper right*) is often planted as an ornamental.

CATCLAW MIMOSA (*Mimosa biuncifera*)
FABACEAE (legume)

Overview: large shrub to small, multi-branched tree.

Flowers: white to whitish pink; globose, flower head on a thin pedicle. *Inflorescence*: borne on spikes that emerge from the leaf axils.

Leaves: twice-pinnately compound, 15 to 30 pinnulae with 3-19 compound leaflets.

Stem reddish-brown; sharp, individual or paired claw-like spines (to 0.5") at the base of the leaflet. Light colored lenticels (organs for the exchange of gases with the internal portions of the plant). Young: smooth and gray-brown; older: much darker, fissured and scaly.

Fruit: pods to 2", flattened and constricted, reddish-brown. Look for downwardly curved spines on the margin.

Notes: another legume that can respond to summer rain with a fresh flush of flowering. Favors dry, rocky slopes and washes.

Sought after by Gambel's quail (for sustenance and cover) and honeybees for its nectar; yields a prized honey. Spines are more numerous, and even more treacherous than catclaw acacia.

Gambel quail (*Callipepla gambelii*), feed primarily on seeds, less frequently on insects. A monogamous mating pair can have an annual clutch of as many as 15, but when food is scarce, this number falls dramatically. In an atypical year of abundant rainfall, a second brood can be produced.

This is a non-migratory bird which allows us to enjoy this delightful desert inhabitant throughout the year. A highly leery and vigilant avian, a large, fleeing group can startle the hiker as they scatter with an explosive noise at the slightest sound.

RONWOOD (*Olneya tesota)*
FABACEAE (legume)

Overview: massive, grayish legume that can be a substantial tree.

Flowers: banner: pale whitish pink to darker purple, much larger than the companion petals; wing: lavender on a field of white; keel: lavender with a more reddish hue. *Inflorescence*: a horde of racemes bearing flowers that can festoon the entire tree in spectacular lavender color.

Calyx: 5 uniform sepals, fused basally, brick red, fuzzy pubescence.

Leaves: pinnately compound with 8-18 pinnae. Tiny spines, positioned at the node, are curved slightly, paired, *and very sharp*.

Bark: young, light gray, bearing thorns; fissures and darkens with age.

Fruit: persistent legume with 1-3 seeds; pod indented between seeds.

Notes: this tree can reach 40-45 ft. A favorite habitat is dry washes that are soaked periodically. Its wood is so dense (66 lbs/ft^3) that it sinks in water; highly resistant to decay, which explains its desirability when long-term use is required. Most of the living trees display signs of prior harvesting of its wood.

Frost-sensitive legume that avoids lower, valley floors and northern exposures. Named to honor S.T. Olney, a 19th century American botanist.

"The ironwood in the wash has undergone many changes over the course of the summer. In May it lost most of the leaves on its outer twigs and replaced foliage with flower buds. The buds burst in the first week of June, converting a ratty-looking tree to a plant of exquisite beauty, a temple seemingly composed entirely of radiant red-purple blooms aflame with color in the early morning light. The ironwood sustained its flowers for two weeks, during which it was visited daily by hundreds of digger bee females that harvested the pollen and nectar.

As the flowers were pollinated and set seed, the faded petals dropped to the ground to carpet a circle of sand beneath the tree. Here once flowers bloomed, green seed pods grew, each just large enough to hold a couple of leguminous beans within a slightly furry case. Rock squirrels abandoned their boulder retreats and became arboreal again to pull the ironwood's seeds into their mouths.

By July, the green pods had turned mottled brown, then deep chocolate, as the surviving beans matured and dried. The seeds and their covers fell to earth amidst the few remaining grey fragments of flower petals. Woodrats and pocket mice came at night to gather what the peccaries left untouched. The ironwood's outer limbs became bare again, with only a few curled pods dangling from branch tips and a collection of dusty green leaves on its inner arms. The dormant tree had joined the rest of us in waiting for the monsoon."

John Alcock from *Sonoran Desert Summer*

BLUE PALO VERDE (*Parkinsonia florida*)
FABACEAE (legume)

Overview: large shrub to small tree with *bluish-green* bark, spiny twigs, and a broad crown.

Flowers: yellow; corolla: 5 petals, four are yellow but one can have a splash of orange. Length: 12-17 mm.

Leaves: twice pinnately compound, 6-10 pinnulae with 1-3 compound leaflets. Compound leaflet supported by a *petiole. Spines borne at the nodes.*

Fruit: flattened pod (see *P. microphylla*).

Handlens: 10 fertile stamens form a ring encircling the pistil; reproductive structures project well above the corolla. Less common than foothills paloverde, it is also much bluer in coloration.

Notes: Blue palo verde has a single, sharp spine at the leaf nodes—a feature absent in foothills palo verde.

The flower color of this legume in the early spring can be an intense, deep yellow. Favors sandy soils of bajadas and flat washes. When found in desert washes, it is usually growing at its margins.

Generally, flowers before *P. microphylla.*

FOOTHILLS PALO VERDE (*Parkinsonia microphylla*)
FABACEAE (legume)

Overview: large shrub to a small tree with conspicuous yellowish-green stems.

Flowers: yellow; corolla: 5 petals, four are yellow but the upper, banner petal is often white. Length: 10 mm or less.

Calyx: uniform, campanulate.

Leaves: twice pinnately compound, 6-10 pinnulae with 4-8 compound leaves. *Sessile. Often, many or even most twigs are devoid of leaves.* When present, pinnae are petite and circular. Multiple compound leaves can project from a common node.

Branches: end in a *sharp point. Spines are not borne at the node.*

Handlens: stamens: 10, orange, basal portion bears white pubescence as does the pistil.

Notes: arguably, the most ubiquitous Sonoran Desert tree, particularly prevalent on rocky slopes. This legume is yellowish-green due to the presence of chlorophyll-laden woody tissues.

Parkinsonia microphylla is aptly named because the pinnulae are so tiny. An important nurse tree for young saguaros. One still finds this genus referred to as *Cercidium*.

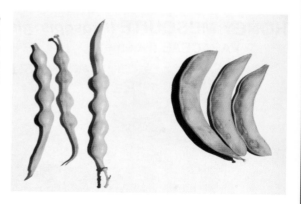

The seedpod of *P. microphylla* has distinct indentations along the fruit that seem to squeeze sections into constrictions *(left)*. *Parkinsonia florida* fruit is squat, curved and shorter *(right)*.

The seeds of legumes typically are a rich source of amino acids, proteins and other nitrogen-containing compounds. Daily consumption of such nitrogen-rich materials is critically important to all mammalian life. Thus, the pods were always highly sought after to sustain a multitude of human and other animal consumers— especially in a desert environment where such materials are always in short supply.

The benefit of moving the green, food-producing chloroplasts from the leaves is demonstrated by the fact that about three fourths of the plant food produced by some desert legumes is secured by its woody tissues

Bruchid beetles [Coleoptera] are a group of insects, worldwide in distribution, that specialize in attacking the fruit of legumes. Some bruchids lay their eggs on the outside of the pod; the newly emerged larvae bore through the pod wall and into the seeds where they develop into adults. Sometimes, the gravid female will deposit her eggs within the pod.

Often, the eggs are deposited on a young pod; larval growth continues while the pod matures and expands. In this way, there is adequate seed development when the first instar larvae emerge. By late summer, virtually every pod shows boreholes— evidence that an insect, arguably a bruchid beetle, has pierced the pod wall *(left)*.

The bruchid beetle, *Caryedes brasiliensis*, oviposits her eggs on the outside of a legume pod. Her newly emerged larvae bore through the pod wall (pericarp) to gain access to the seeds.

HONEY MESQUITE (*Prosopis glandulosa*)
FABACEAE (legume)

Overview: *heavily* branched, large shrub to small tree with a wide crown.

Flowers: creamy yellow; *Inflorescence*: spike-like raceme. *Petals free.* Fragrant.

Branches: sharp, straight, stout thorns (1-2"), that can reach 3", housed at the nodes; arched and curved branches.

Leaves: twice pinnately compound, 7-17 pairs of pinnulae with 2 (occasionally 1) compound leaflet(s). Six or more leaflets can emerge from a single node.

Pinnulae are oblong (0.5"); compound leaflet reaches 2 to 3"; petiole (0.75-1.0").

Fruit: *green*, flat, narrow, terminates at a point, and is similar in size to *P. velutina*. Pod (up to 8") can be constricted between the seeds which are separated by spongy matter.

Notes: this mesquite and other *Prosopis* are a favored host of desert mistletoe. Deep and extensive root system confers significant resistance to drought. Prized for the honey produced from its pollen.

Native Americans dried and roasted the mature pods which were pounded into flour. Intact seeds were given a second grinding. In southern Sonora, this legume can grow to 30-35 ft.

Interesting use: as a bark infusion to curb child incontinence.

A favored habitat of *P. glandulosa* is sandy arroyos whose grandular and loosely packed soil is sought after by the digger bee, *Centris pallida*. Over an 11 month period, these insects develop subterraneously beneath such friable soil.

The newly emerged but still buried female must await an amorous male who detects the female and eagerly digs an excavation channel to free the virgin bee. Not surprisingly, available males fight aggressively to free these entrapped females. On occasion, the males release a male bee that was slow to develop.

Research has established that it is the largest males who prevail from such competitions. Smaller flies still have recourse. They respond to their size limitation, by developing hovering behavior that enables them to intercept a fleeing female able to escape from a burrowing suitor.

SCREWBEAN MESQUITE (*Prosopis pubescens*)
FABACEAE (legume)

Overview: tall, deciduous shrub to a small tree.

Flowers: yellow; corolla; cylindrical. *Inflorescence*: spike-like raceme (groups of 2-6).

Leaves: twice-pinnately compound, 6 to 9 pair of pinnulae with one or two compound leaflet(s), covered with a delicate, gray pubescence.

Stems: paired, white spines (to 1") on gray-barked twigs.

Fruit: lightly greenish, tightly coiled, distinctively shaped, and spiral pod that reaches 2".

Notes: the smallest of the 3 mesquites, characterized by spiny, twisted, and ascending branches that are softly pubescent. This is an unusual legume in that its fruit does not open naturally (indehiscent). Flowers in late spring to early summer and favors sandy washes and riparian habitats.

Interesting use: the shredded bark is employed as a nest-building material by the crissal thrasher, a bird with a sharply curved beak.

Mesquite fruit. *Top*: *Prosopis velutina* (*left*), *P. glandulosa* (*right*); *bottom*: *P. pubescens*

The ripened fruit of the mesquites tends to fall synchronously over a brief period. Since the pods remain closed while on the tree; seeds are not lost before the pods fall and cover the desert floor. These features facilitate collecting and storing of this important food source by desert dwellers.

VELVET MESQUITE (*Prosopis velutina*)
FABACEAE (legume)

Overview: arborescent, desert plant with scaly bark and a circular crown.

Flowers: yellow; *inflorescence*: slender and cylindrical spike.

Leaves; twice pinnately compound, 5-10 pairs of pinnulae typically with *four* compound leaflets (can be two, see top right). A fine, gray pubescence covers the blade.

Stems: solitary or paired spines at the nodes.

Fruit: the pod is slender, *brown*, up to 8 inches in length, and bears a velvety pubescence. Often more markedly constricted and can be thicker than *P. glandulosa;* often their fruits can be difficult to distinguish.

Notes: another abundant leguminous tree, its dark-brown bark cleaves into narrow strips. The wood is highly desired in cooking and other uses. Favors a moist habitat; however, its roots can penetrate deeply into the soil (record depth is 160 ft.) with a taproot as large as the trunk of the tree.

One source claims that an average-sized tree can produce 12 million flowers in a single year. Its pods open along the sutures with sufficient force to eject the seeds far from the plant.

A desirable plant for people who wish to encourage hummingbird visitations. The seeds are ground into a sweet meal and eaten by native people.

The male phainopepla (*Phaino-pepla nitens)* and his female companion are avid consumers of the fleshy berries of the mistletoe (*Phoradendron californicum*).

It is reported that these birds consume on the order of a thousand berries in a single day. Thus, there is little surprise that this food source is of such importance that they will not produce off-springs if mistletoe is not abundant. As a result, they favor sites such as arroyos that support mesquite bosques—a primary source of mistletoe hosts.

These birds carry the mistletoe fruit to the top of the tree where they feed. Defecated seeds, which can survive the digestive system, often fall onto a tree limb. The seed sprouts and the parasite grows into the living host tissues (see p.192). This phainopepla feeding behavior is believed to be a principle means by which mistletoe is distributed throughout the community of desert legumes.

A sprawling velvet mesquite bosque has developed along the creek floodplain. Bosque, a densely packed grouping of trees, is taken from the Spanish fo woodland.

SMOKETREE (*Psorothamnus spinosus*)

FABACEAE (legume)

Overview: a large shrub to small tree with sharply tipped branches and ephemeral leaves. There is a silvery-blue caste to the entire plant.

Flowers: dark purple to deep blue; corolla: *banner*: particularly massive, blended with whitish zones; *wing*: paired, solid coloration; *keel*: solid coloration and whitish spur at its base. Petals rest in a single, flattened plane. *Inflorescence*: borne as a small raceme.

Calyx: supports a row of amber colored glands, gentle pubescence.

Leaves: lanceolate, glandular, small leaves appear in response to summer monsoons.

Twigs: bear a terminal, sharp spine.

Fruit: short, stubby pod, glandular.

Handlens: all the stamens are fused into a large, white basal structure.

Note: unopened flowers display a green calyx with amber glands. Can be a dominant plant in washes; leaves are lost by early summer. Gained its common name from its appearance as a wisp of gentle smoke.

SHRUB LIVE OAK (*Quercus turbinella*)

FAGACAEAE (oak)

Overview: compact, dense shrub to small tree whose leaves, on first inspection, are reminiscent of holly.

Flowers: monoecious; tiny, inconspicuous flowers. *Inflorescence:* male: drooping catkin; female: small spike.

Leaves: oblong to elliptical with rounded base, thick. Upper members: gray-green; lower: yellowish. Leaves are dense; each lobe ends in a very sharp, piercing bristle.

Twigs: red, covered with white pubescence.

Node: little, green bud scar and a red bud.

Fruit: an acorn, with a sharply pointed tip, that requires a year to reach maturity. The nut is housed in a cup-shaped and scaly involucre.

Note: shrub with densely packed, pubescent twigs. Acorns are an important food source for numerous birds and other wildlife; consequently, it is extremely difficult to find a mature acorn on the plant.

American holly, *Ilex opaca;* its wax-laden cuticle, retarding water loss, glistens from reflected sunlight.

WHITE RATANY (*Krameria grayi*)
RANGE RATANY (*Krameria erecta*)
KRAMERIACEAE (krameria)

Overview: intricate and densely branched, perennial subshrub armored with barb-tipped spines on its fruit.

Flowers: reddish purple; 3 upper petals are elongated and spatulate, while the 2 lower petals have lobes that are blister-like oil glands. *Inflorescence*: emerge from the leaf nodes.

Calyx: petal-like sepals with pubescence on the underside.

Leaves: linear and curved, tiny, generally alternate but occasionally opposite.

Involucre: solitary pair of opposite, leaf-like bracts.

Fruit: spherical and spiny.

Notes: there is a *bluish-gray tint to the entire plant*. Bees collect fatty materials (lipids) from this plant for their offsprings. It is valued in human activity for its astringent and antimicrobial activities. Bur-like fruit, with numerous spines, is designed to facilitate animal dispersal. Named to honor J.G.H. Kramer, an 18th century Austrian botanist.

A semi-parasitic plant, it is often associated with triangleleaf bursage and creosote bush.

A less commonly occurring member of this group, *Krameria erecta* (*left*) is no less visually striking.

DESERT LAVENDER (*Hyptis albida*)

LAMIACEAE (mint)

Overview: a multi-branched, woody perennial with an overall bluish-gray cast.

Flowers: violet-blue to lavender; corolla: trilabiate—upper: 2-lobed; lower: 2-lobed; central lobe forms a pouch. *Inflorescence*: borne on a spike that clusters at the nodes. Covered with dense, stellate pubescence.

Calyx: 5 sharply tapered sepals covered in a white and woolly pubescence.

Leaves: ovate to rounded; crenate; fine, woolly pubescence and silvery sheen. Venation pronounced on the underside of the blade.

Stems: densely pubescent on younger members but smooth and grayish with age.

Fruit: angular nutlet that is protected by the calyx.

Handlens: 4 deep purple on white stamens, hairy filaments.

Notes: pleasantly fragrant, lavender-pine aroma. Visitation by various bees and hummingbirds is observed routinely. It grows in washes and desert slopes.

Interesting use: the leaves and fruit were believed to be helpful to insane individuals.

BLADDER SAGE (*Salazaria mexicana*)
LAMIACEAE (mint)

Overview: a perennial shrub that exhibits a tangled mass of sharply tipped branches, many projecting at right angles to the rounded stem

Flowers: deep blue violet; corolla: bilabiate—upper lip: white-pale violet, pubescent lower: 3-lobed. *Inflorescence*: spike-like raceme (2-4").

Calyx: expands to create a greenish white, bladder-like structure with streaks of purple; 2 segments surround and protect the seeds. The resulting "bladder" is persistent for most of the year and functions as a lightweight dispersing agent.

Leaves: ovate to elliptical, opposite, rounded base with a minute petiole.

Handlens: four stamens under the upper lip; lightly-colored filament bearing a much darker anther.

Notes: named to remember Don Jose Salazar y Larrequi, a prominent Mexican commissioner. Flowers in the spring with a second wave possible in the autumn.

GRAYTHORN (*Ziziphus obtusifolia*)
RHAMNACEAE (buckthorn)

Overview: stoutly branched, spiny perennial with fuzzy pubescence, and sharply tipped branches.

Flowers: whitish-green; corolla: 5 petals, inconspicuous. *Inflorescence:* clustered (10-30 units) on the stem at the axils.

Calyx: 5 densely pubescent lobes.

Leaves: ovate to oblong, pubescent, dark green, *Brown stipules and a tiny petiole*; a prominent midvein on the underside of the blade.

Stem: spiny, downy-soft, gray pubescence, and an overall light gray appear-ance. Sharp point at the end of the secondary branches.

Fruit: blue-black and elliptical drupes.

Handlens: olive pistil with a 2-clefted style. Five yellow stamens emerge from regions between the lobes of the calyx.

Notes: drupes are adored by birds, especially white-winged doves and Gambel quail.

Interesting use: American Indians combated rheumatic pain by pricking the infected places with the thorns of the plant.

APACHE PLUME (*Fallugia paradoxa*)
ROSACEAE (rose)

Overview: a deciduous to per-sistent, densely pubescent, white-barked shrub that can attain 6 ft.

Flowers: rose-white; corolla: 5 petals (to 1-1.5"). *Inflorescence*: solitary or bunched at the apex of highly elongated penduncles. Numerous stamens and pistils.

Calyx: 5 sepals, pubescent; 5 bract-like structures are positioned alternately with the calyx segments.

Leaves: ovate, pinnately divided (3-7 lobes), margin reflexed,

Seeds: achenes that support persistent, highly ornate, rosy-pink, plume-like dispersing agents that are derived from the style.

Notes: *Fallugia* recognizes the 19th century Italian botanist: Abbot, V. Fallugi; *paradoxa* is taken from the Greek to describe its unusual plumage. Favors rocky slopes and arroyos.

Interesting use: Hopi Indians prepared a leaf infusion that was used to promote hair growth.

HOPBUSH (*Dodonaea viscosa*)
SAPINDACEAE (soapberry)

Overview: leaf-persistent, viscid shrub that can reach 10 ft.

Flowers: yellow to orange-red; no corolla. Dioecious. *Inflorescence*: produced within leafy clusters, as a raceme, at the stem apex.

Leaves: linear to elliptical (2-3"), persistent, upper surface is glossy due to a sticky resin.

Fruit: showy capsule, 2 to 4 (typically 3) wings, that houses 3 seeds. Red when young but turning brown with age; occasionally pink-tinged, becoming *papery* with age.

Note: world-wide distribution, thrives in different climates and growing conditions. Common name derived from its use in beer making, when hops are not available.

It grows virtually everywhere on the Australian continent. The Maori of New Zealand employed its dense wood to produce a variety of weapons.

JOJOBA (*Simmondsia chinensis*)

SIMMONDSIACEAE (jojoba)

Overview: woody densely branched evergreen.

Flowers: usually dioecious; no corolla.

Pistillate: small, pale green. Calyx: 10-20 mm.

Staminate: larger flower, occurring in clusters. Calyx: 3-4 mm.

Flower buds form only on new shoots emerging from the nodes. Supposedly, these buds remain dormant until they experience a winter chill and adequate spring rain (see p. 23).

Leaves: oval or lanceolate, dull gray-green, opposite. Water loss is minimized by the presence of a waxy cuticle covering the leaf surface. Persistent, can remain on the plant for 2 or 3 seasons.

Fruit: green capsule that can house up to 3 brown seeds (typically only one). Wax accounts for about half the seed weight.

Handlens: pistillate: green, pubescent, 3 styles; staminate: highly pubescent calyx protects a mass of yellow stamens (4-12).

Note: jojoba is desired for its fine, light yellow, odorless, polyunsaturated liquid wax extracted from the seeds. This material is used in many industrial products; for example, as a high-temperature, high-pressure lubricant, and as a low-calorie, non-cholesterol, edible oil. It serves many functions previously served by whale oil. Nearly 40,000 acres are currently under cultivation in the Southwest.

Jojoba is another desert plant that orientates its leaves to track the sun, to minimize surface area exposure. Many desert hikers enjoy its almond-like, astringent but edible seed.

Handlens inspection of the stigma of pistillate flowers shows its relatively large surface area. This is the part of the pistil that is the pollen receptacle. This configuration, which maximizes pollen capture, is a common adaptation by plants which rely upon wind to disperse their pollen grains.

KEY TO LOCAL *LYCIUM*

1A. Calyx lobes can be much less, but not more than half the length of the tube
    1B. Herbage is pubescent to densely pubescent
        1C. Stamens exserted, flowers pendent.......................*L. exsertum*[1]
        2C. Stamens not exserted, flowers not pendent...............*L. fremontii*[2]
    2B. Herbage is glabrous to sparsely pubescent
        1C. Filament base is glabrous to sparsely pubescent.....*L. berlandieri*[3]
        2C. Filament base is densely pubescent....................*L. andersonii*[4]
2A. Calyx lobes are at least half or more than the length of the tube
    1B. Leaves are densely glandular and pubescent....................*L. parishii*[5]
    2B. Leaves are glabrous...*L. pallidum*[6]

    Some of the external features employed in identifying members of this genus include: the size of the calyx and the relative length of its lobes to that of the structure as a whole; the color of the petals, the general overall shape of the corolla, and the size of its lobes; whether the stamens are exserted (strongly as above) or insert, and if their base is smooth or bears marked pubescence (pillose); whether the various structures of the plant lack pubescence (glabrous as above), or are glandular and pubescent.

---

[1] Leaves: oval to spatulate-obovate; stamens: exserted to 5 mm.
[2] Leaves: spatulate to obovate; stamens: not exserted.
[3] Leaves: linear or nearly so; stamens: usually strongly exserted.
[4] Leaves: linear to oblanceolate; stamens: included to slightly exserted.
[5] Leaves: oblanceolate to obovate to spatulate; stamens: slightly exserted.
[6] Leaves: oblong to narrowly obovate; stamens: exserted.

ANDERSON WOLFBERRY (*Lycium andersonii*)
PALE DESERT-THORN (*Lycium pallidum*)
SOLANACEAE (nightshade)

Overview: globose, highly branched perennial shrub.

Flowers: greenish white, often fringed violet to lavender at the tip; corolla: 4- or 5-lobed, tubular and funnel-shaped.

Calyx: 4-5 lobes, campanulate, lobes about 1/4 the length of the calyx tube.

Leaves: linear to elliptic to oblanceolate, finely pubescent to smooth.

Stem: whitish with conspicuous striations and grooves; exceedingly branchy and spine-tipped.

Fruit: small, red, fleshy berry housing many seeds.

Handlens: stamens: unequal in length, only slightly exserted and somewhat pillose

Notes: many birds love the tasty fruit. Most species of this group are edible and served as a welcomed food resource for Native Americans. Pollinators include bees, butterflies, and hummingbirds.

Pale desert-thorn, *Lycium pallidum,* is one of many members of this group of attractive nightshades that can produce a massive shrub resplendent in blossoms.

SALTCEDAR (*Tamarix ramosissima*) *(Tamarix chinensis)*
TAMARICACEAE (tamarix)

Overview: a loosely branched, large shrub to small tree with an open and lacy appearance.

Flowers: pink to whitish; corolla: 5 tiny petals. *Inflorescence*: clustered at the apex as a panicle.

Calyx: 5 lobes.

Leaves: form into a dense cluster that resembles the scale-like foliage of the juniper tree. Both the leaves and the red-purple twigs are deciduous.

Handlens: 5 stamens inserted at the base of the ovary; salt-excreting glands on the leaves.

Fruit: reddish-brown capsules; an individual tree can produce 25 million seeds in a single year.

Notes: an invasive weedy plant that has eliminated much of the native willows and cottonwood trees from riparian habitats. Can grow 9 to 12 ft in a single year—forming dense thickets that deplete critical soil moisture.

First reported within the banks of the Gila River in 1916, this exotic species continues to be a major invasive plant; thickets of salt cedar along the Colorado River divert millions of gallons of water each year. Eradication and containment of this exotic will be a demanding, future necessity. Named for the Tamaris River in Spain.

DESERT HACKBERRY (*Celtis pallida*)
ULMACEAE (elm)

Overview: a densely branched shrub that can reach small tree size.

Flowers: greenish-yellow; corolla: tiny, inconspicuous. *Inflorescence*: small cymes.

Leaves: ovate to elliptical, simple, generally entire when juvenile but gently serrated in older foliage.

Stem: twigs angle in a repetitive manner between the nodes that house two sharp, slender thorns that often have a small barb.

Fruit: orange-red, fleshy, edible berry that develops by late summer to early fall; an important food resource for a host of birds and other desert dwellers. The fruit is edible and sought after by desert hikers who must compete with coyotes, foxes, and javelinas.

Note: favors sandy washes and other open areas. Older plants, enjoying favorable conditions, not only reach tree size but also cover an extensive area.

A watchful, male empress butterfly awaiting the arrival of a receptive female

The desert hackberry is the only plant upon which the empress butterfly (*Astero-campa celtis*) will deposit her eggs. Larvae, developing from these eggs, are sustained by its foliage. In time, they weave a puparium that affords protection during their vulnerable pupal stage. This puparium bears an obvious resemblance to the hackberry; this form of camouflage minimizes danger from predation— particularly important since the pupa is the quiescent stage of their reproductive cycle. The newly emerged female will mate with eagerly waiting males and continue its life cycle on a hackberry plant.

An absolute and irrevocable alliance has been established between insect and desert plant. A question of interest is what is gained by sacrificing all of the available plants that could be used, and rely instead solely upon this single plant? An obvious benefit is that over time the insect has fine tuned its relationship with this hackberry so as to extract maximum resources. This would enhance its chances for long-term survival. Any other thoughts?

NETLEAF HACKBERRY (*Celtis reticulata*)
ULMACEAE (elm)

Overview: sizable desert tree (to 40 ft.) with a stout, shortened trunk; twisted branches and an imposing, spreading crown.

Flowers: pale green; *inflorescence*: emerge (1-4 units) from the leaf nodes.

Leaves: ovate, leathery, entire to somewhat dentated. Lower surface venation: net-like, conspicuous, and elevated. Numerous insect-created galls coat the surface.

Fruit: reddish-orange, globose drupe.

Twigs: narrow with a distinct zigzag pattern; light-brown, adhering buds.

Bark: gray with corky ridges and wart-like structures.

Note: this plant is subject to vigorous attack by insects and fungi. The drupes of this *Celtis* are edible and highly prized for their sweet, juicy taste.

OREGANILLO (*Aloysia wrightii*)
VERBENACEAE (vervain)

Overview: large, multi-branched, and graceful shrub-like plant.

Flowers: white; corolla: 5 lobes divided into 2 larger upper segments

Calyx: campanulate to tubular, deeply 4-lobed, pubescent.

Leaves: ovate to circular, bright green, crenate to finely dentate; upper surface: *wrinkled*; lower: gently pubescent. Petiole: very tiny and pubescent.

Handlens: four unequally sized pairs; 2-chambered ovary.

Stem: slender, brittle with exfoliating bark.

Fruit: 2 nutlets.

Notes: minute flower with a pleasant spice-like odor. Crushed leaves have oregano-like odor. Favored food source for a variety of wildlife.

CREOSOTE BUSH *(Larrea divaricata)*
ZYGOPHYLLACEAE (caltrop)

Overview: highly branched, strongly scented shrub with an open, lacy appearance and foliage clustered tightly around the stem, particularly at their nodes.

Flowers: yellow, corolla: solitary, tiny, 5 clawed petals.

Calyx: 5 yellow-green sepals; soft white pubescent on the inner surface.

Leaves: ovate to oblong, dark and evergreen, opposite, sessile, and composed of 2 fused leaflets that appears as a single, thick, lobed leaf.

Handlens: 10 prominent, golden-yellow stamens. Simple pistil with long, silky, and white pubescence.

Fruit: a small, woolly ball (capsule), about the size of a small pea. At maturity, splits into 5 sections, each bearing a single nutlet.

Notes: when the leaves are crushed, phytochemicals are released to create a pungent fragrance. Highly effective shelter plant for many cacti.

Mormon employed this plant as a cancer remedy, and it is still a part of current-day, herbal medicine.

Named for John Anthony de Larrea, a Spanish student of the sciences.

Creosote bush is one of the most abundant members of the Arizona Upland Subdivision; often forming extensive, homogeneous communities remarkably free of intrusion by other plants. It is also found in the deserts of South America.

This caltrop is repudiated to be one of the most drought-resistant plants of the North American deserts. This favorable property results in large part from its diminutive foliage that is coated with waxy-like materials that minimize leaf surface water loss. Additionally, this shrub grows an extensive root system that effectively scavenges moisture from the soil. During the driest parts of summer, these tissues are able to extricate the last vestiges of soil moisture.

The ability of creosote bush to compete so effectively may also reflect its production of allelochemical(s) that are released into the soil—thereby inhibiting the establishment and development of potentially competitive plants. These presently uncharacterized phytochemicals create a growth-inhibiting zone that simply keeps competitors at bay.

Given its wide distribution and success, it is little wonder that about five dozen species of insect rely upon this shrub for sustenance and shelter; about two dozen bees gain nourishment from its flowers. It is most interesting that another particularly successful desert inhabitant, brittlebush, *Encelia farinosa*, is also reputed to produce growth-inhibiting allelochemical(s).

Many galls result from abnormal plant growth caused by the feeding activity of entrapped immature insects. The immature insect is engulfed and protected by the growing gall, which also serves as a food source for the developing insect. Eventually, an adult emerges from the gall. This gall was created by the creosote gall midge, *Asphondylia auripila* [Cecidomyiidae]; other flies in this family make other galls, primarily on the leaves.

The desert clicker (*Ligurotettix coquilletti*), a brown grasshopper, relishes the creosote bush as a place to feed and mate. Successful, dominant males produce a distinctive clicking sound that is part of their mating-territory defense. Highly territorial insects, they can spend a lifetime in a single creosote bush.

An observant hiker may find this secretive grasshopper by listening for their singing which begins early in the day and lasts well into night. An invading male is greeted with an acoustical outpouring which when ignored escalates to behavior sufficiently aggressive to deter the intruder. Nevertheless, subordinate males continue to reside in a particular shrub governed by a dominant male. It seems obvious that the lesser males would flee to an empty creosote bush where they can sing contentedly and await a receptive female. In fact, the subordinates do not.

Careful analysis of creosote bush foliage reveals storage of a phenol that lowers the nutritional value of the foliage; plants vary in their content of this phytochemical. A female grasshopper eschews such plants since they would provide only minimally for her forthcoming brood. Thus, it is advantageous for the lesser male to remain on a robust plant, and hope to gain access to a female without drawing the attention of the dominant male.

Spectacular sunsets are one of the great joys of living in the Sonoran Desert.

TREES OF RIPARIAN HABITATS

Spectacular riparian habitats occur within the Sonoran Desert; several trees, attaining a massive size, thrive in these hydric sites.

During the Tertiary, when the desert climate was far wetter, great deciduous forests of these riparian trees covered the landscape.

Autumnal coloration of Fremont cottonwood, *Populus fremontii.*

ARIZONA ASH (*Fraxinus velutina*)
OLEACEAE (olive)

A fast-growing and hardy tree that is distinct for the opposite growth pattern of the twigs and leaves. Its leaves are pinnately compound (3-7 pinnae), ovate to elliptical, mostly entire but margins can be dentate or even serrate. Prominent midvein, especially on the lower surface.

It is a dioecious species with yellow pistillate and green staminate flowers. Staminate flowers (in dense clusters) with two, elongated stamens; pistillate: single pistil. The flowers appear in the spring prior to the advent of foliage.

Large clumps of fruit, winged samaras, adorn many branches. A samara is a type of fruit in which the ovary wall grows to create a wing that aids in transporting the seed. A fertile tree can produce 1,000s of seeds in a favorable year.

ARIZONA SYCAMORE (*Platanus racemosa* var. *wrightii*)
PLATANACEAE (sycamore)

Another large, spreading tree with distinctively exfoliating bark that re-veals whitish internal tissues. A massive tree (reaching 80') bearing distinctive leaves and fruit.

The leaves are alternate, simple, and palmately lobed into 3 larger, upper lobes and 2 smaller, lower lobes. Leaf venation is prominent, with a vein terminating at the center and apex of each lobe. Buds are pressed against the stem at the base of the flattened petiole. Bark: smooth, white to greenish and flaking continuously.

Monoecious flowers are borne in a dense head. The fruit is a mass of 4-sided achenes intermixed with hairs to produce a ball-like structure. A major method of reproduction is by the growth of suckers from the roots.

ARIZONA WALNUT (*Juglans major*)
JUGLANDACEAE (walnut)

A highly attractive tree that provides shade and outstandingly edible fruit. The fruit although called a "nut", is actually drupaceous with a fibrous outer skin. The bark is darkly colored and deeply fissured.

Pinnately compound leaves with 9-13 pinnae; the pinnae are finely serrated, alternate, and lanceolate. Monoecious with staminate catkins (thin, drooping, and elongated) and solitary or few pistillate flowers.

The fruit is much sought after by humans and many other animals. Prized for its decorative wood; medicinally-active foliage.

FREMONT COTTONWOOD (*Populus fremontii*)
SALICACEAE (willow)

Very rapid growing tree with a broad, open crown that produces a low density wood and a trunk that can exceed 6 ft. Its leaves are alternate, simple, deltoid, and crenate with a pointy tip. Flattened petiole, about as long as the blade, contributes to the constant state of motion observed with the foliage.

Young stems are green and glandular; older parts are brown with green fissures. The leaf scar houses three bundle scars and a conical, brown bud.

Catkins, borne on separate trees, are the reproductive structures. The fruit capsule contains seeds with a cottony pubescence. During certain times of the year, they can fill the sky with twirling color.

GOODDING BLACK WILLOW (*Salix gooddingii*)
SALICACEAE (willow)

Large, spreading tree that can exceed 3 ft. in diameter; several trunks develop from a common point. Narrowly lanceolate leaves (as much as 4x longer than wide), alternate, simple, finely serrated. Glandular petiole, yellow to yellow-gray twigs.

Dioecious species. Fruit, with fine pubescence, hang in elongated groups on the peduncle; develops from catkins on lateral, leafy branchlets. Seeds are released in late spring to early summer.

GLOSSARY

A _____

Achene-hard, dry, one-seeded fruit that does not open along natural sutures or openings.

Actinomorphic (radial symmetry)-a line drawn through the middle of a structure, along any plane, divides it into mirror images.

Acuminate-ending with a tapering point.

Alternate-pattern of leaf arrangement in which the leaves emerges from alter-nating sides of the stem.

Annual-completes its life cycle in one year or growing season.

Anther-apex of the stamen houses the male sex cells or pollen grains.

Areole-raised portion on cactus surface from which the spines and flowers emerge.

Awn-terminal, slender needle-like appendage.

Axil-space or angle between the stem or peduncle and another emerging plant part.

B _____

Banner-upper most, typically largest, petal of a legume flower.

Basal-occurring at the base.

Berry-fleshy or pulpy indehiscent fruit with one to many seeds. Seeds not protected by a stony structure (pit) as in a drupe. A tomato is an example of a berry.

Biennial-completes its life cycle over two years or growing seasons.

Bilateral symmetry-see zygomorphic.

Blade-the principal part of the leaf, excludes the petiole and stipules.

Bract-modified leaf that is part of the flower head, can be very showy, often below the calyx.

Bractlet-small bract.

Bud-structure that houses the embry-onic tissues that will become a shoot, leaf, or flower; protected by *bud scales.*

Bur-generally a fruit with sharp pro-jections. These pointed structures aid in seed dispersal.

C _____

Calyx-collective term for the sepals protects the internal flower parts. Typically green, more substantial than the petals.

Campanulate-bell-shaped.

Capsule-dry, dehiscent fruit that opens through pores or other openings in the fruit wall. Can be divided into seg-ments or sections.

Catkin-spike-like inflorescence often hangs downward, flowers usually of one sex.

Cauline-above ground, said of leaves located along the upper stem.

Chaff-thin, dry, papery scale or bract on the receptacle.

Cilia- extensions or projections of the leaf margin.

Clasping-attached to or wrapping around the stem.

Clone-genetically identical, resulting from asexual reproduction.

Cohort-an individual in a population of the same species.

Complete-flower possessing all of its floral elements.

Composite-flower of the Asteraceae with ray and/or disk flowers.

Compound leaf-multiple components attached ultimately to a common petiole, not a single blade.

Cordate-heart shaped.

Corolla-collective term for the petals of a flower, inner floral elements.

Corymb-flat-topped, branched inflor-escence, pedicles of unequal length, flowers open from the extremities inward toward the center. It can have a simple or compound structure.

Crenate-leaf margin with shallow rounded or curved teeth.

Cross-pollination-transfer of pollen bet-ween flowers of the same plant.

Cyme (cymose, adj.)-flat-topped, branched inflorescence, pedicles of unequal length, flowers open from the center outward to the extremities.

D_____

Deciduous-the property of falling or separating from the plant.

Decussate-arranged along the stem in pairs, each pair at right angles to the pair next above or below, as leaves.

Dehiscent-fruit that opens naturally along sutures or natural lines of cleavage.

Deltoid- equilaterally triangular.

Dentate-sharp, angular teeth at right angle to the margin. Teeth more pointed than in a crenulated margin.

Dentation (adj.-dentate)-leaf margin bears some type of teeth.

Didymous-occurring in a pair.

Didynamous-generally refers to a group of four stamens, each pair of unequal length.

Dioecious-pistillate and staminate flowers are produced by separate and distinct (independent) plants.

Discoidal head-a flower head (Aster-aceae) consisting solely of disk flowers.

Disk flower-a type of flower (Asteraceae), found in the central core of the composite flower.

Drought deciduous-leaves fall in response to drought.

Drupe-fleshy or pulpy fruit in which the seed is protected by a hard covering. For example, peach, olive.

Dry-said of fruit that is not succulent.

E_____

Elliptic (elliptical)-much longer than wide, tapering at both ends.

Entire-descriptive of the leaf margin, smooth and continuous, without irregu-larities.

Epipetalous-stamens are partially or fully fused to the corolla wall.

Evergreen-plant that appears to keep its foliage throughout the growing season.

Exserted-projecting outward; for example, said of the stamens that project above the plane of the perianth.

F_____

Family-taxonomic unit that refers to a group of genera that share common characteristics.

Filament-slender part of the stamen that supports the anther.

Fleshy-succulent, high moisture con-tent.

Follicle-dry fruit that opens along a single suture in the fruit wall.

Fruit-developed ovary with its pro-tected seeds.

Funnelform-shaped like a funnel, widen-ing upwards.

Fusiform-elongated and widest at its central region.

G

Genera-taxonomic unit that refers to a group of species with common char-acteristics; singular: genus.

Genus-see genera.

Gland-structure that exudes or secretes various substances.

Glandular-bearing a gland.

Globose-rounded, spherical shape.

Glochid-fine hairs on the pads of some *Opuntia* cacti; easily detached, barbed tip. Arises from a tubercle.

H

Habitat-place, surrounding, or setting where an organism lives.

Hastate-arrowhead-shaped, but the basal lobes are expanded (see sagittate).

Head-found typically in flowers of the Asteraceae; organization of the flowers on the receptacle.

Herb (adj. *herbaceous*)-composed of soft tissues, succulent plant lacking woody, persistent tissues.

Herbage-leaves and stem of an herb, but not the floral parts.

Hood-deeply concave, used to describe the shape of certain flower petals.

I

Imperfect-flower that lacks either stamens or pistils.

Indehiscent-not opening along sutures or pores in the fruit wall.

Inferior ovary-ovary positioned below the sepals, petals, and stamens.

Inflorescence-arrangement or grouping of the flowers on the peduncle.

Involucre-collective term denoting all of the bracts, commonly found in flowers of the Asteraceae.

Irregular- not all of the entities are of the same size and shape, said of the petals. Contrasts to regular form.

K

Keel-lower-most petal section of a legume flower, composed of two fused petal sections.

L

Lanceolate-lance shaped, broader at the base than the middle or the tip; length much greater than the width, tapering at the apex.

Leaflet-part of a pinnately compound leaf, pinna (plural: pinnae).

Legume-dry fruit that opens naturally along two sutures in the fruit wall.

Ligule-blade of a ray flower, flattened strap-shaped corolla; found in the Aster-aceae.

Linear-narrow and elongated, nearly uniform in width.

Lip-upper or lower portion of an unequally or irregularly divided petal or sepal.

Lobe-curved or rounded segment divid-ing a leaf or corolla; larger structure than any type of indentation on the margin.

Lyrate-rounded terminal lobe that is larger than the remaining segments.

M____

Mid-vein-vein in the middle of the leaf.

Monoecious-pistillate and staminate flowers *are separate* but located on the same plant.

N____

Nectar- sugary reward for the pollinating animal.

Node-position at the axil where a bud or some other plant part such as a leaf would be positioned.

Nut-dry, indehiscent fruit containing a single seed protected by an indurate covering.

O____

Oblanceolate-lance-shaped but broader at the apex than the base.

Obovate-leaf shape that is broader at the tip than the base.

Opposite-paired leaves attached directly opposite each other at nodes along the stem.

Ovate-leaf shape that is oval but broader at the base than the tip, egg shaped.

Ovary-basal portion of the pistil that grows into the fruit, houses the ovules.

Ovule-female sex cell (gamete) housed within the ovary, embryonic structure that will develop into the seed.

P____

Palea (plural: paleae)-chaffy, dry, scale-like bract.

Palmately compound-complex leaf in which components radiate from a central point like the fingers of a hand.

Palmately divided-leaf blade segments emerge from a common point.

Panicle- compound raceme.

Pappus-appendage that connects to the achene, aids in its wind dispersal.

Parasite-organism that derives its sustenance from another organism.

Pedicle-structure that supports the flower head.

Pendent-hanging downward.

Peduncle-structure that supports the pedicles.

Peltate-petiole attaches to the lower surface, not the end of the blade.

Perennial-persistent, completes its life cycle over many growing seasons.

Perfect-flower with functional stamens and pistil(s).

Perianth-collective term for all of the petals and sepals.

Petal-normally showy parts of the flower, part of the corolla.

Petiole-structure (stalk) which attaches the blade to the stem.

Petiolule-structure (stalk) which attaches the pinnula of a compound leaflet to its rachis.

Phyllary-bracts of the involucre.

Pinna-(plural: pinnae) leaflet of a pinnately compound leaf.

Pinnately compound-complex leaf made of many pinnae.

Pinnately divided-highly disrupted margin, highly segmented, numerous lobes, and clefts extend from both sides of the midvein.

Pinnula-a basic unit of a twice pinnately compound leaf.

Pistil-all of the structures of the female reproductive system, includes the stigma, style, and ovary.

Pistillate-flower contains only the pistil(s), no stamens.

Pod-dry fruit containing the seed(s).

Pollen-material carrying the pollen grains or male sex cells.

Pollination-process whereby the pollen grain is attached to the stigma of the pistil.

Prostrate-growing on the ground, not erect.

Pubescence-a variety of hairs or hair-like structures.

R_____

Rachis-structure that supports the pinnae or pinnula, an extension of the petiole in a pinnately compound leaf.

Raceme-unbranched inflorescence in which flowers, supported on a pedicle, emerge along the peduncle.

Radial symmetry- see actinomorphic

Ray flower-type of flower (Asteraceae), made of ligules. Flattened, strap-shaped corolla.

Recurved-bent backwards.

Regular-all of the entities are of the same size and shape, said of the petals; contrasts to irregular form.

Replum-a membrane-like structure that divides the sections of certain fruit.

Rosette-said of a radiating assemblage of leaves.

S_____

Sagittate-leaf shape that resembles an arrowhead. Two lobes directed down-ward.

Scale-thin, hard, plate-like structure.

Scorpioid-one-sided inflorescence with a coiled axis; resembles a scorpion's tail.

Seed-fertilized, mature ovule; contains the embryo of a future plant.

Sepal-part of the calyx, protects the internal flower parts.

Serrate-coarse teeth that are directed forward toward leaf apex.

Sessile-attached to the stem directly, no petiole.

Shrub-woody plant, less massive than a typical tree, typically lacks a woody trunk.

Silicle-a specialized fruit of the mustard family. Seeds remain fixed to a replum, an internal, central membrane; generally no more than twice as long as wide. Far more globose than a silique.

Silique-dry, narrow, and elongated seed pod that separates into two segments with the length being more than twice the width. A persistent, membrane-like structure divides the segments.

Simple leaf-a single blade.

Solitary-said of a flower; single flower on a stem.

Spatulate-spatula shaped.

Species (plural: species)-plant that breeds true from seeds.

Spike-unbranched inflorescence in which sessile flowers are borne along a common stalk.

Spine-common in cacti, a sharply pointed outgrowth from the stem or pad; produced from a modified leaf.

Stamen-male part of the flower made of a supporting filament and an anther.

Staminate-flowers contain only stamens, no pistil.

Staminode-an infertile stamen.

Stem-primary, above ground structure of the plant that supports various appen-dages.

Stigma-pistil apex, where the pollen grain must reach for successful fertilization.

Stipules-leaf-like appendages typically found at the base of the leaf.

Style-central portion of the pistil between the stigma and the ovary.

Subshrub-a plant consisting of a woody, perennial base with annual, herbaceous shoots.

Succulent-moisture-laden plant with fleshy leaves and stems.

Suffrutescent-possessing woody basal stems.

Superior ovary-ovary is positioned above other flower parts.

Suture-natural cleavage plane or open-ing, a seam.

T_____

Taxonomy-the science of classification of organisms.

Tendril-a slender, organ, typically part of the leaf or petiole, used for support as the plant grows.

Thorn-woody, sharply pointed structure; modified stem.

Tooth-small projection on the leaf margin, far less massive than a lobe.

Tuber-starchy, underground storage organ.

Tubercle-protuberance of the stem of a cactus from which the areoles arise.

Twice pinnately compound-an individual pinna is replaced by a compound leaflet.

Twining-said of the stem; coiled or winding spirally around a support.

U_____

Umbel-flat-topped inflorescence, all pedicles radiate from a common point on the peduncle; flowers open from the extremities inward toward the center.

V_____

Vein-tissues through which water and other materials move. For example, the veins of the leaf blade.

Vine-a plant that grows on a supporting structure.

Viscid-sticky.

W_____

Whorled-two or more leaves attached commonly at the stem.

Wing-one of two lateral petal sections of a legume flower.

X_____

Xeric-a dry environment.

Z_____

Zygomorphic- a structure that can be divided, at its middle, along only a single plane to produce mirror images. Compare to actinomorphic.

INFORMATIONAL SOURCES

Alcock, John, 1990. *Sonoran Desert Summer*, The University of Arizona Press, Tempe, AZ, 187 pp.

Bowers, J.E., and Wignall, B., 1993. *Shrubs and Trees of the Southwest Deserts*, Western National Parks Association, Tucson, AZ,140 pp.

Epple, A. O., 1995. *A Field Guide to the Plants of Arizona*, Falcon Press, Helena, MT, 347 pp.

Gilkey, H. M. and Dennis, L.J., 1967. *Handbook of Northwestern Plants*, Oregon State University Bookstores, Inc, Corvallis, OR, 505 pp.

Hickman, J.C., ed. 1993. *The Jepson Manual—Higher Plants of California*, University of California Press, Berkeley, CA, 1400 pp.

Hodgson, Wendy C., 2001. *Food Plants of the Sonoran Desert*. The University of Arizona Press, Tempe, AZ, 313 pp.

Jaeger, Edmond C., 1941. *Desert Wild Flowers*, Stanford University Press, Stan-ford, CA, 322 pp.

Kearney, T.H., Peebles, H., and collaborators, 1960. *Arizona Flora*, University of California Press, Berkeley, CA. 1085 pp.

Moore, M., 1989. *Medicinal Plants of the Desert and Canyon West*. Museum of New Mexico Press, Santa Fe, NM, 184 pp.

Munz, Philip A. *California Desert Wildflowers*. 1969. University of California Press, Berkeley, CA. 122 pp.

Quinn, M., 2000. *Wildflowers of the Desert Southwest*, Rio Nuevo Publishers, Tucson, AZ, 88 pp.

Spellenberg, R., 2003. *Sonoran Desert Wildflowers*, The Globe Pequot Press, Guilford, CT 246 pp.

Turner, R.M., Bowers, J.E., and Burgess, T.L., 1995. *Sonoran Desert Plants—An Ecological Atlas*. University of Arizona Press, Tucson, AZ 504 pp.

FROM THE WORLD WIDE WEB:
James M. Andre & Michelle Cloud-Hughes: *calphotos.berkeley.edu*

Michael Charters: *www.calflora.net*

Al Schneider: *www.swcoloradowildflowers.com*

Stan Shebs: *commons.wikimedia.org/wiki/User:Stan_Sheb/GalleryPlants*

Flora of North America: *www.eFloras.org*

Wildflowers and Other Plants of Southern California: *www.calflora.net*

Wayne's World: *waynesword.palomar.edu*

Burke Museum of Natural History and Culture: *biology.burke.washington.edu*

Desert Plants & Wildflowers: *www.desertusa.com*

McGraw-Hill Resource Library: *http://www.mhhe.com/biosci/pae/botany/vrl/images1.htm*

Edward H. Mertz: *www.edmertz.com*

Integrated Taxonomic Information System: *www.itis.gov*

ACKNOWLEDGMENTS

Seldom can an effort of this type be brought to fruition without a significant contribution by others. Indeed, many individuals gave generously of their time and creative efforts. The required plant images could not have been assembled without the willingness of a group of generous individuals who permitted unencumbered access to their digital pictures. James A. Andre contributed most significantly; Michael Charters, Al Schneider, Michelle Cloud-Hughes, Stan Shebs, Ed Mertz, John Alcock, Stephen Buchmann, Ben Legler, Steve Matson, Ernie Buchanan, Ronald Rutowski, Richard Old, Linda Covey, Wayne P. Armstrong, Thomas Eisner, John Gunn, Fred Hrusa, Ralph Arvesen, William Hart, Ethan Saul, Gilbert Muth, Aaron Schusteff, Bouncing Bear Botanicals, and The Lady Bird Johnson Wildflower Center provided material from their digital image library. Al Schneider carefully proofed portions of the text; he impressed me with his expertise and attention to details. McGraw-Hill Education, The Royal Society of New Zealand, The Kentucky Native Plant Society, and Wikipedia generously permitted reproduction of a variety of drawings or images. I am indebted to Nadine Ifrah Leo for creating the botanical drawings.

I thank Diane Berney as well as Gretchen and Dave Mills for being ever watchful for plants that appeared in this work. Dr. Leslie Landrum of Arizona State University and personnel of the Desert Botanical Gardens provide their expertise for plant identification; responsibility for accuracy in this regard is entirely mine. Finally, I am grateful to Pamela Slate, Botanic Coordinator of the Wallace Desert Gardens, for unencumbered access to the plant collections; the US Forest Service (Tonto National Forest); the State of Arizona (State Trust Lands); and Maricopa County Parks and Recreation (Spur Cross) for permission to collect plant materials within their areas of responsibility.

I received continued encouragement from my wife, Carol, and our daughters, Amy Saul and Randi Korte. This book is deservedly dedicated to Amy—who throughout her ordeal never gave first expression of her own needs, only those of her family.

TECHNICAL ASPECTS

The digital photography primarily employed a Cannon Rebel XT and the newer XTi coupled with a Canon 100 mm MACRO and a 17-85 mm EFS lens. Organization, storage, and image manipulation of the digital inventory was achieved with ULEAD Photo Explorer 8.5 and PHOTOSHOP 7.0 software.

The digital photo of a *Caesalpinia pulcherrima* flower (about 1" diameter) is noteworthy for the remarkable depth of field that was achieved by the photographer, Edward H. Mertz. I asked Mr. Mertz to explain how this was achieved. He wrote: "The flower image is a composite of 21 individual exposures, each taken at slightly different focal planes. The camera was first focused on the closest parts of the anthers and stigma and then the focus was moved further away for subsequent exposures. Individual exposures then were layered one on top of the other; only the sharpest parts of each layer were kept via a masking process. The result is an image with a depth of focus field far greater than could be achieved with a single exposure. A Canon 1DsMII (16.7 MP) was the in-studio camera (ISO 100, f/18 at 1.3 sec.) equipped with a Canon 100mm macro EF lens".

THE AUTHOR

Gerald A. Rosenthal, a retired Professor of Biological Sciences and Toxicology, earned is doctoral degree in Botany from Duke University. Dr. Rosenthal spent his career engaged n distinguished research and teaching in Botany and Plant Biochemistry; topics n which he has authored several highly regarded technical treatises.

The author has traveled the world for nearly four decades observing and photographing s major plant communities. A resident of Scottsdale, Arizona, he has lived in, hiked, and tudied the Sonoran Desert for 10 years. This work reflects his insightful observations and een understanding of this special and unique ecosystem.

A FINAL SUGGESTION

A 10X-hand lens opens a world of internal detail and color that is fascinating and bsorbing. Children are mesmerized by the beauty and wonder of the Lilliputian world found vithin a typical flower or the forest-like hair on the leaf. Often, there is an insect or two vithin the flower, and this is a delightful sight. These instruments, sold on-line, are available or $5-35. I prefer a two-element hand lens (10X and 5X); when overlapped they produce a 5X magnification. This item can be obtained for less than $5 on the Internet.

PLANT FAMILY CHARACTERISTICS

ACANTHACEAE (acanthus)
FLOWER: annual to perennial shrub, often red, regular to irregular corolla, perfect; cyme spike or raceme (bracted)

        <u>Ovary</u>: borne on a disc, superior, 2-celled
                Pistil: compound (2 carpels)
                Style: 1, slender, elongated
                Stigma: 1 or 2
        <u>Stamens</u>: 2 or 4 as unequal pairs, staminode possible
                Filaments: fused to corolla throat (epipetalous)
        <u>Sepals</u>: 5, persistent
        <u>Petals</u>: 5-lobed or 2-lipped (2 upper, 3 lower)
LEAVES: simple, entire, opposite, no stipules
STEM: four sided
FRUIT: 1-4 seeds in a 2-celled, dehiscent (violently) loculicidal capsule

ASTERACEAE (sunflower)
        Composite flower of disk (tubular and actinomorphic) and ray (zygomorphic) flowers; either type may be absent *Many flowers closely aggregated into a head that is supported, at its base, by a calyx-like involucre of small phyllaries (bracts); often, the whole structure appearing as a single flower*
FLOWER: generally arranged in cymes; disk flowers form a central core; larger, petal-like (ligules) ray flowers form the outer region Flowers borne in a head on a receptacle surrounded by imbricated phyllaries
        Disk: tubular, either staminate or perfect; ray: commonly pistillate, can be perfect or neutral

        <u>Ovary:</u> inferior, 1 chamber
                Style: 1, divided into 2 distinct branches
        <u>Stamens</u>: usually 5, simple or 2 lobed
                Anthers: 4-5 typically fused into a cylinder surrounding the style
        <u>Sepals</u>: 4 or absent or modified into pappus of bristles, scales or awns
        <u>Petals</u>: lacking or 4-5, generally white or yellow or both
LEAVES: often undivided and spoon-shaped, can be serrated or pinnately divided, may be prickly, lacks stipules
FRUIT: achene, often having a persistent pappus of bristles, awns, or scales

BORAGINACEAE (borage)

Bristly or pubescent shrubs

FLOWER: scorpioid cymes or racemes; bracts between are to one side or opposite the petals; funnel-formed and campanulate

Ovary: superior, 2 chambers

Style: elongated

Stigma: 2-lobed

Stamens: 4-paired (5th vestigial); epipetalous; inserted, alternates with corolla lobes

Sepals: 5, lobed, can be 2-lipped

Petals: 5, lobed, bilabiate

LEAVES: 1- to 3-pinnately or palmately compound

FRUIT: 1-4 nutlets, elongated and cylindrical 2-valved capsule

BRASSICACEAE (mustard)

Generally herbaceous with a pungent sap, four look-alike and separated petals form a cross, often white or yellow, actinomorphic

FLOWER: Typically arranged as a terminal raceme or corymbs, tend to cluster at the apex, perfect and regular, rarely solitary and terminal

Ovary: superior; 2 chambered (separated generally by a replum)

Style: 1

Stigma: entire or 2 lobed

Stamens: 6 (4 are long and 2 are short), attached at ovary base, generally 4 nectar glands

Sepals: 4, separated and morphologically distinct

Petals: lacking or 4, generally white or yellow, commonly clawed and diagonally disposed

LEAVES: generally basal and cauline, usually alternate, entire, no stipules; often pinnately divided and lobed

FRUIT: silique or silicle (modified capsules)

CARYOPHYLLACEAE (carnation)

FLOWER: annual to perennial herbs, perfect, regular, usually has an entire perianth; generally no involucre; solitary and axil or a cyme

Ovary: superior (1 cell)

Pistil: compound (2-5 carpels); equal number of styles

Style: 2-5

Stamens: 4-10 in 1 or 2 whorls, free

Petals: often absent, outer whorl of stamens can be petal-like

Tepals: 4-5, imbricate, appears as the "petals"

Calyx: when present: free or united into a tube

LEAVES: opposite, entire, without stipules, generally lacks petiole

FRUIT: many seeded, dry capsule (opening by valves or apical teeth) or a utricle (achene with a loose, outer envelope)

EUPHORBIACEAE (milkweed)

Milky sap, *unisexual flowers,* many toxic members.

Corolla can be absent or entire; perianth may not be present

FLOWER: cyme, panicle, raceme, or spike, monoecious or dioecious

Ovary: superior, 1-4 chambers

Style: 3, generally fused at the base

Stamens: 1 to 10 or more, free or filaments fused

Sepals: often lacking, replaced by green involucres; when present—generally 3-5 (free or fused)

Pistillate: calyx and corolla are both of 5 separated parts

LEAVES: generally with petioles and stipules, usually simple, alternate, opposite

FRUIT: capsule, usually 3 compartments, each with 1 seed

FABACEAE (legume)

Alternate, pinnately or twice pinnately compound leaves, flower composed of banner, wing, and keel petals Lupines (*Lupinus*) and clovers (*Trifolium*) have palmately compound leaves

FLOWER: mostly in terminal or axillary racemes

Ovary: superior, 1 chamber

Pistil: simple, 1 locule with marginal ovules

Stamens: typically 10 with 9 filaments joined and 1 independent; surround ovary and hidden inside the keel petal

Petals: none or 5; typically: banner, 2 wings, and 2 fused to form the keel

Sepals: 4-5 tooth and funnelform

LEAVES: pinnately or twice-pinnately compound, alternate, stipules

FRUIT: typically a legume; usually 1 but may be 2 chambered, typically opens along two seams (sutures)

HYDROPHYLLACEAE (waterleaf)

Stamens project above perianth plane, flowers often blue or purple; campanulate funnelform or rotate (like a wheel)

FLOWER: cyme (reminiscent of a scorpioid raceme) or solitary, perfect

Ovary: superior, 2 carpels

Stigma: 2

Stamens: 5, at base of corolla tube; usually a scale-like appendage at the base of the filament

Sepals: 5 united and deeply lobed

Petals: 5 united at base, often exserted

LEAVES: simple to pinnately compound, typically a basal rosette, no stipules; typically pubescent or glandular; mainly alternate

FRUIT: 2-valved, loculicidal capsule with 1 to multiple seeds

LAMIACEAE (LABIATAE) (mint)

Erect, square-shaped stem, often aromatic, flowers in whorls around the stem.

FLOWER: Cyme, clustered about the stem, typically irregular and bilabiate

Ovary: superior, deeply 4-lobed

Pistil: compound (2 carpels); 4-lobed ovary with 4 cells and a single ovule

Stigma: generally 2

Stamens: generally 4, inserted in corolla tube, exserted; unequal pairs, 2 can be sterile; 1 anther sac is completely or partially aborted

Petals: 2 lipped—upper lip: entire or 2 lobes forming hood over the bottom lip; lower lip: 3 lobed creating a place for visiting pollinators; united as 4 lobes; hypogynous, nectar-bearing disk between the pistil and the stamens

Sepals: 5-toothed or 5-lobed; united and pointed, equivalent or 2 sepals from upper lip and 3 produce the lower lip

LEAVES: opposite, generally glanded and pubescent; pairs at right angle to its neighbor pair, simple, no stipules; entire or dentated-rarely lobed

STEM: quadrangular

FRUIT: three-sided structure, at the base of the calyx, containing 4 nutlets; no seedpod, ripe seeds fall from the calyx

LILIACEAE (lily)

Perennial herbs that over winter as bulbs, corms, or rhizomes

FLOWER: regular, perfect (mostly), white to greenish, radially symmetrical,

Ovary: superior, 3-celled

Pistil: 3

Stigma: can be 3 lobed

Stamens: 6 distinct or 3 that emerge from the perianth tube, may lack anthers

Anther: 2-celled

Petals: 2 series of 3, distinct segments or tubular

Sepals: 3 (may be petaloid)

LEAVES: often a basal rosette, simple, parallel venation

FRUIT: capsule or berry

MALVACEAE (mallow)

FLOWER: large, regular, and perfect; herb or shrub with muscilaginous fluid and stellate or branched pubescence

Ovary: 3, 5, or 8-15 chambers

Pistil: compound (2 to many cells-usually equal to styles or stigmas)

Stamens: united at their base to create a tubular, exserted structure that surrounds the pistil

1-celled anther

Sepals: 5, partly united; often surrounded by bracts

Petals: 5, separate, tubular, fused to the united stamens

LEAVES: Simple, alternate, petiole, stipule, stellate pubescence, palmate lobed or ribbed, or undivided and tooth; leafy growths were these organs join the stem

FRUIT: capsule, follicle, or berry-like

NYCTAGINACEAE (four o'clock)

Perennial herbs or shrubs with delicate stems

FLOWER: Perfect or dioecious with calyx-like involucre; lower portion of perianth: persistent and covers the developing ovary, corolla-like, often brightly colored

The perianth consists of single row of 3-8-lobed petaloid sepals that are subtended by bracts that range in appearance from large and brightly colored to reduced and calyx-like

Ovary: 1-celled with 1 ovule

Pistil: simple (one locule with one ovule)

Stamens: 1 to 30 unequal stamens that can be independent or fused into a basal tube

Petals: none, but corolla-like upper portion; lower: campanulate, funnelform, or salverform

Sepals: 3-8 lobed

LEAVES: simple, entire, usually opposite, no stipules

FRUIT: achene-often protected by the calyx tube; anthocarp: fruit is fused to the perianth or receptacle

ONAGRACEAE (evening-primrose)

A large assemblage of annual and perennial herbs The stigma of *Camissonia* is round while that of *Oenothera* is four-parted

FLOWER: Spike or raceme, sometimes in clusters, terminal or at axils, perfect; corolla fused to the ovary

Ovary: inferior, 2-4 chambers

Style: one

Stigma: 4 lobed

Stamens: 4 or 8, attached to a portion of the calyx

Anthers: 2 chambered

Sepals: generally 4 (2-7) usually equal in size, not fused

Petals: generally 4, (2-7) not fused; perianth often forms a tube

LEAVES: simple; alternate, opposite, or whorled; no stipules, entire to pinnately divided

FRUIT: capsule (loculicidal), 4 chambered; berry or nut-like (indehiscent)

PAPAVERACEAE (poppy)

FLOWER: regular or irregular, perfect, solitary or in small clusters, irregular corolla, milky or colored sap

Actinomorphic, attractive and perfect

Ovary: superior, compound, 2 or more carpels

Pistil: 1 or more

Stamens: 6 or more, can be 2 groups of 3, group around a prominent pistil

Sepals: 2-3 (caducous), enclose the flower bud

Petals: 4-12 segments in 1-2 whorls, distinct or inner petals cohering at the apex, inner and outer petal groups often differently shaped

LEAVES: alternate, simple, often lobed or dissected, no stipules

FRUIT: capsule that often opens by apical pores, valves, or longitudinal slits

POLYGONACEAE (buckwheat)

FLOWER: small; green, pink or white; perianth not divided into calyx and corolla (no corolla); regular; usually perfect; borne on slender pedicles; radially symmetrical; axil or as cymes or panicles

        <u>Ovary</u>: superior, 1-celled (1 ovule); 3 carpels and 2-4 styles

        <u>Stamens</u>: 6-9, often 8 independent or basally fused in two whorled sets inserted at base of calyx

        <u>Perianth:</u> 6 tepals or fused to give 5 tepals Arranged in 1 or 2 series

LEAVES: simple, basal or cauline, entire, stipules absent or fused into a thin sheath that surrounds the stem at its axils; usually alternate The membranous, structure sheathing stipule is an *ocrea*

FRUIT: 3-winged or 4-angled achene or nutlet often protected by persistent perianth tissues

PORTULACEAE (purslane*)*

        Often a succulent, juicy plant

FLOWER: perfect, regular, radially symmetrical

        <u>Ovary</u>: 2-3-celled

            Pistil: 1

            Style: 2-8 branched, united at base or free

        <u>Stamens</u>: 5, equal and opposite to the number of calyx segments or 2-4 more abundant than these segments

        <u>Sepals</u>: 2 or none(members are bracts)

        <u>Petals</u>: 2, 4, 5, or 6 (actually petaloid sepals)

LEAVES: simple, entire, alternate or opposite, hair-like stipules or absent

FRUIT: capsule (dehiscent), can open via an apical lid

RANUNCULACEAE (buttercup)

        Generally white to yellow flower, nectar gland near base of petal; generally actinomorphic but some are zygomorphic and typically perfect

FLOWER: cyme (axils or terminal; may be solitary but frequently in clusters or spikes)

        <u>Ovary:</u> superior, 1 chamber but can be 5 or more

            Pistil: one to many, fused

            Stamens: 5, spirally arranged

        <u>Sepals</u>: typically 5, more or less petal-like (colored and showy)

        <u>Petals</u>: 5, often with a basal nectary (can be lacking or inconspicuous)

        Tepals: can be 4 to numerous tepals, distinct and imbricated

LEAVES: highly variable, base of petiole flat, usually no stipules

FRUIT: aggregate of achenes, follicles, berries or capsules

SCROPHULARIACEAE (figwort)

Typically herbs with rounded stems

FLOWER: Usually borne on spikes or panicle, 1-2 in axils, perfect, nearly regular to dramatically irregular with 5 petals (campanulate and bilabiate), when conspicuous: usual 2 upper and 3 basal lobes

Ovary: superior, 2 chambered

Stigma: two lobed

Pistil: 1

Stamens: 2 long and 2 short; occasionally a 5th, sterile; attached to petals

Sepals: usually 2-lipped, tubular to campanulate or forming 4-5 lobed structure, irregular-enlarges around and protects the fruit

Petals: lobed; upper, 2 lobed; lower, 3 lobed

LEAVES: variable, simple to pinnately compound; no stipules, alternate or opposite, sessile or petiolate

FRUIT: capsule, 2 chambered, or berry

SOLANACEAE (nightshade)

Often climbing with pubescent stems and leaves, petals united to form a bilaterally symmetrical corolla

FLOWER: perfect, regular, terminal or axillary, solitary or cyme, panicle, or umbel

Ovary: superior, 2-celled

Style: 1

Stamens: 5, inserted within and attached to the corolla tube

Sepals: 5-tooth or cleft, can be fused, grow around and protects the fruit

Petals: 5-lobed, tubular, campanulate, funnelform, or rotate

LEAVES: alternate, usually simple but can be pinnately compound

FRUIT: berry or 2-chambered capsule

INDEX

Palo Verde 252